A Lucky Life

A Lucky Life

RICHARD B. GOLDBLOOM

Formac Publishing Company Limited
Halifax

Formac Publishing Company Limited recognizes the support of the Province of Nova Scotia through the Department of Communities, Culture and Heritage. We are pleased to work in partnership with the province to develop and promote our culture resources for all Nova Scotians. We acknowledge the financial support of the Government of Canada through the Canada Book Fund for our publishing activities. We acknowledge the support of the Canada Council for the Arts which last year invested $157 million to bring the arts to Canadians throughout the country.

Cover image: The Chronicle Herald Archives
Photo credits:
All photos from the Goldbloom family album except the following:
P. 235, Top – contributed, Bottom right – The Chronicle Herald Archives
P. 236, Top –The Chronicle Herald Archives; photographer Wamboldt/Waterfield,
    Bottom – The Chronicle Herald Archives; photographer: Darren Pittman
P. 239, Top – Karen Purcell
P. 240, Bottom – Courtesy of The Halifax Herald Limited
P. 242, Scott Munn

Library and Archives Canada Cataloguing in Publication

Goldbloom, Richard B., 1924-, author
    A lucky life / Richard B. Goldbloom.

ISBN 978-1-4595-0284-0 (bound) — ISBN 978-1-4594-0285-7 (epub)

    1. Goldbloom, Richard B.   2. Pediatricians--Canada--
Biography.   I. Title.

RJ43.G64A3 2013   618.9200092   C2013-905055-8

Formac Publishing Company Limited
5502 Atlantic Street
Halifax, Nova Scotia, Canada
B3H 1G4
www.formac.ca

Printed and bound in Canada.

In memory of Ruth —
the open secret of my success — and happiness

The day is short, the task is great,
The labourers are lazy, the wage is abundant
And the master is urgent.
It is not incumbent upon you to
Finish the task [of saving the world] . . .
Yet you are not free to desist from it.
— Rabbi Tarfon Talmud Mishna Pirkei Avot
(Ethics of the Fathers)

Contents

Introduction

The late movie mogul and master of malapropisms Samuel Goldwyn is reputed to have said: "I don't think anyone should write their autobiography until after they're dead." For several reasons, I decided not to wait. First, I've been incredibly lucky over almost nine decades . . . and what good is luck if it isn't shared? By any standard, my childhood was privileged, without being truly wealthy in the monetary sense. The real riches included a loving, supportive family and parents who believed that education, in all its forms (including travel) was the greatest gift they could bestow on their children. Another was exposure, from earliest childhood, to an incredible succession of characters, famous, infamous and obscure, from widely disparate backgrounds. The *dramatis personae* of my life included colourful relatives, some remarkable musical and theatrical personalities and a parade of medical heroes who taught me many subtle secrets of how to become a good doctor — especially the importance of treating the illness (i.e., how the patient feels) as well as the disease (what is wrong with the patient) — and understanding how families work, the factors that strengthen or weaken family function and the family characteristics that determine emotional health and resilience in children.

It is hard to imagine a career more rewarding than that of a pediatrician: to become part of the lives of so many families during moments of joy and sorrow and to watch infants and children grow up to become impressive adults. Besides, not a day goes by that a pediatrician is not confronted with new experiences and challenges, often calling for innovative solutions.

Having lived through the conquest of so many children's diseases — polio, meningitis and the common childhood infectious diseases — people today might expect a marked decrease in a pediatrician's daily workload. But that has not happened. New challenges have appeared in the form of previously unrecognized conditions, including the so-called new morbidity, the psychosocial and developmental problems that present major challenges for parents and doctors alike. But despite these dramatic changes in the patient spectrum, the fundamental needs of parents and families are unchanged, and the physician's mission has also remained unchanged since the beginning of time: to relieve anxiety.

My good fortune has not been confined to a medical career. This book presents a highly varied assembly of relatives and a parade of phenomenal characters from the worlds of medicine, music and theatre who have added a riot of colour to my journey. I can't imagine anyone having a luckier life.

Richard B. Goldbloom,
OC, MD, FRCP, D.Litt (Hon.)

Family History

From Russia to Montreal

There are two lasting bequests we can give our children. One is roots. The other is wings.

— Hodding Carter

The roots of all four of my grandparents were thinly embedded in the hostile soil of Eastern Europe, specifically in that narrow band of western Tsarist Russia that came to be known as the Pale of Settlement, within which Jews were confined by decree. Part of that area later became Lithuania, and Jews who came from that region are still known as *Litvaks*. No matter where people live, in which country, or even in different regions of a particular country, there seems to be a universal need to identify some definable group — national, provincial, religious or defined by colour — to whom they can declare themselves superior.

We Jews were no exception. Thus, although all Jews in Eastern Europe shared difficult lives, many *Litvaks* considered themselves intellectually superior to their co-religionists from Poland, the Ukraine and other parts of Eastern Europe. They also believed Kaunas (which they called *Kovno)* was the Jewish-intellectual epicentre of Eastern Europe.

Both my maternal grandparents came from Kovno. My

maternal grandfather's name was Samuel Ballon. The original spelling may well have been Baline, and my mother's older sister, Miriam (a.k.a. Mamie) claimed with absolute conviction that we were related to Irving Berlin, whose original name was Israel Baline. (Not once did I hear of the great composer claiming a relationship with *us*, but he may have had his reasons.)

My maternal grandmother's maiden name was Klein. One of her brothers had three sons and a daughter, Celia, all of whom, for reasons now lost in history, emigrated from Lithuania not to Canada, but to what was then called Southern Rhodesia (now Zimbabwe), where they settled in the town of Bulawayo. Celia later married a man named Leo Levy who, with Celia's three brothers, initiated large-scale cattle ranching in the region, developing it into a major industry. At one time they owned four large cattle ranches, one covering over four hundred acres. Leo Levy received the Order of the British Empire for his contribution to the development of the cattle industry in Southern Rhodesia. For some reason, my grandmother's family name, which everyone in Europe and North America pronounced "Kline," was pronounced "Klayne" in Southern Rhodesia.

In 1986, my wife Ruth and I visited then-renamed Zimbabwe during a six-month, nine-country lecture tour I had undertaken during a sabbatical leave as the Sir Arthur Sims Commonwealth Travelling Professor, under the auspices of the Royal College of Physicians and Surgeons of Canada. To this day I regret that my tight schedule precluded a side-trip to Bulawayo to visit my sole surviving cousin, Israel Klein, who was in poor health. His wife, Hazel, however, travelled from Bulawayo to Harare to greet us at our hotel. More precisely, she floated into the lobby followed by two servile-appearing black porters, bearing gifts.

Hazel was elegantly attired in a billowing white dress, beautifully mannered but "delicate." Her blonde hair was pulled back and neatly arranged in the style of a ballerina (which she had once been). The black "native bearers" who accompanied her were burdened with lavish gifts, including a magnificent briefcase for me made of elephant hide (now an illegal export). The scene resembled an African version of *Gone with the Wind*, suggesting in a single frame why the subservient black majority felt such resentment toward the wealthy white minority landowners.

As in the southern US decades earlier, many white Southern Rhodesians rationalized their privileged status by claiming they were providing much-needed employment to the black population. The inter-racial gap in Zimbabwe came into even sharper focus the following day. Ruth and I had been invited to visit the St. Paul Musami Mission Hospital seventy-five kilometres from Harare. This rural hospital had gained international attention seven years earlier as the site of a horrible massacre of several missionary nuns and priests by terrorists. A large memorial to the victims had been erected on the hospital grounds.

As a courtesy, I invited Hazel to join us, and she agreed eagerly. Next morning she appeared, again in a lovely, billowing white dress, as if en route to a garden party. We were driven to the mission hospital in an open jeep, much of the trip bouncing over very rough, unpaved country roads. We were warmly received at the mission hospital, and I went on ward rounds with the nursing and medical staff to see the children under their care. One apprehensive little fellow was about to be transported to a Harare hospital for removal of a lemon seed that was stuck in his ear canal. I asked if I could have a look at the boy, and, luckily was able to dislodge the offending seed and save the lad a rough ride to the big city — my sole heroic deed of the six-month sabbatical. After hospital rounds, Ruth, Hazel and I were invited into the small hospital dining room to have lunch with members of the nursing and dietetic staff. After lunch, it was time to return to Harare. As we said our goodbyes, Ruth and I were hugged and kissed by the nurses and dieticians. Back at our hotel in Harare,

Hazel confessed she had never *in her entire life* dined at the same table as a black person, and had never, *never* been kissed by one. She confessed her astonishment at how comfortable Ruth and I seemed to be. It was a striking insight into the depth of racial segregation in that country. Parenthetically, I was deeply troubled that Jews, of all people, should be a party to it.

The Southern Rhodesian branch of my mother's family underwent a second exodus in the late twentieth century, along with many of the country's other white settlers. Many were farmers who lost their land in the uprisings and social upheaval that gripped the country. Not one of my cousins remains in Zimbabwe today. Like so many members of the white population, most left for South Africa or North America.

While growing up, I often envied the sentimental, nostalgic pride so many anglophone Christian families expressed when speaking of their ancestors' countries of origin — mostly England, Scotland or Ireland — and how they loved to revisit their ancestral homelands to view the family homesteads and visit remaining relatives. Not one of my four grandparents ever expressed the faintest twinge of nostalgia for their country of origin. Their Eastern European past was virtually never mentioned. I recall a single occasion when my maternal grandmother, Charlotte Ballon, told me how she had hidden in terror under the bed when Cossacks rode through town brandishing their sabres, looking for more Jews to slaughter. There is a moment in Woody Allen's classic film *Annie Hall* that always recalls that brief conversation with my grandmother. Early in the film, the neurotic *nebbish* (nerd), Alvy Singer, played by Woody Allen, admires an article of clothing his new gentile girlfriend is wearing. Annie tells him it was a gift from her Grammy Hall. "Didn't your Grammy ever give you presents?" she asks. "No," he replies. "She was too busy being raped by Cossacks."

My Goldbloom and Ballon ancestors were as different as chalk and cheese. My paternal grandfather, Samuel Goldbloom, came from a small shtetl known as Neustadt (or *Naishtot,* in its Yiddish pronunciation), in the southwestern part of what is now Lithuania, close to the German border.

In 1835, the village had 4,413 residents, 76 per cent of them Jewish. Jews had settled there in the beginning of the eighteenth century. Between 1865 and 1889, the village survived four major fires, which destroyed many homes. It also endured two cholera epidemics. After 1918, when Lithuania became an independent republic, many Jews (especially the younger ones) began to immigrate to North America and to South Africa.

Between 1941 and 1944, Neustadt was under Nazi rule. On July 1, 1941, the Germans arrested all Jewish males fourteen years of age and older, forced them to march to the cemetery and shot them in groups of fifty, throwing their bodies into previously dug graves. In August of that year, the remaining Jews were herded into a ghetto; and on September 16, 1941, all remaining Jewish women and children, as well as men who had hidden during the first extermination, were taken a few kilometres from Neustadt, shot and thrown into mass graves. The following day, Lithuanian neighbours looted their homes and pillaged their belongings. Only fifteen Neustadt Jews survived, and only because they happened to be out of town. I have a hand-drawn map of the town, sketched from memory by a former resident of the village whose grandson was a pediatric colleague in Montreal. He had drawn the location of each house in the town and inscribed the name of the occupant family. Not one had survived.

In 2008, two of my grandsons, Daniel and Will Goldbloom, journeyed to Neustadt — the first such visit by anyone in my family since World War II. On a map of the city they found a Star of David, which they assumed marked the Jewish section of town. They walked there and found only a mass grave.

In the late nineteenth century, persecution was more than sufficient reason for Jews, especially those of the younger generation, to try to emigrate. Aside from keeping the Jews strictly confined to the Pale of Settlement, Tsar Nicholas I had decreed all Jewish males had to serve in the Russian army. Officially, they could be drafted at twelve, but sometimes children as young as eight or nine were seized for conscription. They were placed in special training units and required to serve another twenty-five years. To avoid such a fate, many parents hid their children in the forest or spirited them across the frontier. Some even amputated their children's fingers or toes to avoid conscription. Although Tsar Alexander II, son of Nicholas I, abolished child recruitment, Jews continued to be conscripted as young adults. Such hardships were more than enough to convince young Jewish men and women to flee the country.

My paternal grandfather, Samuel Goldbloom, and four of his siblings fled persecution in Russia — but their persecution was of a totally different variety. Having produced several children, my paternal great-grandmother died in a subsequent childbirth. Shortly thereafter, my great-grandfather remarried. His new wife, at least according to my grandfather and his siblings, was a shrew. After her arrival on the scene, my Grandpa Sam, along with his two brothers and two sisters, decided to move as far away from their "wicked stepmother" as was geographically possible. William, Isaac, Sarah and Freda Goldbloom emigrated first, with Sam following in the early 1880s. Sam was just sixteen at the time. According to my father, Sam's "total education when he left for Canada consisted of his ability to read the Hebrew liturgy, understanding scarcely a word, and being able to read and write Yiddish."

William and his two sisters settled first in Winnipeg. Before 1900, Winnipeg consisted of a collection of scattered storefronts, jerry-built homes and muddy streets. The population, numbering less than two thousand, included homesteaders, traders, remittance men, Aboriginals and Métis.

By the time Sam arrived, his brother Isaac had already moved on to Denver, Colorado, and set up a furniture business. Like many other immigrants, William initially became a peddler. His sister Sarah, however, was the real breadwinner of the family. She sold coal door to door, with a horse and wagon.

From the moment of his arrival in the New World until his death, my Grandpa Sam personified the eternal optimist. He had a unique talent for laughing in the face of adversity. His extroversion and good humour, gifts for which I thank him daily, propelled him through good times and bad. In his own autobiography, *Small Patients*, my father described Grandpa Sam succinctly:

> *My father had two sure gifts . . . the one was of making money; not fortunes, but quite enough to keep his family in comfort; the other was for losing money, at poker, in wilderness investments, and on the Winnipeg grain exchange. He could not resist a game of poker, and he was a very poor poker player. He sank a modest fortune in early Alberta oil ventures, in worthless gold mines, and in wheat futures, as to which he invariably guessed wrong. The result was that we were always living on a hand-to-mouth basis.*[*]

Grandpa validated Woody Allen's definition of an investment broker as "someone who takes your money and invests it until it's all gone." My father's brother Tevye[†] shared his father's extroversion and his capacity for laugher; and like several other

---

[*]   Alton Goldbloom, *Small Patients: The Autobiography of a Children's Doctor* (Toronto: Longmans, Green & Co., 1959).

[†]   Tevye abjured the Russian-Jewish pronunciation of his name, "Tevya" (as in the hero of Sholem Aleichem's stories, Tevye the Milkman, now widely known from the musical *Fiddler on the Roof*), in favour of a more anglicized version he pronounced "Tevvy." In later years when he toured the northern BC lumber camps as a salesman, many of his logger customers had difficulty even with "Tevvy." They called him "Ted."

family members, Tevye was also a compulsive scribbler. He described my Grandpa Sam and his early career as follows:

> *He had a fantastic sense of humour, was extremely gregarious, and loved a good time. He had arrived in Winnipeg penniless. To make a living, he borrowed a little money and got some credit from one of the wholesale houses. He filled a suitcase with household goods . . . pins, needles, thread, thimbles and other odds and ends that would appeal to housewives, and began peddling door to door. Soon he added other items, such as gold rings and cheap watches. He was so likeable that in no time he had worked up a loyal following. Later he added gold watches and an occasional small diamond. Before long he became acquainted with a few lumbermen who had camps in the Lake of the Woods district in Ontario. By this time he was pretty fluent in English. The logging camp operators took a great liking to Dad and invited him to their camps to do business with the crews. So he gave up house-to-house selling and started making rounds of the logging camps. Soon he was able to sell on credit, with the offices making deductions from the loggers' pay cheques. During the winter, Dad would rent a team of horses and go from camp to camp by sleigh. On one such venture, the ice wasn't quite thick enough, and Dad and the horses went through the ice. Luckily, this happened close to shore and they survived.*

At some time during his Lake of the Woods era, Grandpa Sam contrived to get his name attached to an obscure island in that district: Goldbloom Island, no less. Inexplicably (and unforgivably), Goldbloom Island seems to have disappeared from Ontario's cartography. Grandpa may have sold it or, much more likely, lost it in a poker game. My son David went to the land claims office for Lake of the Woods in Kenora in the early 1990s and tried to lay claim to our family lake; a bored and unimpressed clerk spent at least thirty seconds checking the files before telling him no such body of water existed.

Two of Sam's close friends in the logging camps, Donald Mann and William McKenzie, would go on to form the Canadian National Railway (CNR). During the building of the railway, Sam, known to everyone as "Sammy," became the only salesman allowed in the camp. They also conferred on Grandpa an impressive title: "Travelling Watch Inspector." It was a sinecure, but the title came with a railway pass that remained in effect until he became too old to travel.

One of our family's favourite stories about Grandpa's incurable optimism concerned a trainman who confided to him he had come home unexpectedly and found his wife in bed with another man. "It wasn't even someone I knew," the trainman reported. "I tried to comfort him," Grandpa explained. "I said: 'Don't worry. Maybe she didn't mean any harm by it.'" That phrase subsequently became incorporated into the Goldbloom family's regular conversation. We would invoke it as a rationale for almost any heinous deed we heard about, from bank robbery to serial killings. We would respond to such horrendous tales with the comment: "Maybe he didn't mean any harm by it."

On one of his return trips to Winnipeg from the Lake of the Woods logging camps, Grandpa met a young woman named Belle Goldstein. She had emigrated from a shtetl called Aleksot, just a few kilometres from Neustadt, and had arrived in Montreal in the early 1880s. They had many mutual friends. They soon became engaged and married and lived in Montreal where they had a flat with cold running water but no toilet or bath. There was a latrine in the backyard. For this princely estate they paid a rent of six dollars a month.

As always, my grandfather could see humour in their situation but my grandmother could not. Three children arrived in rapid succession, a boy followed by twin girls. But all three died, as so many infants did at that time. Following an ancient Jewish superstition, it was common practice not to name a subsequent child after a deceased relative (the usual practice) but to give the child a name contrived to deceive the Angel of Death, who was a real presence to many Jewish families in those days. Under such circumstances, the name given was often *Alter* (in Yiddish, literally, "the old one"). Thus, when my father was born, on September 23, 1889, he was named Alter. He later anglicized this name to "Alton."

To make doubly sure the Angel of Death was thrown off track, my grandparents followed another ancient Jewish tradition and "sold" the baby to a great aunt for a gold coin to be redeemed on my father's wedding day. Other life-preserving, closely held superstitions included not showing the baby undue affection or offering him too much praise, not cutting his hair and not allowing him to see himself in a mirror. My father later remembered: "In spite of these precautions, during my first year of life, I fell ill with pneumonia." For several days he lay close to death. My grandmother called on Dr. William Alexander Molson, a member of the famous brewing family who cared for many of Montreal's poor immigrant Jewish families, often with no expectation of being paid. When my father recovered and grew older, his mother reminded him regularly she wanted him to become a doctor "like Dr. Molson" and to take care of poor people as Dr. Molson had done. Molson achieved the status of virtual sainthood in the family.

In the early 1900s, Grandpa must have been doing pretty well because he sent his wife, Belle, and their three children, Alton, aged eleven, Eva, eight, and Tevye, five, to spend a year with their maternal grandfather in the Lithuanian village of Aleksot, just a few kilometres from Neustadt. Grandpa did not go with them.

Aside from having to look after his business in Canada, he would have been subject to military service had he reappeared on Russian soil. The family sailed from Montreal in the Cunard ship *Corinthia*, occupying an inside, four-berth cabin. My father recalled it was on this trip that he first tasted non-kosher food and was amazed to discover it did not taste different and no heavenly wrath descended upon him. This was the beginning of his digression from orthodoxy, and he remained a practising skeptic throughout his life. The transatlantic voyage took twenty-one days, via Belfast and London, to Hamburg. From there they travelled by train to Aleksot. Tevye‡ recalled some of their experiences in the ancestral home as follows:

> When we first met our grandfather [Belle's father], he embraced us and gave us the Lord's blessing. He seemed very old, though he may have been only sixty or sixty-five at the time, because he was severely bent over with arthritis of the spine. We created quite a sensation in the little village. Word spread quickly that people from America had come for a visit. My Uncle Morris in particular liked to show us off. He took us across the bridge to Kovno to let the natives have a look. We were quite a sight, all dressed up in our Sunday best . . . Little Lord Fauntleroy suits for Alton and me, with lace-embroidered collars,

---

‡ I remember my uncle Tevye for several reasons: Like most of the Goldblooms, he laughed a lot, told a lot of jokes and encouraged his nephews and nieces to go forth and do likewise. He also did a few rudimentary magic tricks, like making a cigarette disappear into one ear and then having it mysteriously reappear from the opposite ear. He also played (and loved) the violin, and what he lacked in musical talent he made up in enthusiasm. He did, however, play well enough to perform in a Vancouver community orchestra, and this brought him untold pleasure. Tevye was an addicted cigarette smoker through most of his life and, as a result, developed severe emphysema in his later years and became very short of breath. Nevertheless, his sense of humour never abandoned him. A few months before he died, I phoned him and asked how he was feeling. "I'm fine," he replied, "as long as I don't breathe."

velvet coats and pants; and Eva, her long hair in curls, wearing an accordion-pleated skirt. Evidently the locals had never seen a North American. They followed us everywhere, yelling to one another, "Amerikanski!" as though we were freaks . . . and to them, we probably were. When we passed a barber shop, my uncle suddenly decided he needed a haircut, so we took refuge there.

Dad's father lived in the small nearby village of Neustadt, so we took a horse and wagon and went there to meet him. He had a small fruit orchard and lived in a tiny cottage with a sunken fireplace where all the cooking was done. He was an uneducated man. I remember him, wearing a soiled *kaftan, standing in the corner of the room, bracing himself between the two walls, and falling fast asleep. That, incidentally, turned out to be a unique Goldbloom talent.*

My father added his own description of his paternal grandfather:

He lived in a shanty near the town square. It had no more than three rooms, barely furnished: the floor was earthen. He lived there with his second wife, the vixenish stepmother from whom my father and his siblings had escaped to Canada in his early youth. She was, in fact, a simple, mild-mannered and apparently innocuous old lady who probably breathed easier and more peacefully when my father left. My grandfather was a tall, thin man with white hair and an unkempt white beard who dressed in the Russian manner . . . cap, rubashka *and high*

boots to his knees, into which his trouser legs were
tucked. He was totally uneducated and uncultured.
He had no conversation and no interests; when he
was not working he slept.

My paternal grandparents were, in many respects, the odd
couple. Grandpa Sam Goldbloom was gregarious and fun-loving,
a bit on the rough side, invariably laughing in the face of adversity.
After Grandma Belle's arrival in Canada, she lived with relatives
who were already well integrated into Canadian society and, as my
father put it, "determined to make a lady out of her." She learned
to wear fashionable clothes, to cook and to knit. In fact, she later
became a prodigiously skilled knitter whose work was once exhibited in the windows of the Hudson's Bay Company, Vancouver's
largest department store. While Grandpa was rough and tumble,
Grandma was dignified. In her younger married years she strictly
observed the Jewish dietary laws and followed a traditional lifestyle.
But for reasons still unclear, she experienced a kind of epiphany in
late middle age. At age sixty, she stopped keeping a kosher home,
began smoking cigarettes, and learned to drive a car! My father
reflected on the ultimate impact of his odd parental couple:

The total disparity of temperament, interests and
social attitudes between my parents was perhaps the
chief reason why my father could never abandon his
restless, nomadic habits. He was fond of his family
and was, according to our needs, a good provider,
but he wanted none of the responsibility of our care
or education beyond providing the means. He was
the foreman. We escaped a great deal of punishment
because the threat "just wait till your father comes
home" was much like the adjournment of a court
action sine die. The return date was vague, and

indefinite until one day there would come a letter
or a telegram saying that he was on the way home.
Occasionally, he would pop in out of nowhere,
unexpected and unannounced, see that all was in
order, leave my mother a supply of money, and in
two or three weeks was off again. This was my life
until I was over thirty.

During my own childhood, we would visit Grandma and
Grandpa Goldbloom periodically in Vancouver, where they
spent their latter decades, as did my father's brother Tevye
and, for a time, my grandfather's sister Eva, and their families.
My memories of Grandpa were overwhelmingly of a man who
loved to laugh. We would sometimes visit him at the offices of
"Goldbloom and Son" (Tevye) on Hastings Street. Their devoted
secretary, Betty Hicks, whom Grandpa referred to as "Miss Eeks"
was there, but I don't remember ever seeing a live customer. My
cousins and I knew exactly how to turn Grandpa's crank. We
would ask him: "How's business, Grandpa?" His standard reply
was: "Pretty damn good — and rotten, denk you — and the same
to you!" And we would all dissolve in laughter. Our laughing
genes descended directly from him.

When Grandpa became too old to travel to the logging
camps, Uncle Tevye took over. An excellent salesman, he
shared Grandpa's love of laughter and developed innumerable
friendships in the camps.

My maternal grandparents, Charlotte and Samuel Ballon, like
my Goldbloom ancestors, came from Lithuania, but the simi-
larity ended there. Before my earliest memory of him, Samuel
Ballon had operated a couple of businesses, the Montreal Broom
Factory and the Montreal Iron Works.

As a young woman, my mother, Annie Ballon, served as
her father's bookkeeper, which possibly gave rise to her life-

time of meticulous habits. Her brothers included a well-known otolaryngologist, or ear, nose and throat specialist (David), a quiet, scholarly but unsuccessful lawyer (Isidore) and a surgeon (Harry). Her three sisters were Mamie, Ellen and Florence, Harry's fraternal twin. Ellen was a spectacularly talented pianist from earliest childhood, and other siblings were musically talented, too. Mamie played the piano in her younger days. Isidore was a competent pianist who later became my piano teacher. Florence was a very good cellist who, in her younger days, played in the Dubois Trio and the Dubois Orchestra in Montreal. So did her fraternal twin, Harry, who was an above-average violinist, at least until he entered medical school.

The young Harry must have been a truly promising violinist because at nine or ten he auditioned for the great Mischa Elman, who was in Montreal to give a recital. Details of Harry's audition and Elman's reactions are lost to history, but apparently the audition got off to a shaky start. Elman asked Harry, "Vell, my boy, vat are you going to play?" "The violin," replied Harry. This exchange may well have played a pivotal role in Harry's ultimate decision to abandon the violin and become a surgeon.

David Ballon, the oldest of the siblings, had a highly respected career as head of the Department of Otolaryngology at Montreal's Royal Victoria Hospital (RVH). He and my father were the first two Jewish physicians to head departments at a McGill teaching hospital.

Like both his parents, Uncle David was diminutive (no more than five feet). He had to stand on a crate to reach the operating table at the RVH, but what he lacked in height he made up for in potency, fathering an array of six children, three boys and three girls. (In that context, I can't erase the memory of Groucho Marx, who, late in his career, hosted a popular TV program called *You Bet Your Life!* Contestants had to answer a test question, and if they answered correctly, they won some money. Before posing the question, Groucho would quiz his guests about their personal lives. When one young man stated that he was married, Groucho asked if he had any children. "Sixteen," the man replied. "How do you explain that?" asked Groucho. "Well," he said, "I love my wife." Groucho countered: "Listen, I love my cigar, but I take it out of my mouth once in a while!")

David Ballon enjoyed a well-deserved reputation for extraordinary gentleness and dexterity. He could insert an instrument far up your nostrils and you would hardly know he had been there. He was equally famous for his skill in removing foreign bodies (peanuts or bits of toys) from the bronchi of small children, often succeeding when others had failed.

Uncle David was also a bit of a worshipper of the rich and famous. Among his prized possessions was a huge framed etching of US President William Howard Taft, inscribed in appreciation for medical services David provided to Taft during a presidential visit to Montreal. The etching hung prominently in David's waiting room. Others who loomed large in his trophy collection included two young princes of Luxembourg who had been sent by their mother, the Grand Duchess Charlotte, to spend the war years in the safety of Canada and had been cared for by my father (who, in turn, had referred them to Uncle David for throat and ear problems); and Grace Moore, then an internationally known soprano whom he had treated for a so-called singer's node, a papilloma of the larynx.

David had been a fierce promoter of his younger sister Ellen's career as a child prodigy, and later held similar aspirations for his second daughter, Margot, a talented pianist. Margot, however, did not share her father's dream of becoming a soloist. She became a piano teacher and subsequently an academic gerontologist and married a fine violinist, David Nadien, who became concertmaster of the New York Philharmonic under the baton of Leonard Bernstein.

My maternal grandparents lived at 1511 Bishop Street, one block to the west of us in downtown Montreal. The Ballon home, a substantial three-storey red sandstone and granite home, housed, at various times, an assortment of children, in-laws and grandchildren whose presence resulted from marital disruption, financial difficulties or other adversities. One long-time resident was my mother's brother, Isidore Ballon, a quiet-spoken bachelor and, as far as I could tell, Montreal's least successful lawyer. The secret of the absence of clientele was never entirely clear. Family legend held that he was "too honest," a curious accusation applied to a lawyer. He was inordinately passive and studious, having taught himself several languages. He read foreign-language dictionaries "for fun," or so we were told. He occasionally played chess with one or two equally passive male bachelor acquaintances, but his life was otherwise painfully quiet and uninteresting. To the family's amazement, in late middle life he met and married a nice woman and decamped from his parents' home. Aunt Florence and I played at his wedding. Incidentally, Isidore's unanticipated marital venture also resulted in a modest but unexpected upturn in his professional income, since a newly acquired brother-in-law who owned a large radio and furniture store pushed some legal work his way.

Another long-term occupant of my grandparents' home was my mother's older sister Miriam — Aunt Mamie — who lived there with her three sons. What had led to her move home from New York was usually referred to in whispered conversations and vague allusions (in my presence, at least). As far as I could determine, she had taken up with and married a man in New York who had turned out to be "no good." I suspect they may have been united in what we would later refer to as a "military" (a.k.a. "shotgun") wedding, that is, she may have been pregnant at the time — but I have no proof. There were plenty of rumours and thinly veiled hints about Mamie's husband (whom I never met), including that he had had an affair with her sister Ellen and that he had run afoul of the law. After her marriage failed, Mamie and her children were supported by various family members, including Ellen, David and my father . . . who eventually came to be considered equivalent to a blood relative whenever someone from my mother's family was in difficulty and needed money.

Of my Ballon aunts and uncles I was closest to the two young-est, the twins Florence and Harry. At regular intervals I would persuade Florence to dust off her old cello so we could play duets. Typically, she would express reluctance ("I haven't practised in years") but usually capitulated, upon which we would "render" (in both senses of that word) performances of old chestnuts such as "La Cinquantaine" or Bach's "Air on a G string" (a G string had a very different meaning in those days).

During my pre-teen years Florence would always get me in a corner and ask me to tell her "any new dirty jokes." I was always pleased to oblige and she would pretend to be revolted. "That's disgusting!" she would say, all the while convulsed with laughter. Florence was also capable of witty commentary. At one of my mother's tea parties, a certain third cousin had the habit of sitting with her legs pretty wide apart, revealing her pink silk underwear to all who dared to sneak a peek (myself included, of course). Florence commented that Cousin S was "revealing the entire *Outline of British History*," a popular school textbook of the time.

Another major source of amusement for Florence and me was another cousin from Chicago who appeared periodically at our house wearing a brassiere that sculpted her ample breasts into shapes totally unknown in nature — two pinnacles whose apices came to dangerously sharp points. One glimpse of her two most prominent features was all it took to reduce both of us into uncontrolled fits of laughter.

Florence's twin brother, my uncle Harry, like most other Jew-ish medical graduates of that era, found it difficult or impossible to obtain postgraduate training positions at the McGill teaching hospitals. He therefore turned for surgical training to major European centres. Following his training in Vienna and Budapest, he began a promising career as a chest surgeon at the Barnes Hospital in St. Louis. While still a young man, he co-authored a major textbook, *Surgery of the Chest,* with his renowned chief, Dr. Evarts Graham, and another colleague, Dr. Jacob Singer. Two years before it was published in 1933, Graham had performed the world's first successful total pneumonectomy (surgical removal of an entire lung).

Harry's promising career in St. Louis was interrupted by a strange (by today's standards) turn of events. He had a romantic liaison with a nurse and wanted to marry her. Unfortunately for both, she happened to be a *shiksa* (gentile). In those days, marriage "out of faith" in observant Jewish families was considered tantamount to a death in the family. Some Orthodox families would even sit *shiva*, the mourning ritual for the lost soul, whose name would never again be mentioned. (Judaism holds no monopoly on the horror of interfaith marriages. Many decades later in Montreal, the mother of one of my Protestant patients informed me with utter horror that her daughter was going to marry a Catholic! She whispered to me: "I'd rather she marry a Jew!" I assume she meant this as a compliment . . . but I still can't be sure.)

After Harry's precipitous return to Montreal, he lived in his parents' home prior to and for some time after he married a nice young *Jewish* girl who'd been his secretary. He established a successful career as a surgeon, ultimately becoming chief of surgery at the Jewish General Hospital.

I was very fond of Uncle Harry. For one thing, he would take my brother Victor and me to Delorimier Stadium in east-end Montreal to watch our beloved Montreal Royals play baseball. I remember seeing Jackie Robinson, the person who broke forever the colour barrier in major league baseball, and Chuck Connors, a lanky, agile first baseman who went on to stardom as hero of the shoot-'em-up TV series *The Rifleman*. Uncle Harry also took us fishing at Chateauguay, on Lac St. Louis, where perch and bass were in abundance, and "catch and release" would have been unthinkable.

After I became a medical student and married Ruth, Uncle Harry and his wife, Gertrude, a fabulous cook, took pity on us and often invited us to dinner. Harry, a superb teacher with exceptional clinical skills, would also take me on hospital rounds — and he introduced me to many funny ("dirty") jokes.

One of the unforgettable clinical lessons he taught me took place in a family context. Harry's older brother Isidore was close to death from extensive gastric cancer. As Isidore lay in bed, unconscious, Harry asked me to lay my hand on his abdomen. I never forgot the stony hardness of the cancerous tumour that filled most of his abdomen.

From earliest childhood, as I passed through our ground floor hallway that served both my father's office and our home, my nostrils filled with aromas of the various solvents then used routinely in pediatric practice — alcohol, ether or acetone. These and listening to the howls of infants were part of my daily sensory experience. I don't know whether such early exposures influenced my career choice, but by the time I was old enough to write, I would scrawl my name ostentatiously: "Richard Goldbloom MD." No one in the family, or the profession, objected.

I was born on December 16, 1924, a birthday I share (though not in the same year) with Beethoven, Jane Austen, Noel Coward, Liv Ullman, and other notables. I was delivered into the world, screaming, in a small, five-bed private obstetrical suite on the top floor of Montreal's Medical Arts Building at the corner of Guy and Sherbrooke Streets. My father would one day have his office there. He would eventually share it with my brother and me. My *accoucheur*, who had established this small obstetrical suite as his private preserve, was Dr. James ("Jimmy") Duncan, the very first obstetrical specialist to practise in Montreal.

Precisely twenty-five years to the day after that event, I was a very green intern in a very white, starched outfit, serving on the obstetrical service of Montreal's Royal Victoria Hospital. I was paged to report to the case room where a woman was about to deliver. In those days, our duty as interns in the case room was mainly to observe. Eventually we might be permitted to cut the umbilical cord and, finally, to deliver the occasional baby, under close supervision, typically in uncomplicated "grand multiparas," that is, women who had had six to ten previous babies without difficulty and who probably could have delivered themselves without our help.

When I arrived in the case room the charge nurse informed me the baby was to be delivered by Dr. James Duncan, who would also arrive momentarily. I had no idea Dr. Duncan was still alive, much less delivering babies, but I was struck by the auspiciousness of our reunion on the anniversary of his attendance at my own birth.

It was a snowy, windy night, and Dr. Duncan arrived at the hospital clad in a heavy floor-length raccoon coat, *de rigueur* among wealthy men in Montreal in those days. I detected a faint whiff of alcohol on his breath. (A nurse later informed me he was known to have a tendency toward "elbow flexion.") Nevertheless, he seemed in full command of his obstetrical skills. Standing next to him and his breath gave me an instant flashback to the 1939 movie classic *Stagecoach* in which a wonderful character actor named Thomas Mitchell played the part of Doc Boone, a physician who was usually under the influence but was always able to come through in a crisis.

Once the baby was safely delivered, I couldn't wait to impress Dr. Duncan with the significance of our reunion. For some reason, he seemed less moved by the historic significance of the event. Still, he took the opportunity to sit down and reminisce about his early days. Most babies were then delivered at home by general practitioners. He told me his fee for a home delivery was five dollars, reduced to two if he arrived after the baby was born. Soon after setting up practice in Montreal, a young man brought his wife, seven months pregnant, to see him. "I told him the minute his wife began to have labour pains, he was to come and get me *immediately!*"

The father did as instructed and arrived on a snowy winter night to collect Dr. Duncan with a horse and sleigh. By the time they arrived at the door, however, "I could hear the baby crying in the bed," said Dr. Duncan. All those decades later, Duncan was still in mourning over the three dollars he had been cheated out of by that impatient baby.

I grew up in our family home above my father's office at 1543 Crescent Street, three blocks from the Medical Arts Building. Nowadays, if I tell anyone familiar with contemporary Montreal I grew up on Crescent Street, they look at me with total disbelief. Crescent Street is now lined with chic bars, restaurants and upscale boutiques. But between the 1920s and 1960s, there was nary a bar or boutique to be found there. Many, if not most, of the houses were occupied by doctors and their families. Both sides of Crescent Street were studded with physicians', surgeons' and dentists' offices. Typically, the doctors had offices on the ground floor, and their families lived on the two upper floors. It was a downscale version of London's Harley Street. Our former home is now an elegant jewellery store, but the façade is unchanged.

Next door to us was a photographic studio operated by two unmarried brothers whom we referred to privately as "the girls," since both spoke in high-pitched voices. Next to them lived another physician who maintained a private hospital of five beds. Rumour had it abortions were performed there.

Growing up on Crescent Street had its magical moments, especially in winter. This was decades before huge motorized ploughs and snow blowers. In winter, snow was simply pushed from the road to the sidewalk by horses pulling small ploughs. The snow accumulated to heights that often precluded a view of the opposite side of the street. The wooden ploughs were hinged so that when full they could be inverted, adding to the mountains of snow that lined both sides of the street. Residents would dig out narrow passageways between the huge piles of snow to gain access to the street.

To young boys, those snowy mountains were treasured assets. We dug out large caves in them, providing great places to hide. And when the piles grew really high they provided a kind of mountain-climbing experience that gave us enormous pleasure.

Decrepit old men drove horse-drawn carts up and down the back alley, shouting, "Rags, bones and bottles!" and on June 24, St. Jean Baptiste Day, truckloads of French-Canadian children from rural Quebec would drive into town and park in front of our house, just below Sherbrooke Street, to watch the annual parade. Some would ring our front doorbell and plead: "*Excusez, Monsieur, est-ce-que je peux faire pipi?*"

There was no shortage of neighbourhood kids to play with. Uncle David Ballon's tribe of six children lived just down the street, and other cousins lived in my grandparents' home. A quick dash through the lane that ran next to our house through to Bishop Street and we were there.

After Grandma and Grandpa died and the assorted aunts, uncles and cousins moved elsewhere, the Bishop Street home remained in the family's possession. During World War II the family loaned it to the Canadian Jewish Congress to be used as a rest and recreation centre for Jewish servicemen on leave. It was known as Ballon House.

Buffalo Bill

My great uncle William Goldbloom (a.k.a. Buffalo Bill) was over eighty and I was only fourteen when we first met, but I had never encountered anyone even vaguely like him. He lived in Prince Rupert, BC, where he was a fur trader. He had a white moustache and Vandyke beard and wore a wide-brimmed Stetson at a rakish angle. Across his vest, which *partially* restrained an impressive paunch, hung a heavy silver chain from which was suspended a solid gold 1897 coin featuring a profile of Queen Victoria, commemorating her Diamond Jubilee. The ensemble was completed by an impressive cane and an ever-present cigar. He carried a straight pin in his coat lapel, with which he would impale the cigar butt when it became too short to hold between his thumb and forefinger, ensuring every stogie was good to the last puff.

We met in the late 1940s in my parents' Montreal apartment on Côte des Neiges Road. By then they had moved from their Crescent Street home. William greeted my mother — whom he'd never met before — with a hearty smack on her well-corseted backside. My mother, a woman who had refined Victorian propriety to a religious observance, was the one woman in all of Canada who should *never* have been saluted with that particular gesture. Mother was predictably incensed: "Get that man out of my house!" she hissed at my father.

Before this visit, my father had only encountered William on the rarest of occasions, and his mere existence seemed to have been concealed by a veil of silence. I learned later his relationship with his brother Sam (my Grandpa) had been punctuated by an endless cycle of arguments, followed by short-lived reconciliations. The culmination of such arguments would occur when Grandpa would revive (for the umpteenth time) the memory of an episode from back in the *shul* in their Lithuanian shtetl. Uncle William had farted, and Grandpa had never forgiven him the sacrilege. For decades thereafter, Grandpa would issue the *coup de grâce* to any argument by recalling that scandalous event from their boyhood. Uncle William would invariably have the last word: "OK, Sam, so I won't come to your funeral, and don't you come to mine!"

Notwithstanding my mother's horror of this unmannered boor, I took an instant liking to Uncle William. No one this colourful had ever crossed our threshold, much less claimed membership in our family. Uncle William had come to Montreal by train, via Vancouver. He had left Prince Rupert bearing gifts . . . three pairs of good-sized gold nuggets, salvaged from the gold rush days, each pair mounted as elegant cufflinks. When he stopped to change trains in Vancouver, he presented one pair to my cousin Ted. He brought the other two sets to Montreal as gifts for Victor and me. On the return trip to Prince Rupert, Uncle William almost certainly got into a poker game (as was his custom) and probably lost heavily (as was *also* his custom) because, during the stopover in Vancouver, he repossessed my cousin Ted's cufflinks. Ted never saw them again.

William Goldbloom's history was as colourful as he was. He was just thirteen years old when he came to Canada in 1857. He trekked to Fort Garry, later renamed Winnipeg, where he worked for a while as a peddler. Later, he travelled to New York, where he met a beautiful teenaged girl named Rachel Silverson. William reportedly swept Rachel off her feet and brought her to Fort

Garry where they married. What attracted Rachel to William in the first place was never clear. William was illiterate, a rough-and-tumble guy, with a keen eye for women who spoke English with a Russian-Jewish accent. Their first daughter, Nellie, was (I was told) the first Jewish girl to be born in that outpost. A second daughter, Flo, was born in 1885, the year Louis Riel was hanged.

I remember Flo and Nellie well. Nellie was a bit of a marital athlete, getting hitched at least twice. Many years ago I attended a party at which Flo, already elderly, was present. A guest remarked to her: "You know, your father was one of the early settlers of the Canadian West." Cousin Flo, in family tradition, was never at a loss for a witty response: "That's true" she said. "He was an early settler. He usually settled for fifty cents on the dollar . . . and sometimes twenty-five!"

In 1905, William and Rachel moved to Vancouver where he opened the first ladies' dress manufacturing plant in that city at 210 Pender Street East. Rachel, who was highly principled, stubborn and refined, and spoke flawless English, soon became the matriarch of Vancouver's tiny Jewish community. Several Jewish philanthropic organizations came into existence in her home, including, in 1910, the first Vancouver chapter of Hadassah, which bore her name for many years. Rachel was also well connected politically. She knew many officials of the Canadian Pacific Railway and would often intervene on behalf of some travelling salesman who had come west from Montreal and had failed to earn his train fare home.

In 1916, William took leave of Vancouver and moved eight hundred kilometres north to the fledgling community of Prince Rupert, while Rachel stayed behind to run their dress shop. He began his career in Prince Rupert selling general merchandise and trading furs, which became his full-time occupation. He acquired a permanent location on Third Avenue where he had an eye-catching sign emblazoned on the window. It featured, in profile, a large, handsome beaver under the inscription: "Prince Rupert Fur and Hide Co. Ltd." Beneath were inscribed the words: "W. Goldbloom, The Trapper's Friend."

Rachel moved to Prince Rupert for a short while, but the experiment was doomed to failure. Their marriage deteriorated and she returned to Vancouver. William continued to visit periodically to see his two daughters and, later, his grandchildren, whom he adored and indulged.

William's fur business had two components. He traded in raw furs he bought from the Indian trappers and sold them at retail in his store. Whenever he got word skins were available at some coastal Indian village, he would use any available means of transport — horse, canoe or dogsled — to be the first on the spot. After accumulating a quantity of raw skins (mink, marten, beaver, fisher or otter) he would bundle them in burlap sacks and ship them off to fur auction markets in Vancouver, Winnipeg and Montreal.

Years later, when coastal cruises to Alaska became popular, the ships would stop at Prince Rupert for a few hours, and tourists would descend on his store. When an upper-crust lady tried on a silver fox cape, William would comment she looked very nice, but that she would look *really* nice in bearskin. Invariably, the woman would be struck speechless, uncertain of his precise meaning. William would simply stand there with his disarming smile and twinkling eyes.

William was an inveterate card player and gambler. No sooner had he boarded one of the small Union Steamship vessels that travelled up and down the British Columbia coast visiting the tiny inlets and fish-canning plants than he would parade up and down the decks, bellowing out his customary invitation: "Any poker players? Any pinochle players?"

Dr. Geddes Large, a respected Prince Rupert physician and chronicler of the town's history, reported that William was also "the butt of many a joke, in some cases an effort on the part of the prankster to even the score for Goldbloom's biting tongue." On one occasion, two members of the Department of Fisheries stole a mink skin out of William's pack on a boat and gave it to a waiter, with instructions to sell it back to William. After the sale had been made, they broke the news to their victim. But William took these pranks in his stride and invariably gave as good as he got.

In his 1960 book on the town's history, Dr. Large mused: "What Rupert old-timer will forget William Goldbloom sitting in his armchair on the sidewalk outside his fur store on Third Avenue, exchanging banter with all and sundry as they passed his door?" Unfortunately for Canadian history, the full measure of William's wit was a bit much for the good doctor. He continued: "His cheerful vulgarity was the source of numerous stories, not all of which, unfortunately, lend themselves to the printed word."

I remember one story that would certainly have qualified for Dr. Large's X-rating. Uncle William had visited a local bank to negotiate a loan (possibly to compensate for a business failure or gambling losses). He was ushered into the bank manager's office. William opened the conversation as follows: "Tell me, did you take a bat' [bath] this morning?" "Why do you ask?" replied the manager. "Because," William explained, "I have to ask you for a thousand dollars and I know I'll have to kiss your ass to get it."

Uncle William lived in the back of his store, cooking his own meals, until he was in his eighties. He then moved across the continent to spend his last few years in his daughter's home. His appetite for food was as prodigious as his appetite for life. His daily diet included four basic food groups: black bread, highly spiced salami, pickles and whole, raw cucumbers. When he visited Montreal at age eighty-three, my father noticed his huge appetite and insatiable thirst. Suspecting diabetes, he arranged for him to be seen by Dr. Ezra Lozinski, who confirmed the diagnosis and admitted him to the Jewish General Hospital in a vain attempt to control his diabetes.

When William was about to be discharged from hospital, Dr. Lozinski reiterated his instructions about diabetic care, warning him about his diet, smoking, drinking and other misdemeanors. Lozinski's parting words were: "Now, Mr. Goldbloom, be sure to do as I say." William replied: "You know me, Doc . . . anything you say, Doc." Predictably, he immediately returned to his pre-diabetic "unhealthy" lifestyle. He was not a heavy drinker, but like his brother, my Grandpa Sam, he loved his glass of *schnapps* (whisky), straight, in a single gulp.

From a medical perspective William could never have been categorized as the ideal patient. On one occasion he spent Christmas in hospital in Prince Rupert. He rallied several other patients and they threw a party that became so rowdy they were all thrown out of the hospital — possibly the first time in Canadian medical history that hospital patients were given a "dishonourable" discharge.

He paid no attention to the dire warnings about his diet. He continued his daily regime of salami, steak, whole cucumbers and sometimes several eggs at a time. We learned later that Uncle William had two important characteristics in common with the late comedian George Burns: the ever-present cigar and the fact that he outlived his doctors. He died at age ninety-two.

Paradoxically, in contrast with his wildly unpredictable, rowdy lifestyle, his illiteracy and lack of formal education, he had his own version of strong emotional attachment to synagogue liturgy and to religious observance. Although there were only three Jewish families in Prince Rupert, William managed to round up more than fifty Jewish members of the Canadian and US military stationed near the town during World War II and hosted a Passover Seder for them. A large photograph of the event shows William standing proudly in his Stetson at the head table, beaming down at long tables of happy servicemen. His annual holiday from Prince Rupert was a trip to Vancouver to attend Rosh Hashanah (Jewish New Year) and Yom Kippur (Day of Atonement) services. His grandson recalled how William would come to synagogue "fortified with his small, gold-plated snuff box." In those days, to raise enough money to maintain the synagogue, it was customary to auction off *aliyahs* — the honour of being called up to participate in a part of the service such as reciting the blessings before and after a reading from the Torah. The locals knew William would be good for a bid of about $150 for an *aliyah*, so they would use a couple of strategically located shills to bid him up to that price.

Given his striking appearance, his colourful turn of phrase and his love of a good time, Uncle William attracted attention wherever he went. He reminded people of other striking characters, including Buffalo Bill Cody (whose first two names were so often applied to him), Colonel Harlan Sanders (of Kentucky Fried Chicken fame) and French President Poincaré. On one of his visits to Montreal he was spotted by a news photographer and written up in a local newspaper. Uncle William had all the raunchiness and vulgarity that also marked so many other pioneers of the Canadian West. To well-bred folks like my mother and my grandmother Goldbloom, he was a fearsome old reprobate to be avoided at all costs . . . and certainly *never* to claim as a family member. But I found his irreverence and *joie de vivre* highly infectious. He was never mean-spirited. Above all, he never took himself or anyone else too seriously. He truly believed laughter was the best medicine. I hope I inherited a smidgen of his philosophy.

Eva

Another interesting family member, a generation later, was Eva, my father's younger sister. I remember her with tremendous affection. Born in 1893, she was a compulsive performer and a devastating mimic. She learned to dance when very young and my grandparents put her on display at every opportunity. She went on to a professional career in the theatre, and for many years, using the stage name Eva Goodrich,[§] was the leading lady in a stock company. She never lost her sense of the dramatic or her sense of humour.

Her recollections of her own parents (my Goldbloom grandparents), written in her diary, were colourful and precise:

> *They were without question the two most mismatched people in the whole wide world. She was a strict disciplinarian à la Queen Victoria. She went by all the rules. And my father was a devil-may-care guy . . . a wonderful man, really . . . terrific sense of humour, full of life. They absolutely didn't belong together. My mother had no sense of humour . . . everything was on the line. But she produced some pretty good kids.*

[§] My father also adopted the name, calling himself Alton Goodrich during his years as a professional actor.

When we came back from Europe [the aforementioned stay in Lithuania, living with relatives] and went to live in Worcester, Mass., I had shown some talent for acting. I was very emotional . . . weeping and crying a lot. My father thought I was God's gift to the theatrical world and I was sent for elocution lessons (they didn't have acting lessons in those days). There were two other girls at elocution school . . . one was May Collins, a redhead; the other was Zara Cully, a black girl. Black people were rare in Worcester at that time. We were ten or eleven years old and were very good friends. I didn't realize until many years later that she played the mother on the TV program The Jeffersons.

We moved from Worcester to Winnipeg, where we stayed for three years and where I graduated from high school. After that, we moved to Vancouver. A theatre stock company (The Empress Stock Company) had opened there, so I applied for a job and was accepted. I was with them for seven years. The leading man (who became my leading man) was Ray Collins. He became a famous actor on Perry Mason, *throughout the whole series. If I had had any sense (or guts) I would have followed him. I had a very good radio voice, which I had tried out in Vancouver . . . but of course I was a good girl and stayed at home because my mother was desperate. She couldn't be left alone, because my father was away all the time and she was so dependent on me that I couldn't leave.*

At the theatre, I performed every week . . .
in crappy plays, like East Lynne, Little Lord Fauntleroy *(I played the mother) and* A Tale of

Two Cities. *I was living at home then. My mother
loved to come to the theatre, but when she left the
theatre, she was home.*

Several characteristics made Aunt Eva a favourite of mine.
She loved to laugh, was an excellent mimic and raconteur, had
colourful friends and enjoyed life to the fullest. Although her
greatest pleasure was driving her car — she owned one until her
death at age eighty-nine — she was a terrible driver. Five-foot-
one and shrinking, she kept two pillows on the driver's seat so
she could see over the steering wheel. Her driving style featured
a unique combination of speed and inaccuracy.

Her 1971, two-door, fire-engine-red Chevy Nova was her
most precious possession, symbolizing the mobility she maintained all of her life. But its fenders were bashed in from her
many entanglements with buses, streetcars, and parked cars.
Steve, the honest and skilful young mechanic who looked after
her car and for whom she baked cakes, had his hands full keeping
the innards of her car working. He considered body repairs of her
vehicle to be a costly, futile exercise.

The car — and Steve — would play a central role in a unique
romantic episode, long after her husband had died. The story
deserves retelling, and no one told it better than my dear (now
deceased) first cousin, Eva's daughter, Eleanor Haas:

> *If you had predicted that one day, in her declining
> years, my mother would have an affair with a
> gentleman when both of them were close to eighty,
> she wouldn't have believed you. But I'm her daughter
> and I can tell you it really did happen. Sometimes
> I'm afraid my mother wouldn't have liked me
> telling this story . . . but on the other hand, she never
> minded telling jokes on herself.*

It happened at the end of the year my father died and my husband left . . . a bad year all around. Mother and I were picking up our respective pieces. I had three sad, angry children who couldn't understand their father's leaving. Mother had a life alone after fifty years of marriage, a bank statement she couldn't balance, and a car in chronic need of repair.

One day, out of the blue, she telephoned to ask if I would come over after work. She needed to talk to me privately about something. Although I'd learned not to respond to all her urgent summonses, a certain uneasiness in her voice prompted me to make arrangements for my children and comply.

When I arrived at her apartment she poured me a cup of tea and told me that next week a man was coming to visit her . . . someone she had known before she was married.

"Of course, he'll be staying here at my apartment," she said. I couldn't help but glance in the direction of the apartment's only bedroom.

"Where will he sleep?" I asked.

"That depends," she answered coquettishly, with a look seldom seen on the face of one's seventy-nine-year-old mother.

When Eleanor met Charlie Flash at dinner at her mother's apartment soon after, she took in his ultra-suede jacket and white multi-floral tie. "Quite a guy," she thought. Over dinner, he described to her "in excruciating detail, his prostate tumour, his angina, his high blood pressure and his circulatory dysfunction."

The next morning Eleanor dropped off a wicker basket so Charlie and her mother could enjoy a picnic in Inverness, north of San Francisco where she was living at the time.

Charlie answered the door wearing his red striped pyjamas. As I handed him the basket I peeked over his shoulder and saw that his bed the previous night had been the living room couch. But this was to mark his last night on the couch. After Charlie went home, I asked Mother a lot of questions: Where had she met him, what had he been to her, had he known my father (and what did he *think, and other impertinences)?*

They had met in Winnipeg. Charlie was seventeen and a boarder in the Goldbloom family home. Eva never paid much attention to him then, and they never socialized. Charlie was very poor. He had had to leave school after eighth grade, and when he first came to live with them he was working as a bookkeeper with Imperial Oil. Eva was just a schoolgirl, beginning to go to skating and tobogganing parties. "Of course, they were well chaperoned," Eva said. But on coming home from these parties, there Charlie would be, she lamented, waiting at the door in his dressing gown and slippers. That was the first sign of his jealousy.

Mother and the family moved to Vancouver when she was ready for college, and when that happened, Charlie got himself transferred out there too. That was the first sign of his intent. The year was 1916

and men were scarce at home. "Charlie and I
often had dates together," she said, "but he knew I
wasn't seriously interested in him so he soon went
overseas with the Canadian Army."

After the war, when Eva met, fell in love with and decided to
marry a handsome, intelligent ex-RCAF pilot named Mo Brotman, she told Charlie she couldn't see him anymore. "He was
furious, Eleanor," she told her daughter. "He went away and I
never heard from him again . . . until now."

Now . . . Charlie soon became a frequent visitor, buying gifts,
often swooping Eva off to Las Vegas, or Lake Tahoe, or Reno. Eva
was a blackjack *aficionado.* Once they went to Hawaii, on another
occasion a Caribbean cruise.

One day, while talking to Charlie, I said to him:
"You've known and liked my mother for a long
time, haven't you, Charlie?"

"Sure, I've liked her. A lot. But she did something to
me a long time ago I'll never get over . . . I certainly
can't trust her," he said.

I knew he was waiting for me to ask for an
explanation, but I changed the subject once more. I
really didn't want to get that personal with Charlie.
But later I asked Mother if she hadn't left something
out of the Charlie Flash story: "He said you did
something to him years ago that made him not trust
you anymore. What was it?"

She sighed: "I did something that wasn't very nice.
When I told him I wasn't going to see him anymore,

I just couldn't bring myself to tell him I was going to marry your father. I was afraid of what he'd do. But he kept hounding me for the reason, so I promised we'd meet one day and I'd tell him. We made a date, but when the day came, I lost my nerve and didn't show up. I think he's never forgiven me for that."

Charlie's jealousy and his suspicion that my Aunt Eva might be two-timing him persisted to the very end of his life. By a curious turn of events, the object of his final fit of jealous anger was a young auto mechanic named Steve, who for years had somehow contrived to keep Eva's ancient automobile running. On one of the last times she brought her car in for repairs, Steve informed her that she had already spent far too much money on her car; he wanted her to leave the vehicle with him for several days so that he could fix it up properly; and he wasn't going to charge her for the repairs.

When Charlie got word of this plan, he jumped to the obvious conclusion: that Eva and Steve, the mechanic, must be "having an affair." That was the straw that gave the proverbial camel a spinal fracture, and Charlie disappeared from Eva's life without a trace. Some time later he died, several years before Eva did. To her complete surprise, she learned that Charlie Flash had left her a bequest of five thousand dollars. She referred to it as "my inheritance."

Here's the postscript: I visited San Francisco shortly after Eva had received the news of her unexpected windfall. Naturally, I asked her what she was going to do with the money. She thought she might buy "a new, second-hand" car. I suggested that out of respect for Charlie's memory, and knowing of Charlie's consuming jealousy of Steve the mechanic, a car might be the one item she should *not* purchase with that bequest. She never did buy another car.

Unorthodox Jewish Atheist

My convictions about religion — not just my own, but all varieties — have crystallized over a lifetime, partly based on personal experience and partly on exposure to the customs and beliefs of other faiths.

My earliest memories of going to synagogue date from early childhood. I walked with my Ballon grandparents from their Bishop Street home to the Shaar Hashomayim ("Gate of Heaven") Synagogue on Côte St. Antoine Road in Westmount — a twenty-five-minute journey — and back each week. They would never have thought of driving on the Sabbath.

The "Shaar" was nominally a Conservative synagogue, but in practice it was more than halfway to Orthodox. Men and women were seated separately. At least the women weren't segregated behind a curtain, or isolated in a balcony facing the backs of the men below, or kept in even more severe forms of purdah, as was the practice centuries ago. In Prague, for example, women were permitted only to peek *from outdoors* through tiny slits in the thick stone walls at the sacred proceedings inside. Such segregation was presumably designed to allow the men to focus exclusively on their communication with God, without a thought to the female of the species and sins of the flesh. We Jews didn't invent sexism, but we were certainly in on the ground floor.

Two particular recollections are engraved forever in my memory, dating from my earliest exposure to the synagogue services. First, most of the men, especially the older ones, recited their prayers in Hebrew at such supersonic speed — one hundred words per minute, with gusts to two hundred — they could only have learned them by rote (as they *had* done) and certainly had no time (even if they had actually understood the words) to reflect on their actual meaning. Teaching children to recite prayers by rote is an unfortunate feature of many of the world's so-called great religions.

But my second, and most vivid visual (and aural) memory of my childhood *shul* attendance was of a certain elderly gent, Mr. H., who sat directly behind my grandfather (*and* my brother and me). Mr. H. kept a very large brass cuspidor, or spittoon, under the footrest of his pew (that meant right under our pew). When we least expected it, he would slide one foot forward, extricate the cuspidor from its hiding place under our pew, and expectorate loudly, raising great volumes of secretions from the depths of his bronchi. (In a classic example of onomatopoeia, the pre-expectorant "wind-up" that cleanses the entire bronchial system is known in Yiddish as a *chrakë*, the "*ch*" pronounced as in Lo*ch* Lomond.) To this very day I cringe as I recall the experience.

It was the first in a series of events and reflections that would crystallize my opposition to organized religion in any form, while I remained unalterably and proudly Jewish in other respects.

My father had given me valuable insights into the why and how of synagogue services. In Eastern Europe, in the eighteenth and nineteenth centuries, people (primarily men) went to synagogue to engage in a strictly personal communion with the deity. This relationship was so individual every man prayed in his own way. While there was a traditionally prescribed sequence to the prayers, the rate of recitation was highly individual — every man for himself — and, unlike today's "modern" services, simultaneity was not considered a particular virtue of religious observance. To the unfamiliar onlooker, the impression was one of chaotic babble or bedlam. Between prayers, worshippers would talk to each other about whatever (or whomever) they wished.

Formal sermons, as we now know them, were not part of the Jewish tradition. They were introduced into synagogue services only in the nineteenth century. At the extreme of Reform Judaism, services are conducted largely in a highly orderly (very "churchified") fashion: no rhythmic rocking, no chanting, most prayers recited in unison (*and* in English) with only periodic smatterings of Hebrew. In Reform congregations, hymns are sometimes accompanied by organ music, not unlike Christian church services. Some Jews, of course, particularly the Orthodox, feel Reform Judaism has gone totally overboard to a degree they find totally foreign. This notion was immortalized in a wry joke about a synagogue that was "so Reform" (Christianized), it featured an outdoor sign proclaiming: "Closed on the High Holidays."

My unorthodox views on religion and its observances were further shaped by two medical school teachers. In the 1940s, during my medical student days, Dr. Karl Stern, an eminent and erudite psychiatrist, spoke to us about the role of ritual in preventing and relieving anxiety in our everyday lives. He reminded us of the silly, ritualistic games we played as children: avoiding stepping on cracks in the sidewalk ("step on a crack, break your mother's back"), or not inhaling when you passed a graveyard. As we grow and mature, we think of such rituals as meaningless, childish games. But Karl Stern pointed out that, while we may abandon the rituals of childhood as we grow and mature, we simply substitute *other* rituals to relieve our anxieties.

"Adult" rituals can take the form of religious or other observance (say the prescribed number of Hail Marys and your sins will be forgiven). Dr. Stern asked each of us to think about the personal rituals we practised when we retired to bed at night or got up in the morning. Perhaps, he suggested, you lie on your right side for three minutes, then turn on your back for a few more minutes, then roll over onto your left side, then fall asleep. He pointed out that if we induced anxiety by altering a simple quasi-religious ritual of our daily lives, we would probably have difficulty falling asleep.

In most religions — Orthodox Judaism, Islam and Christianity, especially Catholicism — ritual plays a central anxiety-easing role, though many would ascribe loftier, more spiritual purposes to such systematized observances.

Often, religious observances have been trivialized to the point where they have lost any connection with "God." Think about the baseball player who won't stand up to bat without making the sign of the cross before the first pitch; the boxer who does likewise just before trying to pound another man into oblivion; or the Catholic lady sitting next to me on the plane one time who had to "say the beads" on takeoff and landing. As for me, I'm simply "praying" the pilot had a good night's sleep and wasn't boozing it up the night before.

Another of my medical school teachers who influenced my thinking on religion was Hans Selye, who would become famous for his research on stress. We chatted one day about the conflict between science and religion. He repeated an exchange he had once had with a German Jesuit priest. The cleric encapsulated their two different perspectives succinctly:

"Du sagst es ist wie ein Wunder . . . wir sagen es ist ein Wunder." ("You say it is like a miracle . . . we say it *is* a miracle.")

The historical track record of organized religions on issues such as peace, love and brotherhood (actions as opposed to words) has been less than stellar. More people have been slain in the name of God than in any other cause. The Spanish Inquisition and the Crusades are just two examples.

The various concepts of an "afterlife" among the major religions leave me dumbfounded. I've reached an age when I attend more funerals than weddings and bar mitzvahs combined. I have read or listened to too many eulogies replete with the standard euphemisms for death ("passed away," "with the angels," "with Jesus," "at peace," "eternal rest," "in a better place" and all the others). Some clergy and ordinary folk observe, "He [or She] is up there looking down and smiling at us." Hearing this, I can never resist the urge to look upward. Invariably, I am disappointed.

My personal brand of Jewish atheism has been further entrenched by acquaintance with certain folks who are deeply dedicated to religious observance and regular ritual but whose personal moral and ethical lives leave much to be desired. My father used to sing a song he recalled from vaudeville days. "He goes to church on Sundays, and they *say* that he's an honest man."

But notwithstanding my inclination toward the Richard Dawkins and Christopher Hitchens schools of thought, nothing has lessened my attachment to the traditional Jewish way of thinking: the centrality of family, the supreme value of education, the importance of traditional Jewish philosophy in the practice of medicine, the too-often forgotten tradition of anonymity when making charitable gifts and, not least, the central roles of humour and good food. As a Jewish pediatric colleague of mine once put it: "If I had my life to live over, I'd live over a delicatessen."

Add to this the observation by some other forgotten philosopher that the central message of most historical Jewish holiday celebrations (except Yom Kippur) could be encapsulated in three short statements: "They tried to kill us. We won. Let's eat!"

Being a Montrealer by birth, a pilgrimage to Schwartz's Delicatessen on St. Lawrence Boulevard ("the Main" of Mordecai Richler) for real Montreal smoked meat remains a quasi-religious observance, and my daily breakfast features a Montreal bagel (unparalleled in the annals of bagelry). Finally, my addiction to

Jewish humour is of narcotic proportions. In historical terms, hardship and deprivation have always bred humour (humour = tragedy plus time), and wit has served as a survival weapon through centuries of persecution. Thus, the people of Newfoundland and Cape Breton, like the Jews of Eastern Europe, endured hardship over many generations and can always find humour in unexpected places and situations.

There is an important caveat to my cynical view of so many religious observances of all faiths, including my own. As Voltaire is reported to have said, "I do not agree with what you say, sir, but I will defend to the death your right to say it." By the same token, part of our duty to patients is to respect their freedom to follow their personal religious practices and customs, providing they don't threaten their child's health or survival, as occasionally occurs in withholding a potentially life-saving blood transfusion for a child from a Jehovah's Witness family.

On rare occasions, respect for a patient's and family's religion calls for more than mere passive tolerance. When I was a medical student, my father told me that if no Catholic priest was handy, anyone (even a Jew!) could baptize a dying child. In my younger days I did this on a couple of occasions and was able to reassure the grieving parents that I had done so, much to their relief. I recently checked the veracity of my father's view on this issue by calling my friend, Rev. James M. Hayes, retired Catholic Archbishop of Halifax. He unequivocally confirmed my right (and duty!) to perform this ritual when no clergy were available. I can only assume this validation may have spared me (or the patient, or both of us) from eternal hellfire and damnation.

I struggled for a long time with the question of whether religious observances of any kind or denomination could be shown to provide specific benefits distinguishable from the relief from anxiety most of us desire (and often receive) from other types of ritualistic behaviours.

I have, of course, watched respectfully when many families, with or without benefit of clergy, have prayed fervently for the recovery of a sick relative and have asked myself whether such devotion could be proven to improve outcomes or simply gave comfort and consolation to the supplicants. Admittedly, not a worthless accomplishment.

In 2011, the Cochrane Collaboration, an international organization that reviews evidence on a wide range of health issues and employs rigorous criteria for determining the quality of the evidence, published a massive review, "Intercessory Prayer for the Attenuation of Ill Health." In line with strict evidentiary rules, the authors included ten studies, comprising 7,807 patients, in their meta-analysis. Most compared prayer plus treatment as usual to usual treatment without prayer. There was *no* significant difference in the recovery from illness or death between those prayed for and those not prayed for. In one trial that differentiated between high or low risk of death, people at high risk of death were more likely to live if prayed for and less likely to have specific complications. Finally, to confuse the issue further, those who knew they were being prayed for had *more* complications than those with no knowledge of being prayed for.

Admittedly, these complex studies may be difficult to analyze and to compare. But even to a reader biased in *either* direction, the evidence available could never be accorded a higher rating than the Scottish legal verdict of "not proven." As always, many people will reason that if praying does no harm, why not give it a try?

Almost every situation reminds me of a joke, and this one is no exception. The story is told of a famous Russian pianist named Smirnovsky who was scheduled to give a recital at the Moscow Conservatory during the Communist era. The hall was packed, hushed and expectant. Ten minutes after the recital was scheduled to begin, the manager walked out on stage and announced:

"Comrades, I am sorry to inform you that the great Smirnovsky has taken ill and will be unable to play tonight." At that, a man in the balcony stood up and shouted, "Give him an enema!" The manager ignored this rude outburst and marched off the stage. Many in the audience made no effort to leave the hall, as if hoping for a miracle. Moments later, the manager reappeared and announced: "Comrades, with great regret I must inform you that the great Smirnovsky has died. He will never play again." Once again, the man in the balcony was on his feet: "Give him an enema!" he shouted. By now, the manager, enraged, shouted back: "Comrade, I have just told you, Smirnovsky is dead! What good will an enema do?" "What harm will it do?" replied the voice from the balcony.

"Six of the Best"

As Montreal's first fully trained pediatrician, it didn't take my father long to establish an enviable reputation throughout the community — anglophone, francophone, Jewish, Protestant, Catholic, and *les autres* — with a level of veneration that bordered on deification. His clinical skills were legendary, and stories about how he had ferreted out a correct diagnosis when others had failed were told, enlarged and retold. Francophone patients would gush: "*Ah, docteur Goldbloom, après vous, le bon Dieu!*" To some extent, such veneration was rooted in Montreal mythology, which held that if you wanted your family to be *really* safe and secure, you should have "a Jewish doctor and a French-Canadian lawyer." To my knowledge, neither belief was ever put to the test of a randomized, controlled clinical trial. But soon after I started a pediatric practice, I recall asking the parent of a new patient: "*Madame, qui est-ce-qui vous a référé?*" She replied: "*Ah, je ne sais pas . . . j'ai voulu simplement avoir un bon médecin juif.*"

The Montreal Jewish community worshipped with similar fervour at my father's shrine. At social gatherings, Jewish mothers would fawn over him: "Oh, Dr. Goldbloom, you *must* remember me . . . you saved my daughter's life!" More often than not, he could not recall such legendary acts of heroism. Sometimes, out of curiosity, he would check his records, only to discover the child had had nothing more life-threatening than chicken pox or a strep throat. But to many patients, perception is reality.

Partly because of my parents' extensive connections in the broader community, and partly because my brother Victor and I attended a school that was virtually 100 per cent anglophone and Christian (mostly Protestant, with a small sprinkling of Catholics), we soon developed a degree of social comfort with a wide spectrum of friends of all faiths in that larger community.

During that era, many Montreal Jewish families lived out their lives, geographically, socially and educationally, in the secure bosom of their own community. Their children attended parochial schools and went to Jewish summer camps in the Laurentians if their families could afford it.

My brother Victor and I did have a circle of close friends in the Jewish community, most being the offspring of our parents' friends. All of them lived in Westmount, an almost exclusively anglophone preserve. During those years, it was possible to live an entire lifetime in Upper Westmount and never hear a word of French spoken!

My parents clung to the traditional Jewish belief that a good education was the greatest gift they could bestow on their children. After carefully researching the options, my father decided we should be enrolled at Selwyn House, where we were the first Jewish kids to attend. Soon after, we were joined by two first cousins from Crescent Street, Edward and Jonathan Ballon.

But beyond the culture of this classic boys' school with its British traditions, my father could see the writing on the wall when most anglophones couldn't even see the wall. Thus he decided Victor and I should learn to speak French as early and as fluently as possible. He had previously taught himself French (he had a good ear) by reading French classics such as Voltaire and de Maupassant and attending French theatre productions. But most important, he made it a point to *speak* French to *all* of his francophone patients. As a result, he spoke French fluently, and his medical practice included large numbers of francophones from every level of society. To give Victor and me a jump start toward functional bilingualism, he hired a private teacher to come to our house and teach us conversational French. With additional training in school and, ultimately, with daily experience in pediatric practice, we both became quite fluent, Victor more so than I. Years later, he would become a Quebec cabinet minister in the Bourassa government, and still later, Canada's federal Commissioner of Official Languages. Some francophone Quebecers said he spoke better French than they did.

In addition to French, my father wanted us to learn Hebrew, not just to learn the language of prayer but to speak it in the Sephardic pronunciation, as was then spoken in Palestine and, to this day, in the state of Israel. He hired a teacher, a gentle woman named Luba Gordon, to give us private lessons at home. All went well until the day she was preparing my brother Victor to do the Torah reading for his bar mitzvah at Shaar Hashomayim Synagogue, the *shul* attended by many of Montreal's older, upper-crust Jewish families.

Word somehow reached the synagogue board that this Goldbloom boy was going to perform his Torah reading in Sephardic Hebrew. My father was informed, in no uncertain terms, such a break with tradition would not be allowed. He countered that, in that case, Victor's bar mitzvah would be moved to the Spanish and Portuguese Synagogue on Stanley Street, where Sephardic Hebrew was the norm (and where, incidentally, the rabbi, a witty Englishman named Charles Bender, was a close family friend). Possibly because my father was so revered in the Montreal community, the synagogue board reluctantly caved and Victor was permitted to do his Torah readings in the Sephardic Hebrew pronunciation. Nowadays, folks find it impossible to believe such a contretemps over Hebrew pronunciation could take place in *any* synagogue.

This was not the only aspect of our lives in which my father deviated from local tradition. Then as now, around July 1 each year, many middle-class parents, heaving a great sigh of relief, shipped their children off to private summer camps where canoe trips, sailing, swimming, campfires, singsongs and general camaraderie were the order of the day. With our education always uppermost in his mind, my father decided we should travel to Europe *as a family* and see the great sights. This became an annual excursion, beginning when I was only four or five years old and continuing until the clouds of World War II began to gather. Our memorable trips included visits to Europe's great museums and palaces, to Stratford-on-Avon to share my father's passion for Shakespeare, to Holland where Victor and I learned to eat cheese and herring for breakfast and to Scheveningen where we swam and rode donkeys on the beach. On one of our last prewar family vacations, we drove in a rented car from Stratford-on-Avon to John O'Groats at the northern tip of Scotland. In another experience indelibly imprinted on my memory, as we were touring the Royal Palace in Stockholm, our guide (who presumably considered us "cute") allowed each of us to sit for a brief moment on the Swedish throne. I still remember feeling like king for a day (actually for about five to ten seconds). Had I been granted another moment or two, I would have issued an edict of some kind, but we were swiftly dethroned.

Meanwhile, back at Selwyn House in Montreal, we were required to observe a strict dress code: school blazer, white shirt, school tie (yellow-and-black horizontal stripes), grey flannel shorts, grey socks and black shoes. The student body was exclusively male and Christian, mainly Protestant, and white — not a dark skin as far as the eye could see. When we wore our yellow-and-black horizontally striped sweaters for hockey or soccer, we looked like a swarm of bees (and were so nicknamed with derision by some public school kids). Decades later, having travelled in rural Africa and India and having seen even the poorest of children observing a simple version of the school dress code, I realize how much there is to be said for school uniforms, which de-emphasize class distinctions within the school body and eliminate competitive dressing by juvenile *fashionistas*.

Classes were small at Selwyn House, typically fifteen or fewer. Learning was obligatory, sports participation mandatory and discipline strict. By the time I reached the sixth form (equivalent to second year high school), my entire class comprised six boys! There were only two teachers of the female persuasion, both (to the cruel eyes of youth) unsalvageable spinsters: Miss Snead (I still think this a perfect name for a schoolmarm) and Miss Bruce. Both were of severe mien; their pedagogy was strictly limited to the first two grades. Thereafter, we were taught exclusively by "the masters," as they were known. The ultimate form of discipline was the cane, administered by the headmaster for almost any misdemeanour you could name, such as talking or fooling around in class. Miscreants — I was among them periodically — were required to line up in the hall outside the headmaster's office promptly at 3 p.m.

The headmaster, Mr. Geoffrey Wanstall, was a severe-looking man with an iron-grey moustache, neatly trimmed and slightly upturned at the edges, who wore a well-tailored grey pinstriped suit. I don't recall him ever smiling. He would appear promptly at 3 p.m. at his office door and, with a silent crook of his forefinger, beckon the first in the lineup into his office. Once inside the door he would point wordlessly toward a large leather armchair with broad wooden arms. We would march toward it and "assume the angle," that is, bend far forward over the arm of the chair. He would then administer "six of the best," six strokes with a long, narrow bamboo cane that he swished through the air at high speed toward the target buttocks. I remember pulling my grey shorts down after returning home and twisting my head as far as it would go to inspect in the mirror the tell-tale (tell-tail?) red welts. Nowadays, such physical evidence might be photographed and used by social workers in court to document child abuse but, circa 1930, no one — neither the boys nor their parents — complained. The procedure was considered character-building.

The masters at Selwyn House included an interesting palette of characters, each one of a kind, but all effective pedagogues. Mr. Jackson, a tall, loping, forgiving man used to gently reprimand me for "playing the fool" (as was my custom). Mr. Anstey, an elderly gent, had shot off several toes while cleaning a rifle, we were told: He walked in short steps with a rocking, side-to-side gait. His grey-white hair was tousled, and his pants had not been pressed for several decades. He smoked a pipe almost incessantly during class; his teeth and fingers were stained deep yellow. On the left-hand side of the blackboard he inscribed the names of each boy in our class. He had a unique personal system of demerits for poor academic performances and behavioral misdemeanours. For each one he would inscribe what he referred to as a "scrag" opposite the name of the miscreant. Each scrag was symbolized by a small "x" on the blackboard. When a boy had accumulated a predetermined number of scrags, he would be required to pay the price in the form of extra remedial work or other punishment, including being dispatched to the headmaster's office to receive six of the best.

One year in the fifth form, I needed extra coaching in math, so it was arranged I would take the number 65 streetcar to Mr. Anstey's house for private tutoring on Saturday mornings. He lived in a tiny house on a short street that ran off Côte des Neiges Road. The only other occupant was his tiny spinster sister, who padded wordlessly about and greeted me with a nod. She would occasionally bring her brother a cup of tea and a biscuit but never offered me a thing. She never spoke and seemed fearful of her brother.

Mr. Anstey tried valiantly to inculcate in me various mathematical complexities, pacing back and forth as he puffed on his pipe. Occasionally he would digress to show me his various trinkets, including a wooden cigarette box that, he assured me, had been crafted of wood rescued from the hull of the *Royal George,* the wooden ship celebrated in a poem we had all had to memorize. There was no way to certify the authenticity of the box's lineage, but of course I believed him implicitly and reported this treasured relic to my parents. Some years later, I discovered Mr. Anstey was given to spinning rather fanciful versions of aspects of his life, including his personal friendships with the rich and famous. As a result, I still have some doubts about the lineage of his historic cigarette box.

This was not to be the only disillusionment I would suffer concerning one of our masters. The second involved a man I feared and admired, Monsieur Michel Seymour. Monsieur Seymour was from Alsace-Lorraine and spoke English with a French accent reminiscent of Charles Boyer, the film star who usually portrayed elegant Continental lovers. He was tall and impeccably attired, typically wearing a beautifully tailored, checked sport jacket with double vents. Decades later, when I worked as a medical student during the summer in Cape Breton, these were referred to as "fartin' jackets." But to me, he was a model of sartorial splendor and Gallic charm, and I longed to become exactly like him.

He spoke French without a hint of Québécois and was a tough disciplinarian. His system of behavioral control included marking students down to zero (which he pronounced "zayro"), throwing chalk at us at supersonic speed and with deadly accuracy and banishment to stand outside the classroom door where, if you were discovered by the headmaster, you would be invited to appear at 3 p.m. to receive ritual flagellation.

I usually sat in the back of the small classroom, where it was marginally easier to whisper rude remarks to classmates or to commit other indiscretions undetected. But Monsieur Seymour kept a close eye on me. To this day I hear the echo of his voice: "Go-bloom! One more observation of zees kind, zayro and out!" This outburst was typically followed by Monsieur Seymour hauling off and firing a piece of chalk in the direction of my forehead. His accuracy recalled William Tell.

Sadly, my worship of Monsieur Seymour as a model of masculinity and sartorial splendour met a crushing end. Several years later, he left Selwyn House for points unknown. During that period, my father would often take my brother, mother and me to New York for long weekends to indulge his lifelong love of the theatre. During these excursions, my mother would sometimes drag my brother and me along with her to Bonwit Teller's elegant department store, whose silk underwear and corsetry she favoured. We lived in terror of being discovered in a women's underwear department by someone who knew us. On one such occasion, I was standing in this intimidating environment when I spied a familiar-looking, elegantly attired male figure walking in our general direction with a purposeful stride. It was, unmistakably, Monsieur Seymour, working as a floorwalker in this forbidding feminized environment. I took refuge behind a rack of women's underwear and, as far as I could determine, remained undetected. But the devastating disillusionment over my hero's fall from grace lingers to this very day.

From LCC to McGill

The sixth form (graduating class) of Selwyn House was roughly equivalent to the second year of public high school, so we were obliged to transfer to another school to complete the final two years before becoming eligible to enter university. I applied to Lower Canada College (LCC), then an all-boys school, and was accepted. One of my warmest memories of that era was the establishment of an enduring friendship with one of my "masters" — for here too, teachers were addressed in the British tradition. That teacher was Hugh MacLennan. Hugh had been a Rhodes Scholar and had played for the Canadian Davis Cup tennis team.

For reasons now totally forgotten, I decided I wanted to learn German. At that time the only two German words I knew were *Herren* and *Damen,* which I had memorized while travelling with my parents in Europe so as not to stray into the ladies' washroom by mistake.

Hugh MacLennan taught German at LCC, and I was his only pupil. Our friendship seemed to transcend the age gap and become long-lasting. Hugh later gained wide recognition in Canada and abroad as an author, particularly for two novels, *Barometer Rising,* focused on the era of the 1917 Halifax explosion, and *Two Solitudes,* his penetrating novel about the divide between anglophones and francophones in Quebec.

After completing my final year at LCC, I took the matriculation exams, applied to McGill and was accepted. It didn't take long to discover there was more to university life than academics. I indulged my musical interest in several ways. McGill's traditional annual Red and White Revue had been abandoned during the war, but my brother Victor and I decided to replace it with a variety concert as a Red Cross fund-raiser. Naturally, I made sure I was one of the featured performers. I played the piano solo in the Grieg A-minor Concerto, with a fine pianist named Joy Symons playing the orchestral part on a second piano. My other musical interest at McGill involved establishing a series of student subscription concerts, four recitals per year by distinguished musicians. I also joined the McGill Radio Workshop (MRW), which produced radio dramas from time to time. One of the movers and shakers in the MRW was Charles Wassermann, a schoolmate from LCC. Charles was the son of Jakob Wassermann, a distinguished German-Jewish novelist and theatre critic. Charles later became a regular European commentator for the CBC, and his broadcasts from Budapest during the Hungarian Revolution were especially memorable.

By this time I had abandoned any dreams of glory as a concert pianist, thanks to two valuable insights: The first was the modesty of my musical talents; the second was the need for far too much (boring) daily practice to initiate and sustain such a career. Medicine was my fallback position, but not really a second choice. My father had taken my brother Victor and me on ward rounds on weekends at the Montreal Children's Hospital, and during summer vacations I had worked (without pay!) in the pathology department of that hospital where I learned how to carry out routine blood work and assisted at autopsies and in preparing slides of post-mortem tissue samples.

In those days, most students entering medicine had completed an undergraduate degree, but a few geniuses were accepted from

third year. I was not in that category. I applied during my third
year but was not accepted. I did get accepted during fourth year
and entered medical school keen to "get into it." There were a
hundred first-year students in addition to about fifty veterans
returning from the war.

In those days, medical school began with two pre-clinical
years featuring anatomy, physiology and biochemistry. In what
was then considered a daring innovation, we also attended a
course called "Introduction to Medicine" where, once a week,
we were introduced to a handful of live patients. We rarely got
to speak to them or (God forbid) lay a hand on them. They were
wheeled into an old-fashioned, steep semi-circular British-type
amphitheatre in their hospital beds, their shoulders typically
covered in a red wool "pneumonia jacket" dating from a pre-
antibiotic era when red wool was believed to provide protection
against pneumonia.

Typically, 5 to 10 per cent of the first-year class were cast out
of med school by the end of the year, and some of our less philanthropic instructors would warn us regularly of the dark cloud
that hung over us. A notable exception was our anatomy professor, Dr. C. P. Martin, an Irishman with a thick brogue. He was
also visibly distinguished by the fact he had a hole in his occiput,
the back of his skull, where he had been shot during some Irish
uprising. He covered this occipital perforation with a black eye
patch on the back of his head, held in place by a wide black silk
headband that circled his forehead.

Dr. Martin was one of the rare faculty members who offered
some reassurance we might have a future. Periodically he would
advise us as follows:

> Now look here, I know that some of you are worried
> about gettin' through first year, so I'll tell you what
> I want you to do: At five o'clock today, I want yez

to go down to the corner of Guy and Sherbrooke
Streets, stand in front of the Medical Arts Building
and watch them stupid-lookin' *fellas coming out of*
the building and getting into their Cadillacs. Every
one *of them got through first year!*

His reassuring words remain with me to this day and, before
I knew it, I myself had become one of "them stupid-lookin' fellas" — except I was getting into a second-hand Chevrolet.

Coming of Age in Cape Breton

My first encounter with the vivacious young woman who would become my wife was "arranged." Specifically, I was corralled by a bright, strong-minded young McGill classmate and friend named Judy Stoughton, who lived in the McGill women's residence. The year was 1944. Judy told me she had a classmate and friend at RVC who just happened to be Jewish. Judy was convinced I should take her out. In fact, she came close to commanding me to do so. Her friend's name was Ruth Schwartz and she hailed from Nova Scotia.

While considering the possibility of giving this girl a call, I auditioned for a role in a college production of a light comedy entitled *Junior Miss*, when who should I meet at that audition but Ruth Schwartz! Ruth was petite (five foot nothing) and effervescent. Without a second thought, I decided to get to know her better and invited her to join me for a cup of coffee at the local greasy spoon. Blowing twenty-five cents seemed worth the risk. Mutual attraction didn't take long to ignite. Ruth laughed heartily at my jokes, which was more than enough for me to take our newfound relationship seriously. So I decided to go for the gold and invited her out the next Saturday night for a date. She agreed, but with a caveat; she already had a date for Saturday night with another guy. But with an ingenuity that would become a hallmark for the rest of her life, she decided to tell him she had to be back in residence by 9:15 p.m. sharp. She told me to call for her at 9:30. Saturday night came and, at 9:25 p.m., I ascended the long stone steps past the imposing enthroned marble statue of Queen Victoria to present myself to the attendant just inside the front door of RVC. The scene might have been right out of a "B" comedy. As I mounted the steps for our date, "the competition" descended the same staircase. We passed each other, neither knowing the other, and he blissfully unaware of Ruthie's plans for the remainder of the evening.[¶]

In no time, we were going steady. I finally decided it was time for her to meet my parents, who suggested I invite her for Sunday lunch, one of our sacrosanct family meals. Ruth had heard of my parents, especially my father, and for the first and only time in our subsequent sixty-seven years as a couple she was petrified. In retrospect, I think Ruth truly believed that if my parents did not approve of her, it would spell *finis* to our romance. My reassurance that neither of my parents would bite did nothing to assuage her anxiety, which bordered on panic.

Sunday brunch went remarkably well. Ruth's anxiety vanished about five minutes after she arrived at our Crescent Street home. My father fell in love with her on the spot, and his adoration continued unabated throughout his life.

Before long, we decided our relationship was destined to become permanent. I decided to present Ruth with a ring to solidify our relationship and to choose a ring she would never forget. I found the perfect "gem" at Woolworths. Had the stone been the real McCoy, it would have weighed in at about forty carats. I paid three dollars for it and encased it in a beautiful, blue velvet box from Birks & Co., Montreal's most prestigious jeweller. I asked her to marry me and she accepted with unseemly

---

[¶] Most of her classmates called her Ruthie. Throughout our lives together, I called her Ruth. She was already diminutive enough!

haste. When I produced the velvet Birks box she opened it eagerly, collapsing with laughter when she saw the "Hopeless" diamond it contained. Soon after, I replaced it with a genuine diamond, and we began to make serious plans.

I also told Ruth I would like to come to Nova Scotia to meet her family in New Waterford and Sydney.

Despite having travelled extensively in western Canada, the US and Europe as a child and adolescent, nothing prepared me for the culture and ambience of Cape Breton. When I first visited, the only access was by car ferry. Cape Breton was divided into two parts. There was the "dark side" of industrial Cape Breton, whose population was concentrated in the coal mining communities of New Waterford, Glace Bay, Dominion, Reserve, North Sydney and Sydney Mines. In these communities the mine shafts were long and deep, some extending out for several miles under the ocean floor. Part of their production of soft coal went to fuel the large steel plant of the Dominion Steel and Coal Company, Sydney's principal industry. The other Cape Breton was the magnificent northern part of the island, which includes the Bras d'Or Lakes and Baddeck, where Alexander Graham Bell lived and conducted many of his experiments and where he and his wife are buried atop a mountain called Benn Breagh ("beautiful mountain" in Gaelic). North of Baddeck, occupying most of the remainder of the island, is Cape Breton Highlands National Park, which includes some of the most imposing, unspoiled scenery in all of Canada.

Ruth's birthplace and her family home was in the dark side, the coal mining town of New Waterford. Although I was keen to learn more about her family and her community, Ruth shared none of my enthusiasm for that visit. She was certain one look at coal-blackened New Waterford would be the end of our romance. She could not have been more wrong. From day one, I fell in love with Cape Breton, its people, their unique accents and turns of phrase, their wit and their way of life.

You might wonder just how her nice, impecunious Jewish family, escaping Tsarist Russia, had fetched up in such a remote part of eastern Canada. Their story was typical of many European Jewish immigrants who came to North America around the turn of the century. They gravitated toward wherever a friend or relative from the same Eastern European shtetl had put down roots. Thus, around 1900, Ruth's grandfather, Joseph Claener, speaking only Russian and Yiddish, came to New Waterford because a cousin, for unknown reasons, had recently settled there. Equally typical was that he came alone. After he had accumulated a little money, he returned to Russia and brought back his wife and children.

Ruth's mother, Rose, was thirteen years old when she and her family came to Canada circa 1913. Like most Jewish émigrés, she retained not a drop of nostalgia for the land of her birth and childhood. She couldn't wait to get out. She had been a star student in grade school in *Minskaya guberniya* (the province of Minsk) but, when she was ready to enter high school there, she was barred from doing so because the tiny Jewish quota for high school admissions had been filled.

Like many poor Jewish immigrants before and since, Ruth's grandfather began his career in the New World by borrowing a horse and wagon and going on the road, peddling needles, thread and other basics of life door to door. Despite speaking no English, he managed to get along, eventually earning enough to establish a small grocery store in New Waterford.

On one memorable occasion, during his early peddling days, he drove his horse and wagon over rough dirt roads all the way to Ingonish in northern Cape Breton. He became marooned by a freak late-fall snowstorm, but a kindly local farmer took him in and gave him room and board for the winter. In spring, after the snow melted, Joseph drove his horse and cart back to New

Waterford, where he was warmly welcomed by his wife and family. As he recounted the story of his survival, he reported that at least he had learned to speak English. With great pride, his wife invited in a couple of neighbours so he could show off his newly acquired linguistic fluency. However, what he *thought* was English turned out to be Gaelic, which, in those days, was still a living language for rural inhabitants in northern Cape Breton.

At eighteen, Rose Claener met and married Abraham Schwartz of Sudbury, Ontario. She had been briefly engaged to another young man but, after meeting Abe, she gave his predecessor back his ring and showed him the door. The newlyweds moved to New Waterford where Abe opened a small store that sold clothing, furniture and appliances.

I learned a great deal by observing Rose and her relationship with the people of her town. She was a practising egalitarian. Every customer in the store received the identical level of respect and personalized service. She knew everyone — rich or poor, drunk or sober — and would never try to sell anything to anyone without first inquiring about their personal health and that of their families. She genuinely cared about everyone who came into her store and had refined personalized service to an art form. When times were tough, as during a miners' strike, she extended credit generously and would never pressure a family that had fallen on hard times. On numerous occasions, she would "go good" at the bank for people trying to get started and would do so without anyone else's knowledge. If she was not waiting on someone herself, she would handpick the member of her staff best equipped to look after a particular customer. I loved hanging around the store. For one thing, it exposed me to a remarkable parade of characters and to endless examples of the Cape Breton wit.

I was also taken with the unique Cape Breton accents and figures of speech. In New Waterford, as in much of Cape Breton, women often addressed each other as "girl," "girl dear" or "woman dear." Certain grammatical aberrations were commonplace, such as "I should've went." Friends and acquaintances would often greet each other with "How are ya now?" . . . except the phrase would be pronounced as a single word, as in "H'wareyanaow?" The word "right" was regularly used as the equivalent of "very," as in "right good" or "right rotten," the superlative of the latter phrase being "rotten to de core." I learned words and expressions I had never heard elsewhere in Canada, such as "right logey" (tired, listless) and "right owly" (cranky, cross). The word "so," when used to express degree or extent, was often replaced by "that," as illustrated by a local man who described his extreme hunger as follows: "I was that hungry, I could've eaten the lamb o' God."

Another distinctive phenomenon in Cape Breton in general, and New Waterford in particular, was the need for unique nicknames to apply to individuals and often, by association, to all members of a person's family. The majority of the population was of Scottish descent so that, even within a town population of only around ten thousand, there was not only a slew of MacDonalds, MacKinnons and McIsaacs but often more than one person sharing the same first name as well. The only way to distinguish one family member from another was through nicknames. These were sometimes based on a physical or behavioural feature. I recall a few, including "the Big MacKinnons" (all very tall), "Jack the Widow" and "Stumper," who walked with a limp. In one memorable instance, one man in New Waterford was identified throughout the town simply as "Seven-up." He came by his nickname, people said, after he had gotten seven different women pregnant within a short space of time. Whether his designation was or was not supported by genetic testing, it earned him an enviable reputation.

Another novel phenomenon in some New Waterford families was the fairly widespread use of "personal shoppers," not the kind employed by fancy department stores but juvenile emissaries bearing written instructions for purchases. These shoppers were often children who came bearing notes from relatives who were unable (or unwilling) to come to the store in person. Such notes often began with the words "Please give the bearer of this note . . ." and finished with the words "and mark it," which meant "charge it to my account."

The drugstore in New Waterford was run by a rather gentle, wafer-thin pharmacist who had contracted tuberculosis some years earlier. He'd undergone a surgical procedure then used for treatment of pulmonary tuberculosis, thoracoplasty, in which several ribs were removed surgically, causing the lung and part of the chest wall to collapse. The underlying theory held that an airless, immobile tuberculous lung would heal more quickly. The procedure had left this man, thin as a reed to begin with, with a stooped posture. To make his resemblance to Uriah Heap even more striking, he was very obsequious and would wring his hands as he spoke, bent forward over the counter. One popular story was that a small boy had entered his pharmacy and presented him with a handwritten note reading: "Please give the bearer of this note two French safes and a harmonica, as I am going on a picnic."

There was no better place to observe and overhear human interaction in Cape Breton than a store. Ruth's older sister, Edna, a consummate saleswoman, could size up a customer in a split second and instantly assess the style, colour and size of dress or hat that would look best on her and what would not. One memorable interplay took place between her and a rather large lady who had come into the store in search of a hat. In those days, women's hat departments featured a kind of boudoir table with a large central mirror, two smaller, hinged side mirrors and a chair. Women could sit in front of the table, try on hats and survey their appearance from three separate angles. Edna had brought this woman a series of hats to try on, but none met with her approval. Edna finally played her trump card. She produced a large, wide-brimmed felt hat, which had a wide silk ribbon circling the crown and extending into a long tail, which Edna proceeded to drape dramatically across the woman's upper chest, falling loosely over her shoulder. "There now, Mrs. MacDonald," she said, "this is the latest style — this is the *Lawrence of Arabia* look!" "Christ, girl!" said Mrs. MacDonald. "That'd be no good fer me. I don't even gets out to the sandbar at Dominion any-more." (She was referring to a favourite swimming spot, a long sandbar that runs between the nearby mining town of Dominion and Glace Bay.)

In another unforgettable linkage between New Waterford and Hollywood, Ruth and I attended a screening of *The Great Caruso* starring Mario Lanza, at the ill-named Majestic Theatre, the town's only cinema. It was a rainy night, and as we emerged from the theatre we ran into a young man we knew. "How did you like *The Great Caruso*?" I asked. "Aw," he said, "the movie was OK, but there was too much singin' . . ." — possibly the most succinct review *The Great Caruso* ever received.

When I first summered in Cape Breton as a naive medi-cal undergraduate, one of the town's four family physicians, a family friend, asked if I would like to hang around the hospital, attend rounds, observe procedures and spend a little time in the operating room. Since McGill medical students had virtually no hands-on experience with patients during their first two years, he didn't need to ask me twice. I reported for duty next morning.

Many Canadians are unaware that universal prepaid health care had its birth, not in Saskatchewan (as popularly thought) but in Cape Breton, where a system known as "the check-off" had been operating for some time. Under this system, a por-tion of each miner's pay was deducted from his pay each week, and the accumulated funds were used to remunerate each of the town's physicians through a salary proportional to the number of families under the physician's care. The doctors, in turn, were obliged to provide comprehensive health care without charge for the coal miner and his entire family.

I was a bit of a novelty in New Waterford medical circles. They had never had a medical student, intern or resident in their midst. Possibly as a result, the four doctors were incredibly generous in offering me first-hand exposure and, often, hands-on experience in a whole host of conditions and procedures usually off-limits to people with my abysmal lack of experience. They taught me how to administer open-drop ether anesthesia to patients undergoing tonsillectomies and other procedures, how to apply plaster casts to fractured limbs and, most exciting of all, how to attend deliveries and, ultimately, deliver a few babies myself under close supervision. My principal mentor was Dr. Louis Kristal, an excellent physician and the most competent surgeon in town. Some of the local citizenry referred to him informally as "the head cutter". Working with doctors in Cape Breton required me to learn a whole new language in order to guess at the true meaning of patients' complaints. Generally speaking, many of the patients who came to the local clinic or the hospital were fairly clear in indicating what part of their anatomy was giving them grief. The notable exception involved women describing their gynecological problems. These were typically described under the general heading of "inward trouble." In many cases of inward trouble, the therapeutic intervention prescribed was dilatation and curettage, commonly abbreviated as "D&C." Many women in New Waterford referred to the procedure more graphically as "da scrapin'," as in "I was to the 'ostibul fer da scrapin'." One woman, however, reported: "I was to the 'ostibul and got scroped."

While tagging along on hospital rounds, I was taken in to see a seventeen-year-old girl who had been in hospital for some time with a form of extensive, generalized muscle weakness. She had a nasal voice, was too weak to get out of bed, had difficulty swallowing and was unable to open her eyelids more than halfway. The cause of her weakness was a mystery, and I was challenged to see if I could come up with a diagnosis. I grabbed every textbook I could find and, before long, found a description of a condition of which I had never heard, called myasthenia gravis, an uncommon but well-recognized condition that is due to a biochemical defect in the function of the motor end plate (the site where impulses that travel along motor nerves transmit their electric messages to the muscles, "telling them" to contract). Typically, affected patients have generalized muscle weakness that worsens during the day or with exertion. The clinical "giveaway" is often the progressive weakness of the upper eyelids, which droop so much they can interfere with vision. Affected patients may also have a nasal voice. The neat thing is the diagnosis can be confirmed quickly and unequivocally by giving the patient one injection of a drug such as prostigmine or neostigmine, which almost instantly (but only temporarily) improves the weakness. If the patient is suddenly able to open his or her eyes right after the injection, the diagnosis is confirmed beyond the slightest doubt.

I confided my suspicion to Dr. Kristal, who managed to get a small supply of neostigmine from Sydney. We gave her the injection and her response was dramatic. Within a minute or so, she opened her eyes wider, her voice became stronger and her muscle strength improved instantaneously. As a result of this diagnostic "coup," my stock at the hospital rose steeply — despite the fact more luck than brilliance was involved in solving the puzzle.

During my first summer in Cape Breton, home obstetrical deliveries were still performed occasionally. One is indelibly etched in my memory. One of the town's four physicians was called to a decrepit house in one of the poorest sections of town, an area known as "14 yard." Adjacent to No. 14 colliery, it was not exactly the Riviera, and the particular house to which the doctor had been summoned was overcrowded with older offspring. The delivery took place on a stormy night, and an assortment of older siblings was hanging about, presumably to inspect and welcome the newest member of the family. As the mother's labour progressed, one young boy asked the doctor: "Listen, Doc, ow'd dat baby git inside me mudder's stomach?" "Well," the doctor replied, "your father planted a seed there." "G'wan," said the young fellow. "Don't gimme dat shit . . . my old man's too lazy to even mow de lawn!"

Sometimes patients would complain of symptoms of a kind previously undescribed, even in the most comprehensive medical texts. One young woman of about twenty was a member of a large family of Newfoundlanders. She was well known to the local doctors for several reasons: She spoke in a very loud voice; she was very demanding, often insisting she be seen ahead of other patients; and her complaints often had a bizarre twist. Once, she barged into the clinic and demanded to see Dr. Kristal, whom she never favoured with the title "Doctor." She addressed him, always loudly, simply as "Kristal." "Kristal," she said, "I gots a wonderful 'eadache!" (I was aware that, to some Newfoundlanders, the adjective "wonderful" does not have the connotation it enjoys in most conversations. In this context, it implied "awesome" or "huge," as in Elizabethan times.) Using both hands, palms forward, fingers extended as though she were about to dive, to illustrate the trajectory of her 'eadache, she told him: "It starts in the top of me head, comes down, goes t'rough me breasts, then round and round me nabel, then comes OUT me womb and nearly knocks me jeezly head off!" The climax of the 'eadache's trajectory was described with a great forward scooping movement of her clasped hands.

On another occasion, she burst into the clinic and again accosted her physician: "Listen, Kristal. I got to go to the dentist today, and you knows me. I can't take the et'er and I can't stand them needles, so you gotta give me something to take instead." Dr. Kristal prescribed some sedation for her and she headed off to the dentist's office. Two hours later she was back in the clinic, raising hell, as was her custom. "Listen, Kristal," she told him. "I went to the dentist's office, and I'm gittin' sleepy and my knees are feelin' right queer. Anyway, he pushes me down in the chair, and me eyes is gittin' right heavy. Then I sees him comin' at me wit dat goddam needle, and I'm about to open my mouth to say, 'Goddam you, Kristal,' when all of a sudden, me tongue goes numb!"

In New Waterford I had my first exposure to obstetrical deliveries. Later obstetrical training in Montreal revealed some interesting demographic differences. In Cape Breton, painful uterine contractions were not infrequently accompanied by colourful and explicit cursing, typically directed at the man responsible for the impregnation. The other memorable difference was that most patients smoked freely in the hospital (unless they were in an oxygen tent) and women in labour were no exception. In one unforgettable instance, an expectant mother was giving loud vent to her feelings during a particularly strong contraction, cursing her husband who had gotten her into this condition. As the contraction subsided, she addressed the nurse: "Hand me me makin's," she said, pointing to her package of tobacco and cigarette papers on the windowsill. She proceeded to skilfully roll herself a cigarette and light up, to "calm her nerves."

Entertainment value aside, many lessons I learned there served me well throughout my medical career. Besides, they provided me with memories I cherish to this day.

My paternal great grandfather pictured with his "trophy" second wife "The Shrew", who was more responsible for emigration than any pogrom.

My grandparents, Belle and Samuel Goldbloom, with baby Eva and Alton — my aunt and father. Uncle Tevye is missing in the photo.

My maternal grandmother, Charlotte Ballon, hid in terror under
the bed when Cossacks rode through town brandishing their sabres,
looking for more Jews to slaughter.

Uncle Isidore — a quiet, scholarly but unsuccessful lawyer. He was a competent pianist who became my piano teacher.

My great Uncle William (Goldbloom), a.k.a. Buffalo Bill!

My mother, Annie. In
those days photographers
kept "picture hats"
in their studios for
glamorous portraits.

My father as a
debonair stage actor,
replete with a cigarette
and a Lucifer.

When my Uncle Harry auditioned for the great Mischa Elman he was asked "Vell, my boy, vat are you going to play?" Harry replied, "The violin."

Ellen Ballon (my maternal aunt), a child prodigy, is shown at the piano in her parents' Bishop Street home in Montreal.

Uncle David Ballon, a highly respected head of Otolaryngology at Montreal's Royal Victoria Hospital. He and my father were the first two Jewish physicians to head departments at a McGill teaching hospital.

My aunt, Eva Goldbloom Brotman, a compulsive performer and a devastating mimic.

Ellen Ballon, my mother's younger sister, wearing the prescribed attire for presentation at Buckingham Palace, including a headdress of white ostrich plumes.

A charcoal sketch of Ellen Ballon by Kathleen Shackleton

A family photograph with my mother, father, brother Victor and me in 1934.

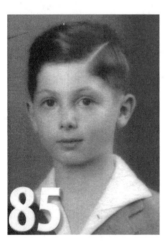

This photo of me was taken at age ten and was used to celebrate my eighty-fifth birthday!

With my brother Victor as teenagers, captured in a rare serious moment.

With Joy Symons, my partner in a two piano duo at a McGill fundraising concert.

My parents on board ship. My father decided we should travel to Europe as a family to see the great sights.

My father's brother Tevye. Uncle Tevye, like most Goldblooms, laughed a lot, told a lot of jokes and performed magic tricks.

Rose Schwartz, Ruth's mother, in the centre
surrounded by her children *circa* 1950 in Barachois.
Ruth is in the foreground.

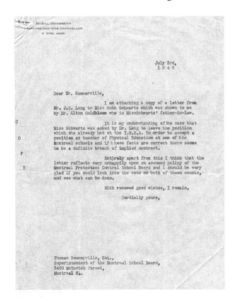

Letter from J. D. Lang,
supervisor of physical
education for the Montreal
Protestant Central School
Board.

Montreal Children's Hospital staff with my father, Dr. Alton Goldbloom, in the front row centre and me in the second row, far right.

Dr. Charles A. Janeway, my mentor and friend, was Professor of Pediatrics, Harvard University and Chief of Pediatrics, Children's Hospital Medical Center, Boston, MA.

My parents, Annie and Alton Goldbloom, visiting in Cape Breton.

Ruth and I were married in Montreal on June 25, 1945 in the presence of family and a few close friends.

The Art,
Science and
Administration
of Medicine

At the Feet of the Masters

For most doctors, the enduring lessons that shape their careers and their individual styles of practice come from listening to and observing great teachers, the true masters of the profession. Whatever success I have had as a clinician and teacher is directly traceable to several inspirational role models. Sometimes the inspiration was sparked by a single encounter or an unforgettable quotation that became part of my daily work and thought.

My earliest and longest-standing role model was my father, Alton Goldbloom. A pioneer of Canadian pediatrics, he was the first fully trained pediatrician to establish himself in Montreal. For decades he practised pediatrics in the community and served as professor and head of the Department of Pediatrics at McGill University and physician-in-chief at the Montreal Children's Hospital. In those days academic full-time appointments were virtually unknown, and even after he became professor and head of the department at McGill, he continued to conduct a busy practice in the community.

Professionally and attitudinally, my father was decades ahead of his time. He recognized he had to become fluent in French to serve the Montreal community effectively. This was an era in the history of Quebec when a deep divide (bordering on a chasm) separated anglophone and francophone society. That division was rooted in two historic phenomena: one economic, the other religious. On the economic side, the average annual income of an anglophone Quebecer was substantially higher than that of the average francophone. Although that differential was largely an accident of history — the original French settlers were mostly agrarian, whereas most anglophone settlers, mainly from England and Scotland, were merchants, hence predestined to receive a larger slice of the economic pie — it was painful.

Besides, the Catholic clergy in Quebec ruled the lives of ordinary citizens in the nineteenth and twentieth centuries with a tighter grip than in most largely Catholic countries of the world. This was also rooted in history. The seigneurs (aristocrats) who brought the early settlers from France to the New World eventually abandoned them and returned to their homeland, leaving them under the stewardship of the Catholic parish priests and bishops. Congregants were instructed weekly from the pulpit, in no uncertain terms, on how to dress, how to behave and how to vote.

As a schoolboy, I remember travelling to the Laurentians for ski weekends. Somewhere near St. Jérôme, a huge billboard featured an enormous likeness of the reigning bishop of the district, Père Labelle. He was portrayed in full clerical garb, with cassock and purple sash. His name did not appear on the poster. It did not have to, because everyone recognized him. Beneath his likeness was the simple inscription: "*Le Roi du Nord*," The King of the North.

In those days, the majority of francophone children attended Catholic schools, many as boarders. In stricter institutions, morality could take bizarre forms. In a few convent schools, girls were permitted to take showers only if clad in a kind of loose nightgown, presumably in the belief that seeing their own naked bodies would lead to God alone knew what kind of evil thoughts or immoral behaviour. Some convent schools were also known for the blandness of their cuisine; I remember one of my francophone friends referring to a rather watery soup as *soupe du couvent.*

I remember with sadness the width of the gulf that separated the two linguistic entities. Segregation between Montreal's anglophone and francophone communities was rooted not only in economic, religious and linguistic domains, but was expressed geographically as well.

In Westmount, then an almost *pure laine* anglophone enclave, you could fire off a machine gun in any direction and never hit a francophone. Many residents' attitudes and communications were unilingual and unicultural. There was a story, undoubtedly apocryphal, but perilously close to reality, about an upper-crust Westmount anglo matron entertaining a few aristocratic lady friends at afternoon tea. The conversation turned to the current initiative to require all anglophone children learn to speak French. The hostess opined she didn't see why French children shouldn't be required to learn English: "After all, my dears," she said, "English was good enough for Our Lord, it should be good enough for them!"

When Victor and I first became practising pediatricians in Montreal, my father allowed us to use his office. We would also do house calls for him periodically. We received none of the deification accorded him. In fact, many regarded us as poor substitutes for the genuine article. Some patients made little distinction between Victor and myself. We were the upstarts, our father the master. My father loved to tell of an occasion when he answered the telephone and a francophone lady said: "*Allo, docteur Goldbloom?*" Father: "*Oui.*" Lady: "*Est-ce-que c'est le père ou le fils?*" My father replied: "*Non, Madame, c'est le Saint-Esprit.*" ("It's the Holy Ghost.")

I was on the receiving end of the second-generation put-down on another occasion. I had been in practice only three or four years when I was awakened one night by the telephone at about

1:30 a.m. The caller was a good friend of Ruth's and mine. One of her sons had come down with a fever. She asked me what to do. After asking a few questions about his symptoms, I felt he should be examined to determine the exact cause of his fever, so I offered to make a house call. "Oh no," she said, "that won't be necessary. I was really phoning just to find out if this was serious enough to disturb your father."

The education I received from my father in pediatric clinical skills really began in my early childhood years. From birth until I was a teenager, when we lived over his office on the ground floor of our Crescent Street home, he kept a telephone on the dining room table. As a result, for years I eavesdropped on the advice he dispensed to anxious parents.

Another source of my early pediatric education came while listening to conversations between my father and colleagues who came to dinner. My father, together with his surgeon brother-in-law, Dr. Harry Ballon, had been caring for a desperately ill eight-year-old girl who had developed recurrent suppurative (pus-producing) streptococcal infections involving the glands in her neck and her lungs. She had endured multiple hospital admissions and repeated surgical procedures to drain abscesses at many different sites. These recurrent, overwhelming infections and hospital admissions had extended over two years, with only brief, temporary improvement. My father and uncle were certain she was going to die. Around that time, reports had just begun to appear describing the effectiveness of two new drugs, Prontosil and Prontylin, which had been developed and tested in Germany with encouraging results. These were the earliest ancestors of the sulphonamide antibiotics and were pretty toxic. My father and Uncle Harry somehow managed to obtain a tiny supply of Prontylin from Germany and used it to treat this girl.

I still recall their excitement over the girl's miraculous

response to this radical treatment, which they later reported in the *Canadian Medical Association Journal*: "Within twenty-four hours, the fever, which now had been running a septic course for many months, fell to normal and has remained so ever since." She gained weight progressively and her life-threatening infections never recurred. Subsequently, they treated three more patients with Prontylin with equally gratifying results. The excitement in our dining room over her miraculous recovery was palpable and is permanently engraved in my memory.

Nowadays, many medical researchers commit their entire time to the laboratory in pursuit of new knowledge. But in my father's time it was not unusual for a few clinicians to devote part of their time to scientific investigation while conducting a busy practice. My father published some fifty-six papers in the course of his career. Early on, he had developed an interest in polio-myelitis and sought some way to prevent the disease. At McGill, he maintained a small colony of macaque rhesus monkeys — the rhesus monkey being the only laboratory animal that could be infected with polio virus — for his studies.

When his practice became too demanding, my father hired a research associate named Maurice Brodie. They tried to determine whether the blood serum of monkeys convalescing from polio (convalescent serum) would contain sufficient antibody to polio virus to protect uninfected monkeys from developing polio after infecting them with the virus.

After some years, Brodie moved to the Rockefeller Institute in New York to continue the work there. One of the few exquisitely painful childhood memories I retain is of being taken by my father to a laboratory at the Rockefeller Institute, where I was approached by a man in a white coat holding what looked to me like a gigantic syringe, full of some liquid, which he proceeded to inject into my thigh. My screams were clearly audible in New Jersey. (In those days the concept of informed consent was unknown. Had that been an option, I would have flatly refused.) In retrospect, I suppose my father's intentions were commendable. He wanted to protect us from polio if at all possible. Eighty years later I have partly forgiven him. Unfortunately, the convalescent serum didn't work, but there was an interesting sequel.

My father presented the disappointing results of the experiments at a meeting of the American Pediatric Society. In closing his presentation, he predicted the ability to protect children against polio would require development of a method of growing the polio virus in vitro, that is, in the laboratory. Among those in the audience was a young man named Frederick C. Robbins, along with another young researcher named Tom Weller, and their mentor, Harvard virologist John Enders. Years later, they would be the first to grow polio virus successfully in tissue culture. Once that feat had been accomplished, developing an effective polio vaccine was simply a matter of time. The trio of Robbins, Weller and Enders were deservedly awarded the Nobel Prize in Medicine in 1950. Thereafter, Jonas Salk and Albert Sabin were in a tight race to develop an effective polio vaccine. Fred Robbins, a wonderful human being, later reminded my father of his prophetic prediction. "Those were wise words, Doc," he said.

When I arrived at Boston Children's in the early fifties to begin my pediatric residency, my very first assignment was to the infectious disease ward, and my first attending physician was none other than Fred Robbins. There could have been no better way to begin my year in Boston. Fred was a superb scientist and clinician, a great teacher and a warm, wonderful, modest human being.

Another of my father's research interests was in exploring the mechanism by which so many normal babies became jaundiced in the first few days of life, a phenomenon known as physiological jaundice. Babies are born with more red blood cells than they need to carry oxygen, once they have emerged from the relatively low-oxygen intrauterine environment to inhale the earth's more highly oxygenated atmosphere. He had produced evidence suggesting the rapid breakdown of the excess red blood cells released hemoglobin, which the liver converts to bilirubin, the bile pigment that causes jaundice, and that this was a big factor in causing physiological jaundice.

Another school of thought held that the principal cause of jaundice in newborns was immaturity of the liver. During my year in Boston I spent two months on the pediatric service of the Beth Israel Hospital under the guidance of Dr. Sydney S. Gellis. Working with colleagues in his laboratory, we were able to show that the red blood cells of the newborn were more susceptible to mechanical trauma than those of older infants, providing additional support for my father's belief that excessive red cell breakdown was a major factor in explaining why so many healthy newborns become jaundiced in the first week of life.

On July 1, 1950, I arrived in Boston to take up an appointment as a senior resident at the Boston Children's Hospital. A popular saying in medical circles at that time held that "Boston is not a city, it's a state of mind," and that statement was not entirely without foundation in medical circles. The city incorporated some of the world's most sophisticated medical centres and attracted some of the best minds in the profession. Patients came from all over the world to seek the opinions and help of Boston's world-renowned specialists.

None of us was immune to that pervasive aura of medical superiority. Boston's Children's Hospital was part of Children's Medical Center, commonly abbreviated to CMC. My resident colleagues and I frequently referred to it, only semi-facetiously, as "CMCW" (Children's Medical Center of the World). I admired the dedication and sacrifice of many of the highly reputed Harvard pediatric faculty members, particularly since

remuneration of medical faculty at Harvard was about the lowest in the country. However, my awe for what appeared to be
their highly principled sacrifice of monetary gain was tempered
somewhat by the discovery several of them had either inherited
enormous wealth or, equally helpful, had married big money.
For them, working for a miserly Harvard salary imposed no com-
promise of lifestyle.

Charles A. Janeway was the chair of pediatrics at Harvard and
physician-in-chief at the Children's Hospital. (We all called him
Charlie behind his back, and much later, to his face, after we had
completed our time at Children's.) Charlie had begun his medical career, not as a pediatrician, but as an internist and scientific
investigator. He had been one of a small group of scientists who
had first isolated the individual proteins of blood plasma, including gamma globulin, which would play a key role in protecting
patients exposed to measles, hepatitis and other diseases and in
offering life-saving protection against infection to children with
immunological deficiencies. When Janeway was offered the pro-
fessorship in pediatrics at Harvard, he transformed himself from
internist to pediatrician with remarkable speed and success.

He was a great teacher, with a deep concern for the human
condition and, in later years, for the health and welfare of children in less favoured parts of the world. He had formidable
bushy eyebrows that moved up and down rhythmically and frequently as he spoke. He had super-keen eyes and ears, a gentle
approach to children and their parents and an abundance of the
greatest of all pedagogical attributes: He taught us to ask the right
questions and to figure out for ourselves how to find the right
answers. After I finished my residency at Children's, Ruth and I

continued our warm friendship with Charlie and Betty Janeway, who would visit us periodically in Montreal with their children.

But one of the greatest lessons I learned from him came unexpectedly during the late summer of 1950. My father was visiting Boston, and Charlie had invited him to lunch. As a courtesy, Charlie asked me to come along. I reported to his office just before noon and no sooner arrived than I was paged. Ruth was calling to tell me that our son, Alan, had a fever and a stiff neck. Boston was then in the midst of a polio epidemic, and polio typically begins with a low-grade fever and stiff neck. Naturally, that was my first thought. I told Dr. Janeway I had to beg off lunch because I had to drive home and check on Alan. "Nothing doing," he said. "I'm driving you out there and I'll have a look at him myself." He packed me into his jeep and we headed off at high speed. When we arrived at our apartment, he examined Alan with great gentleness and skill. He told us that there were no signs of polio, really the only thing we needed to hear.

The lesson was indelible — too often forgotten these days — that the needs of the patient always take precedence over the needs of the doctor. I still cling to the (old-fashioned?) belief that medicine is a serving profession, not a self-serving one. I realize nothing is to be gained by regaling today's physicians with stories of how "in my day we worked every second night and every second weekend for the princely sum of fifty dollars a month," etc., etc. The listeners, if any, quickly develop a glazed look and eyelids start to droop. Some day, I suppose, I may come to accept that times have changed, possibly forever, and that our profession has learned from the labour unions that the only two items we can really bargain for, under the rubric of "better working conditions," are less work and more money.

But several personal and professional heroes have informed much of what I've tried to accomplish as a pediatrician. In addition to my father and Charlie Janeway — and Sydney Gellis, my pediatric hero, about whom more later — several others were sources of inspiration. Here are a few of my heroes:

Bronson Crothers: By the time I arrived at the Boston Children's, Bronson Crothers was ready to retire. He was chief of neurology and was highly reputed throughout the world. The rich and famous often brought their children from great distances to seek his opinion. This was especially so regarding those children who, in those days, were often designated as "retarded" (now more humanely referred to as "developmentally delayed").

I learned one unforgettable lesson from him. One day, a fellow resident asked him: "Dr. Crothers, how do you go about telling parents that their child is retarded?" Crothers replied: "I *never* tell them . . . I help them tell me."

In those few words lay one of the most important lessons concerning physician communication with patients and their families. Understanding is never communicated by pontificating, by making pronouncements, or by transmitting "facts." It is an inductive process, usually accomplished more by asking parents the right questions rather than by giving them the "right" answers. *For the doctor*, it requires far more listening than talking. Most of all, it requires enough time, often more than a single visit.

Anxious parents often begin their visit to the doctor regarding a "problem child," such as one who is developmentally delayed, having behavioural difficulties or experiencing problems in school, with an enumeration of all the youngster's difficulties and shortcomings. If the child is old enough to catch even the flavour of the conversation, I often watch the youngster out of the corner of my eye, sinking progressively lower into a chair and looking sadder and sadder as he or she listens to the parents' recitation of the child's perceived shortcomings. I learned long ago to interrupt such conversations by acknowledging that the parents are worried about their child but, "before we get to those problems, I'd like you to tell me *everything* about him/her that is really wonderful . . . his/her nicest qualities and all the things he/she does best." This helps put the child's problems into context and provides a positive foundation on which to build helpful interventions. In the process, it is heart-warming to watch the youngsters brighten, sit up straighter and even smile as parents begin to recite their virtues. Another element too often absent, or insufficient, in such doctor-family conversations, is the regular injections of expressions of empathy into the conversation.

When dealing with a child with a developmental delay, early in the discussion I always ask parents to tell me *their* estimate of the age level at which their child is functioning, and I never cease to be amazed at their uncanny accuracy. While their estimate may or may not translate into realistic expectations for the youngster's future educational or occupational attainment, it is an essential starting point for further conversation, assessment and intervention.

The other issue far too easily overlooked is discovering what the *parents'* ideas and fears (often unspoken) may be regarding why their child came to have this problem in the first place. Many parents harbour their own, often unarticulated ideas about what might have originally caused their child's problem. These may be unspoken fears that something they did, failed to do or should have done long before the baby was born may have caused him or her to have this problem — like having taken one or two drinks during pregnancy. Such self-accusatory thoughts may seem inconsequential from a medical viewpoint, but they can be all it takes to haunt a parent with feelings of guilt and self-blame.

In the final analysis, uncovering and dealing with such hidden agendas can do far more to relieve parental anxiety than all the MRIs, blood tests and specialist consultations combined. For one thing, parents need to understand it is *normal* for people in their situation to harbour self-accusatory thoughts. Putting their unspoken, often unfounded, fears to rest can be highly therapeutic.

Randolph K. Byers: Randy Byers succeeded Bronson Crothers as chief of neurology at Children's Hospital in Boston. He was a man of mighty few words, but we learned more from watching him than from listening to him. When asked to see a small infant with a neurological problem, he would pad quietly over to the ward, position himself at one end of the infant's crib and watch the baby silently for fifteen minutes, observing every move. After observing the infant, he could tell us far more about that infant's neurological status than most of us could do by handling the baby, testing reflexes and performing a classical hands-on examination.

Alan Ross: When my father retired from his positions at McGill and the Montreal Children's Hospital, he was succeeded by Dr. Alan Ross. Alan was an excellent physician, less theatrical than my father, but a man of great integrity. He was the one who persuaded me to give up community practice and move into the Montreal Children's as a member of the full-time staff, limiting my practice to consultation by referral and increasing my involvement in teaching and research. I have innumerable reasons for remembering Alan Ross with affection and respect, but as is so often the case in one's roster of great teachers, a single episode can be unforgettably instructive.

In those days, when any of us was planning to submit an article to a medical journal for publication, it was standard courtesy to first show the manuscript to the department head for approval and for suggested improvements. On several occasions I had sent Alan manuscripts of a paper I was writing. I knew he read them carefully because the manuscripts would be returned in a few days with suggestions (always good ones) pencilled in the margins. Incorporating his suggestions invariably made for a better paper. But on one occasion, in his characteristic gentle fashion, he taught me a lesson that endured. I had sent him the manuscript of a paper I planned to submit to a pediatric journal. Four days after sending it to him, the manuscript was returned and, for the very first time, not a single suggestion for change was written in the margins. But in the bottom of the brown envelope, I discovered a gift from Alan. It was a small paperback book by two authors named Strunk and White, *The Elements of Style*. The message could not have been clearer. To this day, I'm deeply grateful to him for that gentle hint.

The courtesy of showing papers being prepared for publication to one's department head, once obligatory, has now faded into oblivion. Nowadays, if a medical department head becomes aware of a paper a department member has written, it's more likely to be by accident than by design. Acceptance by department heads of some degree of responsibility for whatever wisdom (or lack thereof) emanates from their department members has declined progressively over decades. At one time, it was obligatory to list the name of the professor/department head as a co-author of every single paper published by a member of the department.

On one unforgettable occasion, that custom led to a volcanic academic upheaval. In the Department of Pediatrics at Case Western Reserve University, someone had conceived the bizarre idea of anastomosing (joining) the common carotid artery in the neck to the jugular vein as a treatment for what we now call Down's syndrome (then referred to as Mongolism). Proponents of that surgical procedure claimed to have documented significant postoperative improvements in intellectual capacity in such children. The issue, understandably, was heavily charged with emotion for parents of affected children, who began to lobby other centres demanding the surgical procedure be performed on their children.

The late Dr. Wilder Penfield, an eminent Canadian neuro-surgeon, was pressured to perform this operation on several children with Down's. He flatly refused. He saw no anatomical or physiological reason why such a procedure could produce the remarkable results claimed. Tragically, it was later revealed the psychologist who had reported striking improvements in IQ in the children who had undergone the operation admitted to falsifying the results. Everyone whose names had appeared on the original published papers had to resign. Dr. Charles McKhann, a distinguished pediatrician, then head of the Department of Pediatrics at Western Reserve, was one of them, although he had nothing to do with the research. Happily, the custom of listing the department head's name as a co-author when the head has had nothing to do with the research has vanished.

Nathan B. Epstein: Nate Epstein grew up in New Waterford, Nova Scotia, the same coal mining coastal town where Ruth was born. His father, Benny Epstein, owned the store immediately next door to the one that belonged to my mother-in-law-to-be, Rose Schwartz. The Jewish population of New Waterford comprised, at its peak, about twelve families. Most were storekeepers, with a single striking exception — a coal miner who was known underground simply as "Harry the Jew." The epithet was more descriptive than derogatory, since the town was remarkably free of racism.

I attribute the fact Nate Epstein, in later life, became a hard-nosed, pragmatic psychiatrist who demanded short-term positive results from his patients to his rough-and-tumble upbringing in New Waterford, where fisticuffs were simply a normal means of communication. As a young teenager, Nate had been Ruth's boy-friend. As Ruth tells it, the romance came to an abrupt end when Nate tossed a brick at her and hit her in the nose. That "friendly" assault was eventually forgiven (but not forgotten) when our son

David married his childhood sweetheart, Nate's daughter Nancy!

I have indelible memories of Benny Epstein's acute anxiety and disbelief when it was revealed that his son had decided to specialize in psychiatry, a career that he associated only with "crazy people" and had little to do with *real* doctoring. (Interestingly, my paternal grandfather had similar misgivings when my father decided to become a pediatrician. For Grandpa Goldbloom, the apogee of medical achievement was to become what he called a "surgent.")

We visited Cape Breton most summers, and Benny Epstein never lost an opportunity to ask the same questions about his son's bizarre career choice. Benny had a tic involving his left shoulder, causing him to suddenly jerk it upward. The tic became more prominent and more frequent whenever he became anxious, which was often. He would stand in the doorway of his store, and when he saw me coming along he would beckon me toward him, his shoulder tic-ing away. It was always the same question about his son, and he would lapse into Yiddish: "*Deek, vos tut mein Neach doh mit die meshugoyim?*" ("Dick, what's my Natie doing up there with those crazy people?") Patiently, I would try to explain to him that psychiatry was an important specialty and not just about "crazy people." At first, he was not easily persuaded.

However, as Nate's training progressed and he began to develop a successful practice, Benny's views on psychiatry underwent a 180-degree turnaround. He not only came to approve of Nate's choice of specialty but became a self-appointed town authority on psychiatry and an apostle for the specialty. When a cousin of his asked what Nate actually did, he had a clear explanation: "My Natie knows when you're lying, even when you don't know yourself!" (To my knowledge, that definition of a psychiatrist has never been equalled.) The final episode in Benny Epstein's coming to terms with psychiatry happened in

New York, where Nate had established an office in his apartment, including the requisite analyst's couch. Benny, accompanied by his wife Shayna, had travelled to New York to visit their son and see for themselves what a success he was becoming. When he spotted the analyst's couch, he commanded his wife: "Shayna, lie down!" She was puzzled by the order, but he was insistent, so she lay down on the couch. Benny turned to his son and said: "Neach, give 'er a lesson!"

Nate joined the faculty at McGill where he collaborated with a sociologist, William Westley, to carry out a landmark investigation of fifty ostensibly "normal," well-adjusted families to identify the specific attributes associated with emotional health and stability in the children. Their observations, published in a small book entitled *Silent Majority*, remain relevant for psychiatrists, pediatricians and family physicians, indeed, for anyone who has to help families deal with problems that affect all family members: behavioural difficulties, a chronic condition in a family member, addiction problems or marital difficulties. In retrospect, their findings may seem fairly obvious, but they are too often neglected or overlooked in clinical practice. Three factors, more than any others, were the main determinants of emotional stability in the children: warm, open communication; shared labour; and leadership.

For generations, the principal forum for warm, open communication was the family dining table. There, kids did their homework while mothers prepared meals (before microwave ovens, frozen foods, pizzas, instant puddings and heat-and-serve meals). The family kitchen was where friends and family members gathered to talk. This was, of course, before the proliferation of electronic distractions — television, smartphones, MP3 players and video games — which, along with discordant parental work schedules in so many families, spelled *finis* to eye contact and to conversation. What has supplanted conversation in many families is, increasingly, a nonverbal electronic form of communication, devoid of traditional and crucial elements such as facial expression or tone of voice, the traditional conveyers of emotion.

Contemplating these societal changes in family life takes me back to Epstein and Westley's delineation of the elements of family function that determine children's emotional health. Those key elements have not changed, and many families require active intervention to resuscitate them.

When Nate moved from Montreal to Hamilton, Ontario, to become head of the Department of Psychiatry at the brand-new and then highly innovative medical school at McMaster University, he and his colleagues continued to refine the family therapy model, later known as "the McMaster Model," as a practical, relatively brief but highly effective model for the treatment of many forms of family dysfunction. The pragmatic elements of family therapy are highly relevant to pediatricians. The method requires a clear, formal commitment by all involved family members — a therapeutic contract. Second, individual family members are assigned clear roles and therapeutic tasks to change how the family works, with progress reports required of all participants at each session. Finally, the process is not open-ended; there is a defined limit to the number of sessions allocated to the family to produce the desired results. Too often, when we are dealing with children with chronic conditions, the caregiving responsibility falls disproportionately on one parent, usually the mother. In such situations, redistributing the tasks of daily living among family members can be highly therapeutic. Nate Epstein's wisdom and his tough, pragmatic Cape Breton approach have served me very well in trying to help families deal more effectively with tough situations. His influence also played an important role in shaping the expertise of my son — his son-in-law —

David, who has become an impressive psychiatrist in his own right.

Heinz Lehmann: Heinz Lehmann was born in Berlin in 1911 and received his MD degree in clinical medicine in 1935. Two years later he arrived in Montreal as a German-Jewish refugee.

Over the years, Heinz Lehmann reminded me periodically that my father had given him his first chance to establish himself in Canada by offering him an internship at the Children's Memorial Hospital. At the end of his long career he recounted to my son David that my father had taken him under his wing as they walked down several flights of stairs together at the hospital. My father taught him on this walk and told him that, by the time they reached the ground floor, Heinz would know all he needed to know about infant nutrition.

In those days, psychiatrists like Lehmann were few and far between. And few Canadian-born, Canadian-trained physicians were interested in working in mental institutions doing work with psychotic patients that seemed singularly unrewarding. Thus, many of the physicians who took jobs in such hospitals, including Lehmann, were foreign-born. For most, these were the only jobs available.

In 1950, during my internship in medicine at the Royal Victoria Hospital, I was assigned to a rotation in psychiatry at what was then the Verdun Protestant Hospital, where Lehmann was the clinical director. It was an enormous institution, housing about 2,500 patients, many of whom had spent or were destined to spend most of their lives within its confines. Lehmann described the atmosphere of the hospital when he arrived as "a snake pit." The various buildings that comprised the hospital were connected by a series of tunnels. One of my responsibilities was for patients housed in a building called East House. That forbidding structure housed the most deteriorated, chronically psychotic women. Many would not tolerate clothing, shouted obscenities or made incomprehensible noises and smeared excrement everywhere. Some were violent. I couldn't help wondering what I had done (or not done) to deserve this assignment and what benefit, if any, I could possibly offer these tragic creatures who seemed entirely out of contact with the world.

Lehmann was convinced even the most severely regressed, psychotic patients could be helped to become quieter, happier and more conventional through the simple process of conditioning. To prove the point, he took on East House as his challenge and documented the evolution of the patients' behaviour in a black-and-white amateur film titled simply *East House* — a historic documentary.

Lehmann had his assistants put dresses on the women. The women would tear them off and the staff would put them on again and again until the patients would eventually tolerate them without complaint. Then his assistants would brush the women's hair. The patients would immediately mess it up; again it would be brushed. The process was repeated until they stopped messing up their hair. Then he introduced mirrors and makeup and showed again that these women would gradually accept a greater degree of "normalization" of appearance and behaviour through this process of conditioning. Further, these changes were accompanied by a striking reduction in wilder behaviours and vocalizations. In the last frames of *East House* the women are playing soccer outdoors. The change toward more socially acceptable behaviour was dramatic, a beautiful example of how pharmacotherapy and behavioural treatment of psychiatric illness are not merely complementary but are synergistic components of successful treatment of severe mental illness.

Lehmann became a true pioneer in the history of modern

psychiatry. In the 1950s, he was the first to use an effective pharmacological agent (chlorpromazine, also available as Largactil) as an effective treatment of schizophrenia. Lehmann was truly the father of modern psychopharmacology. He realized mental illness had to involve a chemical disturbance in brain function, a radical notion in an era when psychiatry was largely dominated by psychoanalysis.

Lehmann later evaluated effective pharmacological treatments for depression. He was an innovator in dealing with every dimension of treating mental illness. He introduced visual arts and music as adjuncts to its treatment and documented how the content and colouration of patients' paintings reflected their response to their therapy.

By any measure, Heinz Lehmann was inspiring. My final encounter with him occurred in 1998. I was then a member of the selection committee of the recently established Canadian Medical Hall of Fame, and we had unanimously selected Heinz Lehmann as an inductee. I came downstairs into the lobby of Ottawa's Chateau Laurier Hotel to take a taxi to the Canadian Museum of Civilization where the induction ceremony was to take place. I spied Heinz and his wife and offered them a ride in my taxi. I had not seen him for years.

He began, as always, by reminding me that my father had given him his first break in Canada. I mentioned my 1950 rotation at the Verdun Protestant Hospital and asked if he remembered several patients whom I named and with whom I'd been involved. He not only recalled them but remembered many fine details about each one I had long forgotten (or never knew). I never saw him again, but I remained indebted to him. Like all great teachers, he taught more by example than by preaching.

There are probably few physicians who have done more to change the way we think about mental illness or about the complementary roles of pharmacological and behavioural therapy in successful management. The duality of that approach applies equally to the management of so many conditions we see in children.

Early Years in Practice

An inevitable result of aging is that nostalgia becomes a way of life, accompanied by loud laments — to the yawns of most listeners — for all the good things that have been swept away by the tide of "progress." Here are a few ancient practices that deserve to be resurrected, at least in modernized versions.

During my father's era, the house call was central to good patient care and continued to be so throughout my early years in community practice. In the earlier half of his career in pediatric practice, my father continued to make many house calls every day. However, finding a parking place near his patients' homes became increasingly problematic, so he was urged to hire a chauffeur, which he did. The first and longest-lasting of these was a short, stocky French-Canadian man named Oscar Chatel, who became a virtual member of the family. Aside from remarkable driving skills, he was an expert mechanic who could fix virtually any problem under the hood. He also taught my brother and me to drive several years before we were old enough to be licensed.

After completing five years of postgraduate pediatric training at the Montreal Children's Hospital and at the Children's Hospital Medical Center in Boston, and a final year as chief resident at the Montreal Children's, I entered pediatric practice in Montreal. The daily routine included ward rounds to see patients in hospital, office visits and house calls.

When I began my own practice, I raised a few eyebrows among my fellow pediatricians. At that time, colleagues were charging five dollars per house call. Even as a brash upstart, this seemed inadequate remuneration for what was often an hour's work (including travel), and I decided to charge seven dollars per house call from day one. Patients did not object, and my fellow specialists soon followed suit.

My house calls took me to every corner of Montreal — from the homes of the poorest of the poor to the mansions of wealthy anglophones. In a perfect world, incorporating a certain number of home visits into the fabric of postgraduate medical education would be of inestimable value in the training of young physicians, especially in the care of children with chronic conditions. But this is unlikely to happen, and I recognize (wistfully) that neither the baby nor the bathwater is likely to be restored to that original status. To quote Peter De Vries: "Nostalgia isn't what it used to be."

I made anywhere from two to ten home visits in an average working day. Nowadays, thanks to the visual clarity of the "retrospectoscope," I appreciate the tremendous educational value of those house calls and how much they taught me about illness, and about children and their families — lessons I would never have learned in the intimidating surroundings of an office or hospital clinic. Children and their parents are much more relaxed and comfortable in their natural habitat than in a professional environment. A home visit also produces an important role reversal. The doctor becomes the guest of the family, not the reverse. Home visits also provide unique insights into how the family "works" under real-life conditions and how these dynamic forces have a major impact on the child's medical management, especially when youngsters are affected by chronic or disabling conditions.

As an added bonus, I would often be invited after the consultation to share a few extra social moments with the family over a cup of coffee and (in those awful days) a cigarette! Those few extra minutes often played a crucial role in achieving the doctor's mission as defined by the late Dr. Harry Gordon: to relieve anxiety. The experience also underlined the importance of the two priorities that parents say they seek in their doctor: "enough time" and "explaining things in words I can understand."

Once in a while, a home visit led to a diagnosis that would otherwise have completely escaped me. A memorable example took place on a cold winter morning when I received a frantic phone call from the father of a seven-year-old patient. She had developed severe episodes of wheezing a couple of years earlier. Investigations had shown her to be acutely allergic to several inhalant allergens, including dust and feathers, and a couple of foods, including peanuts. Her parents had removed those triggers from her environment and she had improved greatly. However, on that Sunday morning, her father reported she had experienced a sudden onset of cough and severe wheezing shortly after getting out of bed. I told her father I would drive out to see her. When I arrived, she was still wheezing and coughing severely. The suddenness of the onset of their symptoms strongly suggested she had either eaten or inhaled something to which she was acutely allergic. So I sat by her bed and reviewed everything she had done, breathed and eaten since the preceding evening. No clues were revealed. Frustrated, I prescribed a bronchodilator medication and prepared to leave, asking her father to call me later in the day to report progress.

He was helping me on with my overcoat when he uttered five words to which I have learned to pay studious attention, because they often preface a revelation that is key to understanding the child's condition. Those fateful words are: "Oh, by the way, Doc . . ." In this instance, that was followed by, "You don't suppose this could be anything to do with the duck?" My hand dropped from the door handle. "The *what*?" I asked, not sure I had heard correctly. "Come here," he said, beckoning me toward a closed door that led to the kitchen. He inched the door open, revealing a large (live!) white duck waddling contentedly around the newspaper-covered kitchen floor. I couldn't believe my eyes. "Where did that thing come from?" I asked him after I regained consciousness. He confessed that early that morning he had taken his daughter to Montreal's Atwater Market where live chickens, ducks and geese were sold. He and his daughter thought the duck would make a wonderful pet, so he bought the bird. For reasons still hard to fathom, he seemed to associate feathers only with pillows, not with birds! In one of my rare dictatorial *pronunciamentos*, I ordered the offending bird and all traces of its presence to be removed from the home "any time in the next five minutes." The girl's subsequent rapid recovery was living proof that removing the cause of an illness is more effective than treating the symptoms.

Migration to the "Far East"

By 1967 I had become an associate professor at McGill University and a physician at the Montreal Children's Hospital. Ruth and I had acquired a lovely home and garden in the comfortable suburb of Hampstead, three captivating children and innumerable friends. We planned to spend the rest of our natural lives in Montreal.

In the mid-sixties I had been approached by folks at the University of British Columbia (UBC) looking for a new head of the Department of Pediatrics. A giant carrot linked to that opportunity was their plan to build a beautiful new children's hospital. It sounded tempting, and I travelled to Vancouver for a further mutual assessment. The dean of medicine at UBC was Dr. John ("Jack") McCreary, a fellow pediatrician whom I had known for some time in his previous position on the senior staff at Toronto's Hospital for Sick Children.

When I arrived in Vancouver, I was lodged in a beautiful suite at the elegant UBC Faculty Club, where, I was told, the preceding occupant had been no less a celebrity than Prince Philip. McCreary welcomed me warmly and spread out on a large table the architectural drawings and plans for a brand-new children's hospital. Back in Montreal, Ruth had advised all three children: "We might be moving to Vancouver." This was one of two occasions when her predictions were wrong.

During my Vancouver visit I had the uneasy feeling their elaborate plans for a new children's hospital were still more dream-like than reality-based. That assessment turned out to be correct. By the time I returned to Montreal I had decided against the move and communicated my decision, and my appreciation, to Jack McCreary.

A few months later, as I was seeing a patient in my office at the Montreal Children's Hospital, the phone rang. The caller was a man of whom I had never heard, but he sounded important and decisive. I recall his opening statement verbatim: "Dr. Goldbloom, my name is Chester Stewart. I'm dean of the Faculty of Medicine at Dalhousie University in Halifax, Nova Scotia, and I've come to Montreal with the sole purpose of sitting down with you to persuade you to come to Halifax as professor and head of the Department of Pediatrics and physician-in-chief of the new Izaak Walton Killam Hospital for Children, whose construction will begin shortly. I'm staying in Montreal at the Ritz Carlton Hotel, and I'm prepared to stay here as long as it takes to get you to come down here to discuss my proposal."

With those few words, Chester Stewart had taught me a couple of lessons about recruiting that would serve me remarkably well in years to come. Never delegate recruitment to lower-ranked personnel. And the value a prospective candidate places on a position is determined largely by the value the recruiter sets on it. Various later personal experiences, good and bad, ultimately led me to publish a short article entitled "Head-Hunting in the Jungles of Academia: A Recruiter's Guide."

That telephone conversation and subsequent face-to-face conversations with Chester Stewart convinced me to travel to Halifax for a site visit and further discussions, so I booked a flight. Meanwhile, Ruth advised our three children: "Don't worry, kids, your father will *never* take a job in Halifax." That turned out to be the second time she was wrong.

The departing head of pediatrics at Dalhousie was an old friend, Dr. Bill Cochrane, who had left for the University of Calgary a few months earlier to become head of pediatrics there. Bill Cochrane had been a key figure in persuading Dorothy Killam to contribute $8 million toward construction of a brand-new state-of-the-art children's hospital as a memorial to her late husband, Izaak Walton Killam, one of the two richest men in Canada.

I never met Mr. Killam, but my father had known him when Killam was a member of the board of the Montreal Children's Hospital. In those days, two basic qualifications were required for appointment to a hospital board: major wealth and willingness to help pick up the hospital deficit. At the end of each fiscal year, board members would sit around the table and each would quietly volunteer a large amount toward balancing the budget. My father remembered Mr. Killam mainly for his silences, which were legendary. Killam's principal form of oral communication was the grunt.

Back to Bill Cochrane. Not only did he play a significant role in obtaining the $8 million from Mrs. Killam, but he also identified several talented young pediatric residents to send away to leading medical centres in North America to train to provide expertise in pediatric sub-specialties in the new hospital.

When I returned to Montreal from that first visit, Ruth later recalled, I had a gleam in my eye as I described the enormous opportunities I visualized for developing and improving pediatric care, teaching and research in Nova Scotia. I soon made a return visit, during which I met with several key individuals and committees. Two meetings were particularly memorable. One followed a luncheon with members of the Medical Advisory Committee of the Halifax Infirmary, then one of Halifax's two main teaching hospitals. The committee comprised six physicians, including a Dr. Laufer, one of the earliest specialists in internal medicine in Halifax. Laufer was short and balding, with tufts of hair projecting laterally from behind his ears. He spoke English with a fairly pronounced Germanic accent. He sounded like a caricature of Sigmund Freud. After a cordial discussion over lunch, Dr. Laufer sneaked up behind me as we exited the dining room and silently tugged at my sleeve. What followed recalled a scene from a World War II British spy movie. Dr. Laufer whispered to me very confidentially in his Teutonic brogue:

> *"Goldbloom — you are ssinking of coming to Halifax?"*
>
> *"Well, yes, sir, I'm thinking about it."*
>
> *"I give you an advice."*
>
> *"What is your advice, Dr. Laufer?"*
>
> *"Tr-r-rust no von!"*

My other indelible memory involved another luncheon meeting, this one with members of the Medical Advisory Committee of the Halifax Children's Hospital, which was to morph into the Izaak Walton Killam Hospital for Children. The luncheon was chaired by Dr. Stewart ("Stu") Wenning, a straight-talking Cape Bretoner from Baddeck who was chief of anesthesia. During our lunchtime discussions he addressed me only as "Doc." Following lunch and plenty of Q&A, he asked me:

> *"Now, Doc, is there anything about this job that you don't like?"*
>
> *"Well," I replied, "there is one thing I'm not very happy about."*

"What's that?"

"It's the name you've chosen for the new hospital: the Izaak Walton Killam Hospital for Children. People might refer to it as 'the I. Killam Hospital.' That doesn't sound too good."

"Doc," he replied, *"eight million bucks you ain't worth!"*

The message could not have been clearer. Thus began the next, and most productive, phase of my life in pediatrics and other pursuits, some allied, others not.

Regional Pediatric Care: Spreading the Gospel

After arriving in Halifax in 1967, I realized the province's entire cadre of pediatric specialists resided in the capital city of Halifax. With two exceptions. The exceptions, both of whom I had known as trainees at the Montreal Children's Hospital several year earlier, were in Yarmouth and Sydney. The remainder of the province was a kind of pediatric wasteland, and families from those regions had no choice but to travel to Halifax if they wanted their child assessed by a pediatric specialist.

Normally, I am not a believer in divine intervention, but in 1969 something happened that almost changed my mind. I met a young medical student named Nuala Patricia Kenny — more specifically, *Sister* Nuala Patricia Kenny. Nuala Kenny had migrated to Halifax from New York City in 1962 at the ripe old age of eighteen. A child of a solid Irish Catholic family, she had come to Halifax with the express purpose of joining the Sisters of Charity, whose motherhouse was in Halifax. In 1912, the Sisters had established a college for young women that later evolved into a degree-granting institution, Mount Saint Vincent University. (Many years later my wife, Ruth, would become chair of the board of that university.)

Reflecting the beginning of the Second Vatican Council, Sister Nuala had entertained the "radical" idea she would like to become a doctor. She was told that, as a Sister of Charity, she could *not* become a doctor; she could, however, become a nurse. But she clung doggedly to her ambition and presented herself to the Mother General of the Sisters of Charity, Sister Irene Farmer, to plead her case. Sister Irene's curt response was: "Thank you, Sister, that will be all."

But, to her astonishment, two days later, she was called before the General Council of the Congregation and informed she would be permitted to go to medical school if accepted. Nuala Kenny became the very first Sister of Charity to graduate from a Canadian medical school. Toward the end of first year she "kicked the habit," as many women in religious orders were doing, in favour of conventional attire, but to this day she remains a deeply committed member of her order, an eloquent speaker and a nationally recognized authority on ethical issues in health care.

When Nuala was a third-year medical undergraduate, she told me she wanted to become a psychiatrist, having worked for a time in a psychiatric hospital. I sensed her deep level of commitment and (perhaps for selfish departmental reasons) told her she could do more good as a pediatrician. If she could affect the life of a child, I explained, she could influence that child's entire life thereafter. By the time she graduated in medicine from Dalhousie, the traditional rotating internship had begun to disappear and so-called straight internships in several specialties, including pediatrics, were becoming available.

Nuala Kenny became one of the first straight interns in pediatrics at Dalhousie and spent her first three years of pediatric residency training in our department. By the end of that time, I felt she would benefit from further training at another pediatric centre. I telephoned my mentor and friend Sydney Gellis in Boston, and he agreed to offer her a residency post. She recalls with awe Sydney's encyclopedic knowledge of pediatrics, though her impression of him was that he was a misogynist. My own interpretation is that this was a bit of Sydney's "front," guaranteed to elicit a reaction.

When Nuala returned to Halifax from Boston I was determined she should become a member of our department. Little did I know she would ultimately become one of my successors as department head. But at that time, aware of her deep commitment to the community and her lack of family encumbrances, I thought she was ideally suited to help develop a system of regionalized pediatric care for the province of Nova Scotia. We sat down to work out how we might convince doctors, nurses, hospital administrators and regional health boards that it was in their interest to provide specialized care and consulting services for infants and children in their own communities and perhaps to have one or more pediatric specialists settle there.

We worked out a plan, beginning with an exercise that, in retrospect, seemed rather primitive, but it worked. We made a totally arbitrary decision that no family in Nova Scotia should have to travel more than thirty miles to consult with a pediatric specialist. We then laid out a map of Nova Scotia on a table, took a pair of dividers and drew circles of a thirty-mile radius around each of the province's main population centres. To our surprise and pleasure, the circumference of each circle was contiguous with that of another centre. Thus we were able to identify every community where, in our view at least, one or more pediatric specialists should be located.

While this was a great idea on paper, there was no way that we could impose such a plan on the regional centres. There was a major selling job to be done, and Sister Kenny was the ideal person to close the deal. She had no material gain to achieve. Together we worked out a program to assess systematically the quality of current pediatric services in any community and to make specific suggestions on how child health care in that region could be improved, reducing for thousands of families the amount of travel to the Children's Hospital in Halifax and the associated disruption of family life.

We called this plan the Regional Pediatric Program, and Nuala was given the prestigious title of Regional Pediatric Co-ordinator. The ground rules and modus operandi of the program were specific: First, she would carry out a regional assessment of pediatric services and facilities, but *only* when invited to do so by the regional hospital or local branch of the Medical Society. Second, there would be no charge for any of our services. Third, the services were to include evaluation of in-patient physical facilities and personnel, including pediatric equipment and pediatric training of personnel; and review of discharge summaries of a representative sample of pediatric patients. Following completion of the survey, a written report would be submitted to the hospital and regional medical society with specific recommendations for improving pediatric services.

Finally, during her regional visits, Dr. Kenny would make herself available for individual pediatric consultations when requested by the family physician. The job required a lot of travel throughout the province. *Mirabile dictu*, the Sisters of Charity agreed to buy Nuala a station wagon, and she hit the road. From then on, I referred to her as my "roaming Catholic"; we had become friends.

Our progress toward establishing a complete regional network of pediatric specialists in Nova Scotia followed what soon became a predictable sequence. At her first visit to a regional hospital, family physicians were often notable for their absence. Those in attendance were mostly nurses. But by the time she had completed her work and presented her assessment of the pediatric facilities and services along with her chart review of children discharged from the regional hospital, and had presented her findings to the medical staff and hospital administration, the atmosphere became progressively more receptive. In some centres she would be told initially: "We really don't have too many pediatric problems here." By her second visit, one or two children began to appear for a "second opinion." The number of patients typically increased as local health care personnel began to realize how much they and their patients might benefit from having a pediatric specialist in the region.

Her evaluations of facilities, equipment and personnel led to widespread improvements throughout the province. Most important of all, her work led to a new appreciation of the worth of pediatric consultants. The final outcome of the Regional Pediatric Program was precisely what we had hoped for: new initiatives to recruit one or more pediatric specialists to settle in each of the province's larger communities. Today, Nova Scotia boasts regional pediatric specialists in eight population centres outside of Halifax.

In 1986, I was honoured to be appointed an Officer of the Order of Canada in recognition of my contribution to the development of regional pediatric services in Nova Scotia. As is so often the case, I may have had the original idea, but someone else did the heavy lifting. The weightlifter in this instance was Sister Nuala Kenny. Both of us still derive great satisfaction from the outcome.

An Ounce of Prevention: What Is It Really Worth?

Before 1976, I had given little thought to the broader issues of disease prevention. Preventive procedures were already part of a pediatrician's everyday practice, beginning at a baby's birth, with the instillation of silver nitrate drops in the eyes of every newborn to prevent gonorrheal eye infection and routine immunization of young infants against smallpox, diphtheria, whooping cough (pertussis) and tetanus (lockjaw). Later, as new vaccines were developed, the list grew to include vaccines against polio, rubella (German measles), mumps, varicella (chickenpox), rotavirus, pneumococcal infections, meningococcal meningitis, influenza and human papillomavirus.

But daily routines soon become automated, and I had not given much thought to high-flown issues such as proof of the validity of advice we were giving to parents and of the things we were doing to their children in the conviction such interventions would stave off an assortment of diseases.

In 1976, though, I received an unexpected phone call from Dr. Walter O. Spitzer, asking me to join a national task force as a pediatric representative. The task force was to examine the validity of preventive interventions then being recommended and practised to prevent a wide range of diseases and conditions.

The newly formed body was called the Canadian Task Force on the Periodic Health Examination. It had been established by the Conference of Deputy Ministers of Health of the ten Canadian provinces.

Walter Spitzer was a bit of a character. An extremely articulate family physician, an intellectual and, incidentally, a licensed airplane pilot, he was one of a small handful of Canadian family physicians with a solid background in clinical epidemiology. He was convinced that, before any preventive intervention could be officially recommended to health professionals and accepted by Canadians, its effectiveness should be solidly grounded in solid scientific proof of efficacy *and* effectiveness.

If you had asked me when I joined the task force to explain the difference between efficacy and effectiveness, I would have either pleaded ignorance or, more likely, tried to fake my way through. Clarifying that vital distinction was the first of many fundamental lessons I learned during my eighteen years with the task force, including my service as chair after Walter Spitzer's retirement.

I was intimidated by the knowledge and competence of my fellow task force members. In developing a modus operandi, we consulted with many experts, the most knowledgeable and pragmatic being Dr. David Sackett, then head of the Department of Epidemiology at McMaster University and, to many, the "father" of modern epidemiology.

North American task forces and expert committees sometimes discourage (or even exclude) people known to hold dissenting opinions. In health care, this is especially likely to occur when the relevant scientific evidence bearing on the issue is iffy or incomplete. Individuals known to hold dissenting opinions are often not invited to the party and thus do not get to present their views to the "experts."

During my first couple of years as a member of the task force, I

experienced a gnawing frustration. After almost two years of meetings and some admittedly fascinating discussions, we had yet to
tackle a single ostensibly preventable condition. But some valuable
insights can be gained only through the "retrospectoscope."

Our first two years of seemingly interminable discussions turned
out to be the secret of our success. That lengthy period was devoted
exclusively to developing a solid methodology — a set of standard-
ized, strict rules — to evaluate the strength of the evidence for
preventability of *any* ostensibly preventable condition and to evaluate the efficacy and effectiveness of the preventive intervention.

Which brings me back to the vital distinction in meaning
between those two words: "Efficacy" describes how well an intervention (such as a vaccine) works among those *who accept it.*
In contrast, "effectiveness" refers to how well that intervention
works among those *to whom it is offered.* The distinction is vitally
important. For example, if regular digital rectal examination could
be proven to prevent all fatal prostate cancers (which it doesn't),
it would be 100 per cent efficacious. However, in actual practice,
if only 5 per cent of males showed up for the dubious pleasure of
undergoing that unpopular examination, its effectiveness would
be far too low (5 per cent) to support an authoritative recommendation for universal implementation as a preventive manoeuvre.

The Canadian Task Force made two contributions that gained
it international recognition and respect: First, it developed a
clear methodology to *evaluate the preventability* of *any* adverse
human condition and the *efficacy* and *effectiveness* of any preventive intervention. Second, it issued graded recommendations
on whether a particular preventive manoeuvre should (or should
not) be incorporated into the periodic health examination. This
type of critical analysis led to one of the task force's idol-shat-
tering recommendations: that the undefined annual checkup be
abandoned in favour of a series of gender-and-age-specific health
protection packages.

The fundamental difference that made the Canadian methodology unique was that *evidence took precedence over opinion.* In addition, the task force graded the *strength* of the evidence for effectiveness of any ostensibly preventive intervention as follows:

Level I: Evidence obtained from at least one properly randomized, controlled trial (a trial in which those receiving the intervention and those not were picked by totally random selection and in adequate numbers for the results to be statistically significant).

Level II-1: Evidence from well-designed cohort or case-control studies, preferably from more than one centre or research group.

Level II-2: Evidence based on comparisons between times and places with or without the intervention. Rare dramatic results in uncontrolled experiments, such as the introduction of penicillin in the 1940s, were considered as this type of evidence. The results had been so dramatic that the conduct of a randomized, prospective trial would have been unethical.

Level III: Opinions of respected authorities, based on clinical experience, descriptive studies or reports of expert committees.

It is worth noting that the task force gave the lowest value in its hierarchy of evidence to the opinions of experts. Throughout medical history, "experts" have been proven wrong far more often than right. The recommendation of bed-rest after childbirth and after surgical operations for the treatment of rheumatic fever or tuberculosis is only one among hundreds of examples.

A distinguished epidemiologist, Dr. Alvan Feinstein of Yale University, once observed: "The greatest mistakes in medical history have been directly traceable to the opinions of experts." Sadly, his statement had little dampening effect on the tendency for professional medical bodies to produce and circulate large numbers of position papers from "expert committees" advising us on how to care for our patients and how to prevent certain diseases, whether the scientific evidence for efficacy and effectiveness was sufficiently solid to justify their position.

Some time ago, Dr. Peter F. Belamarich and colleagues published a piece aptly entitled "Drowning in a Sea of Advice." He and his colleagues had read and coded each of the 344 policy statements published by the American Academy of Pediatrics. From these, they identified 57 recommendations, containing no fewer than 192 specific health care directives the Academy expected pediatricians to deliver to the parents or guardians of their patients during office visits. Topics included safety advice, media use, substance abuse, environmental health hazards, developmental/emotional health, sexuality, pregnancy and nutrition. Not a single policy statement offered a hint of evidence that office-based counselling achieved the desired health or behavioural outcomes. And from a practical perspective, following these recommendations religiously would probably require an office visit of at least two hours!

In an age of phenomenal advances in medical science, including preventive health care, most of us are still captivated by a curious amalgam of fond hope, faith and magical thinking, the kind that convinced us as children that if we didn't step on cracks in the sidewalk, everything would be all right.

There is no shortage of current issues in preventive health care for which the distinction between faith, hope and solid scientific evidence is murky. Breast self-examination for breast cancer and prostate-specific antigen (PSA) screening for prostate cancer are two emotionally charged examples. Understandably, the views of some will be irreversibly shaped by the experience of a single personal experience or that of a close relative or friend: "Ten years ago I examined my breasts religiously every month, and I found a small lump. The doctor removed it *just in time*. It was cancerous, and now I'm just fine. If I hadn't discovered it, I'd be dead by now."

The conviction that breast self-examination saves lives has been nourished by cancer societies and women's groups. But what does science tell us about its efficacy and effectiveness, not in simply finding tumours but in saving lives from breast cancer, a vitally important distinction? In 1994, in a critical review of the evidence, the Canadian Task Force concluded the evidence was "not strong enough to make a clear recommendation on teaching breast self-examination; there is insufficient evidence to either include or exclude such teaching in the periodic health examination for women."

In another example, the man who, on advice of his friendly neighbourhood urologist, has had his PSA measured, found it elevated and had his cancerous prostate removed, now assumes he will remain hale and hearty for years to come. No one will convince him his life was not saved by the PSA test. Far more men die *with* prostate cancer than die *of* prostate cancer; that is, the prostate glands of many elderly men contain nests of cancerous cells, most of which will never cause disseminated disease or death.

It has been said that experience is the greatest teacher. Conversely, it has also been said that clinical experience is "making the same mistake year after year after year with increasing levels of certainty."[**] I tend to revive the latter definition when colleagues express an opinion that begins, "In my experience . . ."

[**] Michael O'Donnell, *A Sceptic's Medical Dictionary* (London: BMJ Publishing Group, 1997).

Compulsive Scribbler

From my earliest years as a pediatrician I was a compulsive scribbler. My writing career, if I can use that pretentious a description, began when I was a mere medical student. I aspired to join the Osler Society, which was dedicated to studies of the history of medicine. To qualify, students had to submit a paper on a topic of medical historical interest. I wrote one that I named "Music and the Physician" and submitted it to Dr. William "Billy" Francis, custodian of the Osler Library at McGill and patron saint of the Osler Society.

"Music and the Physician" was fun to write. At the time, direct, uncluttered writing was hardly my strong suit. Rereading my pretentious opening paragraph a mere sixty-four years later gives me a combination of facial flushing and the dry heaves. But I was admitted to the Osler Society anyway, and a copy of that article, along with others scribbled by new members, gathers dust to this very day in the Osler Library.

From then on I became a compulsive scribbler, producing over one hundred and fifty publications in refereed medical journals, four textbooks, twenty-three contributions to textbooks and ten articles in the popular media, including a series of pieces on pediatric topics for *Readers' Digest*. My output included editing *The Canadian Guide to Clinical Preventive Health Care* and the textbook *Pediatric Clinical Skills*.

But my most rewarding writing experience, bar none, began when I became a regular contributor to *Pediatric Notes,* a weekly four-page publication founded in 1976 by Sydney Gellis, then chair of the Department of Pediatrics at Tufts University in Boston. One of Sydney Gellis's characteristics that endeared him to me forever was that he could see the humour in many situations others took far too seriously. He had a unique ability to balance wisdom and wit. Sydney could also be deadly serious when the situation demanded it.

A prolific author, he had for years edited the *Yearbook of Pediatrics,* an annual compendium of abstracts of the most significant articles in the current literature. He appended to each of the half dozen abstracts a brief, always insightful and often witty editorial comment. Most were written by Sydney, with occasional contributions by experts in particular fields. Because Sydney enjoyed huge popularity among his fellow pediatricians, *Pediatric Notes* attracted many subscribers, and its summary format saved them a huge amount of reading time. Nothing succeeds like succinct.

In the early 1990s, Sydney asked me to contribute an occasional abstract with editorial comment. As time went by, his requests for submissions became more frequent. First, the task required me to keep up with a wide range of topics in the current pediatric literature. Second, it provided me with a unique opportunity as editor to put certain topics (especially current fads) into perspective. Finally, because Sydney and I shared a strong affinity for the humorous side of people and events, neither took himself (or anyone else) too seriously. We also shared a considerable degree of resistance against being suckered into the latest fads in pediatric diagnosis and treatment.

In 2002, when Sydney became seriously ill, I visited him and his wife Matilda in their home in Newton, Massachusetts. He was bedridden. I sat by his bed, and we had a warm, affectionate conversation. He asked if I would be willing to take over as editor of *Pediatric Notes*. I agreed readily and was honoured to do so. My relationship with Sydney had become quasi-filial. In his latter days, Sydney would sometimes address me (in Yiddish) as *"mein sohn"* ("my son"), a term of endearment that always warmed my heart.

The following is an excerpt from the first 2003 issue of *Pediatric Notes*:

Sydney Gellis Remembered

Sydney Gellis died peacefully December 6, 2002, at 88 years of age. Despite having been seriously ill for the past few months, he was still editing material for Pediatric Notes *a few days before he died. Had he known that I would write a few words of praise and remembrance after his death, he would certainly have done everything in his power to discourage me. He wanted to "go gentle into that good night" and, at the end, that is what he did. I miss him enormously and always will.*

I first came under Sydney's spell in 1951, as a young pediatric resident at Children's Hospital in Boston. Every Saturday morning, he presided over a unique conference on pediatric exotica . . . rare syndromes and diseases. Behind his back, he was often referred to as "Syndrome Syd," because his knowledge of these rarae aves was encyclopedic. Each conference concluded with a written quiz of a dozen or so questions. Anyone who could answer more than 50 per cent correctly was assigned to the genius category. No matter how tired we were from working most of the preceding night, Sydney's conference was an event we would never miss. Attendance was a quasi-religious observance. Not all of his pearls were immediately applicable to clinical situations, but many obscure "factoids" stuck in our memories like glue, long after more practical bits of information

COMPULSIVE SCRIBBLER 141

were forgotten. I can never forget, for example, that the opossum has no corpus callosum. In 1951, Sydney was an assistant professor at Harvard and chief of pediatrics at the Beth Israel Hospital, across the street from Children's. He also maintained a research lab there, focusing on jaundice in the newborn and liver disease. There he gave me my first exposure to serious research. After ward rounds each morning we would gather in his office to talk, often for an hour or more. The conversations were wide-ranging, and were never limited to pediatrics or to the current status of our research projects. They included lively discussions of books we had read, concerts attended and plays seen, always with a healthy sprinkling of anecdotes and good laughs.

Sydney had a low tolerance for manifestations of self-importance in others. By the same token, he never took himself too seriously. Innumerable pediatricians throughout the world were beneficiaries of his wit and wisdom, whether in the Yearbook of Pediatrics, *which he edited from 1952 to 1978, or in* Pediatric Notes, *which he founded and edited from 1976 to 2002. Many times I heard colleagues say that they read these publications more for Sydney's comments than for the content of the abstracts!*

He served overseas with the US Army Medical Corps during the Italian Campaign in World War II and played an important role in introducing gamma globulin prophylaxis to stop the outbreak of Hepatitis A that was disabling huge numbers of American military personnel. After the war, he served as Secretary of the Society for Pediatric Research, during the era when the Secretary virtually ran that society single-handedly.

Years later he became Chair of Pediatrics, first at Boston University and finally at Tufts. When he accepted the Chair at Tufts he telephoned his mother to tell her about his latest appointment.

She was not impressed. She wanted to know when he was going to get a steady job.

Current Pediatric Therapy, *which Sydney originally co-edited with Ben Kagan, and which still bears their names, continues to be an invaluable desk reference for thousands of pediatricians. As a result of his prolific published output, I suspect that more of Sydney Gellis' words have been read by more pediatricians than those of any other pediatric author in the modern era. More often than not, his comments left us smiling, but they always left us better informed as well. The other day, I paged through some of the very first issues of* Pediatric Notes, *from 1977. One is immediately struck by his marvelous mixture of wisdom and wit. On March 8, 1977, he commented on the first report documenting that Chlamydia trachomatis could cause not only inclusion conjunctivitis but serious pneumonia in infants as well. He wrote, in part:*

"It is disturbing to have fixed beliefs altered; however, so many of our old concepts are being shattered, we ought to be able to take this one in our stride. Add this agent to the others that can produce a pertussis-like syndrome and give it strong consideration when a young infant has a prolonged pneumonitis."

Three weeks later he was back in whimsical mode. Commenting on a report of Group A streptococcal wound infections in which one source had been identified by an anal culture of one of the surgeons, he wrote:

"Previous papers have reported anesthesiologists harboring group B strep in their bottoms; now we have a surgeon who is an anal carrier of Group A. I can picture a group of haughty surgeons lined up for culture. I'll not laugh too heartily; we're probably next."

His clinical skills were superb, and his patients worshipped him. They were invariably touched by his humanity, and would recall both his care and his caring many years after a single visit to his office.

Sydney leaves an enduring legacy of love for his family — for his dear wife, Matilda, daughter Beth, son Stephen and, not the least, his grandchildren. He adored them all and they have reciprocated in full. Readers everywhere will join in extending condolences to the entire Gellis family in a loss we all share.

Sydney's widow, Matilda, a decisive woman of great intelligence, continued to manage the business side of *Pediatric Notes.* I wrote each issue in Halifax, where a compositor put it into print-ready form and sent it to Boston for printing and mailing to subscribers. I tried to honour Sydney's memory by perpetuating his style of healthy skepticism in editorial commentary whenever appropriate.

Serving as editor of *Pediatric Notes* allowed me free rein to express my sometimes heretical views on a variety of topics and periodically to light the fuse under a few contemporary myths. It gave me the perfect platform to air various personal pediatric pet peeves, such as the over-use of so-called ventilating tubes to treat children with fluid in the middle ear, a transient condition in most children; the over-investigation of children with urinary tract infections; and the eruption in recent years of a hysterical preoccupation with the development of asymmetric head shapes in otherwise healthy babies.

Some of this asymmetry was being attributed to the "Back to Sleep" campaign, which encouraged parents to place their babies on their backs to sleep. It was believed this manoeuvre would reduce the statistical risk of dying from SIDS (sudden infant death syndrome), a classical instance of guilt by association rather than rigorous proof of causality. Whether this campaign ever actually saved any babies' lives was never proven. What it did accomplish with certainty was to produce visible flattening of the back of the head of many otherwise healthy babies. The worst crime in this saga was that someone decided this "condition" deserved a fancy name. Some wretch assigned it the thoroughly scary title of "postural plagicocephaly," no less. Clinics dedicated exclusively to treating this "problem" sprang up to deal with these innocent babies. To make matters even scarier, some evil spirit came up with the idea of putting "moulding helmets" on these poor babies' heads in an attempt to compress their noggins into perfect cranial symmetry. Simply giving it such a pretentious medicalized name was sufficient to strike terror into the hearts of innocent parents.

Over many years as a practicing pediatrician I had seen innumerable infants with noticeable flattening of the back of their heads or of one side or the other. (Some of them slept on their backs.) My late father taught me how to understand and "cure" this condition. Babies' skulls are soft and malleable. When they lie in their cribs they typically turn their heads (and eyes) toward the major light source, usually a window. This produces a flattening of the occiput on the side turned toward the window. My father pointed out that you could "cure" this condition simply by turning the baby around 180 degrees in the crib! Alternatively, you could do absolutely nothing, since the asymmetry would correct itself gradually after the child assumed the vertical posture.

I used to quiz medical students about how to treat this totally benign and transient cosmetic condition — if, indeed, they felt obliged to do so. Most would reason it out, but many would conclude they should turn the crib around 180 degrees! The thought of simply turning the *baby* around 180 degrees never occurred to them!

Finally, when this topic came up in an auditorium setting, usually in the context of a lecture I entitled "Pediatric Non-Diseases," I would ask the audience to look around the room and tell me how many "deformed" asymmetric heads they could count. Invariably there were none. There had to be a message there.

This whole sad story is a classic example of a common phenomenon: the pathologizing of normalcy. The lesson to be drawn is the importance of *never* treating any "condition" before its natural history (what happens to it over time, if you do absolutely *nothing*) has been well documented. Finally, never assign Latin or Greek names to conditions unless they have been proven unequivocally to be harmful to health.

Over and over again, we pediatricians have validated George Santayana's assertion: "Those who do not learn from the mistakes of history are doomed to repeat them." The history of pediatrics is littered with embarrassing validations of that maxim, including:

1. The use of misnamed "corrective" shoes to treat feet turning in or out, most of which have no beneficial effect and no significance for achieving the functional purpose or future direction of feet.

2. Removal of tonsils and adenoids for almost any excuse, the most common being, to paraphrase Sir Edmund Hillary, "because they're there."

3. Excessive and invasive investigations of children (especially girls) who have had a single urinary tract infection. This was a *bête noire* of mine, particularly because many infants and young children were being routinely subjected to an extremely painful, invasive procedure called voiding cysto-urethrography that required catheterization of the urethra and retrograde (very painful) injection of a radio-opaque dye. This miserable procedure was being inflicted on infants and young children, often following a single urinary tract

infection, and infrequently revealing abnormalities that
called for intervention.

After innumerable children with vesico-ureteral reflux (VUR)
had had their ureters surgically detached from their normal point
of entry through the bladder wall and reimplanted at a different
site, it was discovered VUR disappeared or improved spontaneously in the fullness of time in most cases without the benefit (?)
of surgical intervention!

Here are a few more examples of my pet peeves, as published
in *Pediatric Notes*:

On the uselessness of misnamed "cough suppressants": After
a double-blind study showed two such preparations to be totally
ineffective, I commented: "You would think that observations
such as these would cause the bottom to fall out of the cough
medicine market, reduce health care expenditures and cause
venerable practitioners to return to my grandmother's chicken
soup, hot tea and lemon and other sovereign remedies that really
do work. Dream on."

**On the passion for putting infants in the prone (face-down)
sleeping position, ostensibly to prevent sudden infant death
syndrome:** "I've suffered increasing insomnia (in both the
prone and supine position) ever since the American Academy
of Pediatrics (AAP) and the Canadian Pediatric Society (CPS)
published their policy statements on infant sleeping position
because of a nagging suspicion that the available data didn't justify such a global pronouncement. These authors have done us
'yeoperson'[††] service by articulating their doubts and providing
supporting data . . . we haven't heard the last of this hot potato.

[††] The gender-neutral term designed to replace the sexist "yeoman."

And, by the way, isn't sleeping prone in New Zealand the same as sleeping supine in the US?"

On a study of the effect of consuming dairy products on bone composition: "It may be unkind to point out this study was partly funded by the National Dairy Council, whose enthusiasm for greater consumption of the products of bovine lactation is not easily cowed. The fact that we (humans) are the only mammalian species that clings doggedly to the milk of another species raises some fascinating bio-philosophical questions."

On a study of halitosis in children: "Halitology" is a new specialty (to me, at least). We should take comfort in the ancient dictum attributed to Confucius: "Better to have halitosis than no breath at all."

On the treatment of diaper rash: "My late father used to intone the ancient adage that 'diaper rash is not cured by what you put on it but by what you take off it' (i.e. the diaper, followed by exposure to air). Pediatricians who continue to prescribe large quantities of steroids and antifungals for plain, old diaper rash are giving the infants (and their parents) a bum rap."

On the attribution of children's symptoms to teething: "Physicians who persist in attributing any child's symptoms to teething should be given a large dose of reality medicine and labeled as dentally retarded."

And one of my favourites, an article on dyslexia with some important messages:

Dyslexics Have More Fun

(Editor's Note: Some articles must be read in their entirety to be fully appreciated, and this is one such. We summarize it here to encourage our readers to trot out the original journal and devour the full text of this moving report by Mike Peters, a former child dyslexic, now both a life-long dyslexic and a Pulitzer Prize–winning cartoonist.)

He describes himself in childhood as "a stuttering, skinny kid" whose parents had not gone past the eighth grade. He was seldom read to at home. Also, he couldn't see the blackboard, though no one noticed this until he was in third grade. Despite these handicaps, he loved creative activities and art. By the time he went to high school he was still, by his own description, "cross eyed, skinny and stupid." In his final year of high school, his mother was called by the teacher, who told her that her son was retarded. She was urged to send him to trade school. His classmates voted him "least likely to succeed." Nowadays, he sometimes makes speeches to students, telling them that the "dirty secret in society is that learning disabilities often translate into creativity." He concludes "if you can survive school, people then start throwing money at you because you are creative." (Peters, M. J. Child Neurol. 19:827-828, October 2004).

Comment: The foregoing excerpt does not do justice to this very special article. It should be read by all pediatricians who treat children with learning disabilities. They would be wise to remember that therapeutic success, after all, is more often built on children's strengths rather than by trying to beat their deficiencies into submission. Mike Peters' ultimate success seems to have been due to a combination of good luck and the triumph of a long-submerged talent over an intransigent education system. (R. Goldbloom)

Sydney Gellis's lasting contribution to medical publications was his recognition that the humorous touch often strengthened the message, rather than weakening it, increasing the likelihood that it would lodge in readers' minds and sometimes even improve the quality of their patient care. Wit and wisdom need not be mutually exclusive.

Each of us has something wrong with us — more often several things — but not every "abnormality" needs treatment. And the most difficult thing for many doctors to do can be to do *nothing*.

After Sydney Gellis died in 2002, I was happy to become the editor of *Pediatric Notes*. But several years later when his wife offered to sell me the publication, I was well into my eighties and, as Henny Youngman put it succinctly, "When I go into a restaurant and order a three-minute boiled egg, they make me pay in advance." I therefore declined her offer, and on December 30, 2010, the final issue of *Pediatric Notes* was published. The timing of the finale was probably right.

My lifetime association with Sydney Gellis and my years with *Pediatric Notes* made me a far better pediatrician and more critical reader of medical literature. Those years also kept me in close touch with world pediatric literature to a degree otherwise unimaginable. The experience stands high among those that gave me such a lucky life.

Pediatric Hidden Agendas and Myths

It took me several years in pediatric practice before I became fully aware many folks who bring their child to see a doctor carry with them a certain amount of baggage — family secrets that may turn out to be the *real* reason the family has come to see you. When children are brought to the doctor for complaints that may seem trivial to the physician, their *real* worry, often too frightening to verbalize, may be a fear their child may have something far more serious. Failure to root out and deal with such unspoken fears guarantees persistence of the anxiety. Most hidden agendas fall into one of the following categories: fear of serious (or fatal) disease; and parents' guilt feelings and fear that something they did, or failed to do, may have been responsible for the child's problem.

A mother brings her child to the emergency department complaining of abdominal pain. If the doctor asks who else in the family has complained of abdominal pain, it is sometimes discovered the child's grandfather complained of abdominal pain a year or more earlier, was found to have bowel cancer, and died within months.

Such secret terrors may make no medical sense to the doctor but are as real as real can be to the parents. Assuming the doctor has a good idea of what *is* causing the child's bellyaches, it can be helpful to seize the moment and explain to parents that bowel cancer does not occur in youngsters of this age, and the likely cause of his complaint is something relatively benign, such as constipation, which is easily treated. It can be downright meddlesome and counterproductive to order investigations such as x-rays because the mere act of doing so tells parents "the doctor isn't really sure what's wrong; otherwise, why would he be ordering those tests?"

There is no shortage of very common complaints that can make parents fear the worst (while *never* volunteering such terrifying fears). For example, over the years I have seen innumerable children with headaches. Whenever I see such children, who are often between three and ten, I take most of the history from the child rather than the parent; after all, who can describe the symptoms better than the patient? Even with very young children I usually ask them to hold up an index finger and point to the *exact* spot on their head where the headache starts. Typically, many point to a spot very close to or above one of the eyes. I then ask them to tell me what they can do to make their headache feel better. Typical answer: Lie down, darken the room and go to sleep. I also ask them what makes their headache worse. They often identify noise and bright lights (or watching TV). Are there any foods they eat that can give them a headache? Some identify hotdogs, chocolate or processed meats. Having satisfied myself this youngster has typical childhood migraine,‡‡ I turn to the parent(s) with my standard conversational opener for detecting unspoken fears: "I don't know about you, but many parents of youngsters with headaches are really afraid they may be caused by something really serious [I then stop, look and listen for even the slightest acknowledgement, such as a slight, silent affirmative head nod] . . . like . . . a brain tumour." Following acknowledge-

---

‡‡ Many parents mistakenly believe that migraines affect only adults.

ment of that fear, my next question is: "Who do you know that has had a brain tumour?" Parents then may describe a relative, or even someone they had only heard about who "complained of headaches, went to see two or three different doctors but, by the time they found out it was a brain tumour, it was *too late!*"

Having established to my own satisfaction this child has migraine (and often having elicited a history of several "*migraineurs*" in the family), I explain to the parents *why* their child's headaches are typical of migraine and how dramatically they differ from those of youngsters with brain tumours. These are typically much worse (being caused by increased intracranial pressure) and tend to occur first thing in the morning, when spinal fluid pressure is at its highest.

I make a special point of *not* ordering investigations such as brain scans on such children. Merely doing so communicates the message I too am not really sure it *isn't* a brain tumour. Not surprisingly, most parents are far more concerned with what the child's symptoms are *not* than about what the real problem may be. Their palpable relief at such reassurance is clear evidence their real (unspoken) concern has been dealt with effectively.

There is no shortage of equally dramatic examples of hidden agendas that can hang over parents' heads like a huge black cloud. Consider the two-year-old who develops a fever and suddenly loses consciousness, turns blue and goes into a generalized epileptic-like convulsion. So-called febrile convulsions are common, occurring in many otherwise normal children. Years ago, I examined many such children in pediatric emergency departments. They were often brought in by police cruiser, sirens blaring and lights flashing. Often by the time the child reaches the emergency department, he or she has regained full consciousness and normal colour. Emergency department staff have had a reassuring chat with the parents and have given them an informative brochure on the topic of febrile convulsions. As staff physician, I was required to approve the child's management plan before the family was allowed to leave. As the pediatric resident described the management plan, I always asked: "Did you ask the parents whether they were afraid their child was going to die?" Most often, they had not done so and seemed taken aback by the bluntness of my question. I would suggest we return to see the parents before they left the emergency department. After greeting them, I would say to them: "Folks, I don't know about you, but a lot of parents who see their child having a convulsion worry that their child is dying." (I stop, look and listen.) More than one father has said to me at this point: "Doctor, we were sure she was *dead!*"

It has been well documented in the medical literature that most parents who witness their child having a febrile convulsion believe their child is dying. Given such evidence, how can we possibly provide appropriate, compassionate and comprehensive care to such families unless we raise the issue of fear of death and deal with it head on *in every case?*

Another recent widespread variety of unspoken parent anxiety involves the fear that the child may die of SIDS (sudden infant death syndrome). I am convinced we pediatricians have to take the lion's share of the responsibility for creating an epidemic of SIDS-phobia.

Some years ago, the medical literature sprouted with reports of phenomena that were grouped under the vague heading of "apparent life-threatening events," or ALTEs, for short. Babies who had seemed to stop breathing momentarily, or had turned bluish at home, were being admitted to children's hospitals right, left and centre and put through complex protocols of investigation, including round-the-clock monitoring with frightening machines that emitted frequent false alarms, creating panic among parents and staff alike.[§§] I remember counting four such

§§ To raise anxiety levels even further, such infants were often diagnosed (and labelled) as having had "near-miss sudden infant death."

babies on one of our pediatric wards at the same time. To add insult to injury, many of these youngsters were sent home with electronic baby monitors designed to sound an alarm at the first sign of any deviation in breathing or heart rate.

After some time, pediatricians began to realize such fancy investigations and home monitoring had probably not saved a single life. But one outcome was certain; the whole process was guaranteed to induce sky-high levels of parental anxiety.

Nowadays, many, many parents, especially in the upper middle class, are addicted to home baby monitors: a microphone near the baby's crib, with loudspeakers strategically located throughout the home so anxious parents can hear the baby's slightest peep, rush into the room and make sure the youngster is still alive.

We have no information on what proportion of parents who are "addicted" to commercial home baby monitor use actually harbour secret fears their baby might become a victim of SIDS. Presumably, such parents hope that, thanks to the monitor, they will receive a signal that might allow them to "save" their baby. To my knowledge, no one has conducted a quantitative study of how often baby monitor use is a subtle sign of SIDS-phobia, but I have identified the connection in several families. One of these was unforgettable for several reasons.

Several years ago, an especially nice mother and father were referred to me by their family physician. They told me their son, then eleven months of age, was waking ten or twelve times per night and crying. The parents were taking turns rushing into the baby's room, picking him up, soothing him and returning him to his crib, until the next episode, typically within thirty to forty-five minutes.

As we sat and chatted in my office, I looked at the baby, bouncing happily up and down on his father's lap. It did not require a stroke of genius to know this was a healthy boy. But it was also clear the parents' lives (their nights, to be precise) were a living hell. Somewhere in the course of our conversation, they mentioned they had a baby monitor in the room. I "took a flyer" and did something I do only rarely. I pointed my finger at them, accusingly, looked them straight in the eyes and asked: "*Who do you know* that has lost a baby from sudden infant death syndrome?" Their verbal and nonverbal responses to my question are etched in my memory. Mom could no longer maintain eye contact with me and looked as though she was about to cry. In contrast, the father's shoulders relaxed, he smiled and said: "My wife has a second cousin who lost a six-week-old baby from SIDS a few months before our baby was born."

I learned long ago never to postpone discussion of such a "hot button" issue. I said: "Folks, let's stop right here. I can't tell you what either of you is going to die of, or when, and I can't tell you what I'm going to die of, but I *can* guarantee you that *this* baby is *never*, repeat *never* going to die of SIDS." I had good reason to be so dogmatic: Their baby was already far beyond the age range at which almost all cases of SIDS occur, and there is no evidence a child who has a second cousin who died of SIDS is at any greater risk than any randomly selected child from the general population.

The process of helping anxious parents goes far beyond telling them, authoritatively, their child does or does not have the condition that was their number one worry. There are always important issues of context, and I felt they should be explored with this couple.

Their visit to my office took place in November. I asked *when* the last time was the two of them had gone out together: to a movie, to visit friends or relatives or whatever. Father replied instantly: "January fourth." The precision and duration of his memory was, in itself, pathological. I decided to ask about other ways in which this recurrent nocturnal fixation had coloured their lives. I suggested: "I don't imagine this night-time routine has been too good for your sex lives." To this, the father (who now seemed to be enjoying the interview) replied: "Doctor, it's been the best contraceptive we've found so far!"

Having uncovered this hidden agenda and defined its dramatic impact on their lives, it was time to establish a therapeutic contract, that is, to negotiate an agreement with the family (not an authoritarian instruction) about steps to be taken to deal effectively with the problem. We agreed on the following plan:

> Step 1: Immediately upon returning home that afternoon they would remove the baby monitor and throw it in the trash (they agreed readily).

> Step 2: After establishing they knew a babysitter they trusted, they agreed to hire her and leave their house (for whatever social activity they chose) for a minimum of two hours on two specified days during the coming week.

> Step 3: We agreed on a stepwise process of deconditioning the baby from the habit of being picked up at night: progressively delaying going into the baby's room; delaying any moves to pick the baby up; never speaking to the baby during the episodes; and making their visits to the baby's room progressively shorter. Finally, they agreed to call me in one week to report the results of these interventions.

I am pleased to report mother, father and baby lived happily ever after.

Since that experience, I learned to ask many parents if they use a baby monitor. For those who do, I gently explore the possibility of "SIDS-anxiety" and have been surprised at the frequency of a positive disclosure.

I can't help wondering how much SIDS-anxiety may also have been generated by the widely publicized "Back to Sleep" campaign I mentioned earlier. There is, in my view, a real possibility that we pediatricians sometimes create more anxiety than we cure, and we all know the material with which the road to hell is paved.

Another common hidden agenda takes the form of a family secret in which parents believe something they did (or failed to do) may somehow have caused the child's disease or disability. I received a lifelong lesson in this phenomenon many years ago:

A wealthy family brought their daughter, about twelve, to see me. The girl was severely developmentally delayed. I estimated her overall developmental level to be about that of a five-year-old. She had already been evaluated by several highly competent specialists, but the parents were obviously still seeking something. As physicians, it is tempting to issue pronouncements but easy to overlook what *the parents* believe about what may have caused their child's condition.

I used my well-worn "permissive" introduction to the key question: "I don't know about you folks, but many parents who have a child with this kind of problem have their *own* thoughts or ideas about what might have caused it." In response, her father said, "Doctor, I *know* what caused it."

I asked him to elaborate. "It was the time she fell in the swimming pool," he said. I asked for details. They had been visiting friends who had a swimming pool. He had been walking along beside the pool, holding his daughter's hand. For a moment, he inadvertently let go of her hand, and when he looked, she was on the bottom of the pool. She had been resuscitated pretty quickly, and there was no reason to believe this brief immersion could possibly have been responsible for such severe developmental delay. Nowhere in her extensive medical documentation was there a single mention of her having fallen into a swimming pool.

But her father had carried this burden of guilt with him ever since that event. One can only assume he had never revealed his awful secret because *no one had asked him for his ideas* of what might have caused the child's problem. That single revelation turned out to be the key to resolving his deep-rooted feelings of guilt.

A Myth Is as Good as a Mile

There are still a few areas of pediatrics in which folklorish beliefs trump evidence. Some traditional ideas seem immune to any evidence to the contrary, acquiring lives of their own. If only for personal catharsis, here are a few of the false beliefs to which I've been exposed throughout my career as a pediatrician.

Myth 1: Teething is the root of all evil

. . . and the cause of any symptom you care to name. Many years ago, I visited a small Scottish country churchyard. Some head-stones dated back to the 1700s and 1800s, often marking the death of a succession of young children within a single family. Often the cause of death was engraved on the headstone. Many children were inscribed as having "died of a fever," but in several cases, the cause of death was recorded as "teething." From those days right up to the present, the normal, physiological and *pain-less* process of tooth eruption has been accused of causing every symptom and sign ever observed in the very young, including, of course, fever, irritability, diarrhea, convulsions, feeding prob-lems and thumb-sucking . . . you name it. Doting grandmothers throughout the world, frequently regarded as the fonts of all knowledge and experience in child-rearing and diagnosis ("After all, my dear, I raised eight children myself"), observing unusual signs or symptoms, pry the baby's mouth open, find a smidgeon of enamel peeking through a gum and pronounce with unassailable authority the diagnosis of "teething." Typically, Grandma is deaf to any suggestion that dental eruption might *not* explain the baby's crankiness, drooling, fever, skin rash or whatever.

My late father was totally skeptical about the idea teething could cause *any* significant symptoms or signs in infants and toddlers, but even his authority and patrician air frequently failed to convince grandmas, who knew better.

Many years ago, a famous British pediatrician, Dr. John Apley, uttered what should have been the final word on this issue: "The only thing that can be attributed to teething is teeth." Those immortal words should be framed and hung in the waiting room of every physician who cares for the young (and their parents). The final shovel of earth to be heaped on the whole idea that teething could cause symptoms and signs in the very young came from an extraordinarily thorough study carried out by Tasanen and associates in Finland. These researchers maintained scrupulous daily records on a large group of infants in an orphanage, examining them daily and carefully over one month and keeping meticulous records of even the slightest symptoms. They noted every conceivable symptom or sign that might possibly be attributed to tooth eruption: temperature, irritability, skin rashes, bowel disturbances and other deviations. They also checked every child's gums daily for tenderness to pressure with a tongue depressor. Effectively, they left no stone (or tooth) unturned in their meticulous search for signs or symptoms that could reasonably be attributed to dental eruption.

The sum total of their findings linking the process of teething to significant signs or symptoms was a goose egg.

Notwithstanding such conclusive observations, I can safely predict people everywhere (including a few misguided physicians) will continue to invoke the ever-handy diagnostic scapegoat of teething to explain a variety of signs and symptoms, whenever they can't come up with a more plausible explanation.

Myth 2: Pacifier addiction is beneficial

I have long contended that if you took a dozen or so infants, dressed them in identical clothing and shoved a pacifier into each of their mouths, their mothers would be unable to pick their own children out of a police lineup. On more than one occasion I have had the near-emetic experience of preparing to examine a pacifier-plugged toddler when the dreaded object fell out of the child's mouth and landed on the floor. I then watched in horror as the mother picked up the pacifier, moistened it in her own mouth then reinserted it in the baby's mouth!

In the UK, what we North Americans call "pacifiers" are known (far more appropriately) as "dummies," a term that, in my not-so-humble opinion, would be better applied to the adults who insist on inserting these ghastly objects into their children's mouths. It may be hard to imagine, but a good deal of space in the pediatric medical literature has been given over to pacifiers. All this writing has had minimal impact.

In November 1995, a group of researchers at the University of Oulu, Finland, conducted a prospective fifteen-month-long study to examine the relationship between pacifier use and the incidence of acute ear infection (otitis media) in 845 children attending daycare centres. They found using a pacifier was a significant risk factor for ear infection, being responsible for 25 per cent of ear infections in children under three years of age!

Other researchers have documented a statistical association between pacifier use and a shortened duration of breast feeding, though which factor is cause and which is effect has not been clearly established. In a study of 605 rooming-in infants in a large Brazilian hospital, the risk of weaning breast-fed infants at age one month was increased almost threefold among pacifier users compared with non-users. Thus, the World Health Organization and the UN Children's Fund have strongly discouraged the use of pacifiers because of their perceived interference with successful breast feeding and their association with early weaning.

Sadly, to muddy the waters even further, several papers have suggested — although the evidence is highly indirect, and therefore suspect — that pacifier use might reduce infants' susceptibility to SIDS. In my view, this kind of research can best be described as meddlesome, interpreting a vague statistical association as a possible indicator of causality. But this suggestion can be enough to strike terror into the hearts of parents who already harbour a morbid fear their infant may fall victim to SIDS. Such parents will cling to anything purported to hold out a scintilla of protection against that awful (but rare) tragedy.

Misinterpreting a vague statistical association as suggesting a causal relationship is the most fundamental abuse of statistical methods, the pitfall of guilt by association. As a footnote, the causes of SIDS (and there are *definitely* several) are unknown in the vast majority of cases, making any ostensibly preventive measure iffy at best. At the risk of being pilloried in a public place, I include among suspect measures the current officially sanctioned "Back to Sleep" campaign (urging parents to have their young babies sleep on their backs, except for premature babies who, we are told, should sleep on their tummies . . . go figure!). That ostensibly preventive measure against SIDS is, again, based entirely on guilt-by-association reasoning.

Myth 3: White coats scare children

In my years as a postgraduate trainee, the wearing of white outfits by doctors was an edict to be obeyed (and a cost to be borne). Every patient or family member could identify a doctor or a nurse on sight. Furthermore, every one of us in both of those professions wore large, easily readable name tags, large enough to be read without requiring males to peer at unseemly close range at the labelled bosoms of nurses or doctors of the female persuasion.

Then, slowly and insidiously, the cult of anonymity overtook the health professions. In pediatric institutions, it seemed to gain a foothold initially in two specialties: adolescent medicine and child psychiatry. Without a scintilla of evidence to support the change, physicians who specialized in the care of adolescents seemed to latch on to the notion they would be less intimidating to their teenage patients if they dressed more like them. Even at the time, the idea seemed ridiculous. Seeing these docs wearing torn blue jeans, open-necked shirts, neck chains and assorted jewellery, and sporting long, unkempt hair, made them (to me, at least) look ridiculous. I'm certain their teenage patients were neither taken in nor made more comfortable by their mod attire. Along with this costume charade, many adopted the speech patterns of their teen patients, which seemed to me to make them sound ridiculous too.

Since those early beginnings, the cults of anonymity and false informality have permeated many health care institutions. The few physicians who still wear a white coat and tie are usually — like myself — well over sixty. It can be next to impossible in some hospitals to distinguish a nurse from a member of the housekeeping staff! Many health care personnel no longer wear name tags, and among those who do, the names are often unreadable except at inappropriately close range. Some hospitals have even adopted "casual Fridays," during which the entire staff dresses down as a fund-raising scheme. Call me a fossil, but I am convinced if we are to do everything possible to fulfill our fundamental mission of relieving anxiety among patients and their families, everything we say and do, and how we look, should serve that noble mission as thoroughly as possible. In hospitals, no day should be considered "casual."

Almost hidden away in the medical literature are several highly informative studies that bear on this issue, including investigations in which patients, including children and their parents, have been asked directly how they wish their caregivers to dress.

In 1995, Dr. Robert Bischof of Jefferson Medical College in Philadelphia published a brief but important "Viewpoint" piece in *The Lancet,* entitled "White Coats in the Care of Children." Bischof had searched the medical literature for hard evidence bearing on this issue. He found absolutely nothing to support the abandonment of white coats. In contrast, he identified two relevant studies. One showed that patient-physician rapport with adolescent patients was *not* affected by the doctor's choice of attire. The other demonstrated that children aged five years and older did *not* respond adversely to doctors who wore white coats. In contrast, informally dressed doctors were viewed negatively. To my knowledge, no one advocating less traditional, more informal attire for physicians has produced a single drop of evidence to support the practice.

The white coat was adopted early in the twentieth century, partly to legitimize socially taboo behaviours such as rectal and pelvic examinations as part of routine medical care. In 1986, Dr. S. R. Mitchell published his reflections on this issue. He contended that the white coat conferred protection to both doctor and patient, as well as "a sanctity that allows the physician unique liberties within the context of the doctor-patient relationship."

Where pediatric patients are concerned, the published evidence concurs with this perspective. At the Children's Hospital of Cincinnati, researchers showed a series of photographs to parents or guardians of 360 children who had come to the emergency department for care. They were shown eight photographs of physician pairs (male and female), each pair dressed in different levels of attire, ranging from formal (white lab coats, dress shoes and tie) to surgical scrubs and tennis shoes. They were asked to choose the doctors they liked most and least and to indicate whether their perception of competence was affected by the physicians' attire. The majority preferred the more formally attired physicians, and two-thirds identified those wearing no lab coats, no tie and tennis shoes as those they preferred least. Neither the severity of their child's illness, nor the time of their visit, the age, race or gender of the parent or guardian had any significant effect on parental preferences.

On a personal note, I take it as a personal failure if any child older than a few months cries in my office, and I am a dyed-in-the-wool, unabashed white-coated, neck-tied, clean-shaven dresser of impeccable sartorial splendour — if I say so myself.

In Their Own Words

Out of the mouths of babes and sucklings hast thou ordained strength . . .

— Psalms 8:2

One of the special joys of being a pediatrician is the opportunity to talk to children once they become verbal and to listen to them once they become verbose. Specialists who care for children often spend too much of their patient encounters talking and listening to parents when that time would often be better spent (more informative, more entertaining) talking and listening to the children. Children are our best comedians, and their written and verbal communications often deserve to be inscribed in the Annals of Spontaneous Wit and Wisdom.

For the past decade or so, I have been invited to address incoming classes of first-year medical students. During orientation week for new students at Dalhousie, a special assembly is held in the university auditorium. Not only are the students invited to attend but their parents and siblings as well. The medical school chorale sings, the dean welcomes the new class, I recite the Hippocratic Oath and, traditionally, I have been invited to speak briefly to the neophytes about professionalism.

Typically, I do not stick to my assigned topic but speak to them about *why* people choose to study medicine. Some are inspired by role models such as medical family members or personal physicians; some are motivated by pure humanitarianism, the desire to help fellow beings afflicted by illness or injury; and still others believe (correctly in most cases) the life of a physician will bring them significant material and monetary rewards. I then suggest to them that if we are honest with ourselves, most of us enter the study of medicine with some ambivalence between humanitarian and materialistic motivations. I then offer them documentary evidence such ambivalence between the materialistic and humanitarian motivations is demonstrable in children as young as nine or ten years of age. To prove the point, I read them a letter my eldest son, Alan, received when he was a practicing pediatrician in Halifax. It goes as follows:

Dear Dr. Goldbloom,

I would like to be a doctor when I grow up except I can't even look at spit.
I would like to be a doctor so that I could make a lot of money and buy a big house and a nice car.
Do you have to look at a lot of sick things?
I'd also like to be a doctor so that I could help other people.

Sincerely yours,

Stephen

P.S. What kind of car do you drive?

That letter invariably gets a great reception, and I could let it go at that. But I can't help but add a few words about the importance of giving equal attention in *every* patient they see to *illness* (how the patient and family *feel*) and *disease* (what is *wrong* with the patient).

As with graduation speeches, there is little likelihood many will be "inspired" for more than thirty minutes after the event, but it's worth a try. At least I feel better after giving that talk.

After my many decades of seeing children and their parents as patients, several other children's comments are permanently engraved in my memory.

I have often quizzed children over five about their ambitions in life. Whenever a youngster replied he or she would like to become a doctor, I would offer them a future job as my assistant, suggesting I would pay them five dollars a week *providing* they signed a contract right away. Some grabbed at the offer eagerly. One or two tried to bargain the salary upward — to *ten* dollars a week — which I would agree to reluctantly after a moment of thought.

But one day a girl of about eight, whom I saw in the emergency department, put me in my place. She said she wanted to be a doctor when she grew up, so I immediately made her the usual job offer as my assistant at the usual salary as soon as she finished med school. She looked me up and down. "You'll be *dead* by then!" she said. Her mother was mortified, but I was overcome with laughter and admiration for her ability to think analytically, mathematically and prophetically.

The biggest show-stopper among the many youngsters I have quizzed about career aspirations was a serious-looking, serious-minded boy of eight who told me he wanted to become a "herpetologist." I couldn't help wondering if he knew what the word meant, so I feigned ignorance and asked him what a "herpetologist" did. "He studies snakes," he replied immediately. I didn't see the boy again for some time. But when he learned early in 2012 I was going to retire, he told his mother he wanted to come to "say goodbye." He presented me with a handwritten letter, probably the worst-spelled *and* most endearing letter I had ever received from a patient of any age. Here it is, exactly as he spelled it, written in September 2011, when he was thirteen:

> *Dr. Goldblum you have bin in my life for 13 glorys years now that its time for you to retire I thank about the good times we had its time for you to go but now that you haf to go I need you so much more its time for me to grow up and get a new tharapist its to mach to lat you go but over the years we had fun lots of lafs and gigls now its time for you and me to say goodbye and have lots of fun befor we go I don't whant you to leve but Im gating older and your gating younger but your 83 (actually 87. RBG) but you look no older than 30 no one can be 30 and look that good But now its time to say good bye no more laffs no more gigls but some day some ware will meet again my favorit Doctor Goldblum and you will be misset by me and my family will miss you no one is a bater Doctor than you Doctor Goldblum. Ill miss you Doctor Goldblum.*

> *Your best friend,*

> *PS – Ill miss you.*

He seemed quite moved and was a little teary, which, of course, I found moving as well. As I read and reread this letter I think back on my own school days, when spelling and punctuation were paramount, and a letter such as this would have received a really bad failing mark. But I have never received a letter from a child or adult so full of genuine love, emotion and sincerity, pushing all the spelling mistakes into oblivion. This is the most sincere and heartfelt "love letter" I ever received from a patient, and I treasure it.

Talking (and Listening) to Parents

During many decades of teaching medical undergraduates at Dalhousie University, one of my regular tasks was to give groups of second-year students an introductory exposure to the rudiments of family interviewing skills. To make the sessions less didactic, I would tour the hospital wards beforehand to identify parents, preferably both a father *and* a mother, willing to help me in this teaching exercise by letting me interview them in the presence of the students. I always selected parents I did not yet know to avoid any artificiality in the interview. I would seat the parents facing me with our sides toward the students to minimize the distraction of the audience. Most parents welcomed the chance to give students their perspective on how doctors should talk and listen to them.

Following introductions, I would ask the parents *why* they had brought their child for medical attention and *what sort of help* they were hoping for. Then I would surreptitiously measure the duration of their answer to my opening question. Afterwards, I stressed the importance of listening carefully to the entirety of the parents' or family's opening statement, which was rarely longer than one-and-a-half minutes. Then I would point out to the students that many patients are never allowed to complete their opening statement of complaints because they are so often interrupted by the doctor. Not surprisingly, this often results in patients or parents feeling their concerns have not been adequately heard.

I have also made it a point to spring an unexpected question on the parents. Noting that, since they were in a teaching hospital, they must have encountered quite a few doctors, I would ask them to tell us what characteristics of a doctor were the most important to them. The consistency of their answers was stunning. Their priorities were almost always twofold, expressed in words such as: "I want a doctor who gives me *enough time*" and "I want a doctor who explains things to me using *words I understand.*"

I point out to the students that how much time is "enough" is a perception rather than something quantifiable with a stopwatch. When parents or patients have been listened to *without interruption,* they are more likely to feel their concerns have been heard.

On the second matter, I would always ask the parents if doctors had ever explained things to them using words they did *not* understand. Typically, they would reply with vigorous nods of assent. So I would ask: "Why did you not interrupt the doctor to ask for clarification?" Typical answer: "I was afraid he would think I was stupid."

I would point out to the students that much of their time as medical undergraduates had been spent learning a new vocabulary. As a result, they acquire the unconscious tendency to incorporate medical lingo (including abbreviations) into their discussions with parents. Parents often *seem to* understand when they do not; but they are reluctant to request clarification.

On hospital wards, I have sometimes eavesdropped on conversations between students or residents and parents. They tell the parents Johnny "will have an IVP next Tuesday" or "is booked for an EEG." Most parents acknowledge such information with an affirmative head nod, even though they understand little or nothing of the information. It comes back to the importance of listening more than talking and of encouraging parents to ask questions. Once again, the bottom line is the relief of anxiety. Conversations between doctors and parents or patients should be far more concerned with the induction of understanding than with transmitting information.

Transmitting medical information is pretty much a one-way process — doctor to patient. Inducing understanding and identifying patients' and parents' unspoken fears is vastly different. It involves less talking, more questioning, more listening and more observation of nonverbal cues.

Throwing Money at Disease

As a former member of various research organizations and funding bodies, I should be the last person to be skeptical about contemporary fund-raising for research "to find the cure." Our society has become intoxicated with the unstated and appealing, but simplistic, idea that the cure for virtually any human affliction will be discovered if we simply throw enough money at it.

Read the obituaries in any newspaper and you will get a good idea of what killed many of the deceased simply by noting the disease fund for which memorial donations are requested. A specialized fund now exists for almost every major internal organ and for most diseases that afflict the human condition.

But when this phenomenon is viewed from a dispassionate distance, it recalls "primitive" peoples who sacrifice their crops and livestock to their gods in the fond hope of being blessed with a cure for their ills or forgiveness for their sins. In our ostensibly more enlightened society we say prayers, we light candles, we fast and we write cheques. To "cure" assorted diseases, we run, dance, play golf, attend expensive dinners and dress up in bizarre costumes as part of our fund-raising rites. But the ultimate question remains: Have such exercises been shown conclusively to have produced cures?

Most discoveries begin, not with funding, but with astute

observations. Alexander (later Sir Alexander) Fleming, bac-
teriologist, was annoyed by the fact a pesky mould, *penicillium
notatum*, was overgrowing and killing his precious bacterial
cultures in the laboratory. He asked a simple question. What was
it in the mould that was killing off the bacteria? He found the
answer by isolating the substance he named penicillin. It is said
a newspaper reporter later asked Sir Alexander: "What was the
very first thing you said when you discovered penicillin?" Fleming thought for a moment and replied: "Well, I *think* I said, 'I
say, what's this?'"

Nowadays, it is rare the daily mail fails to include one or
more appeals for donations to help cure yet another human
affliction. My wife Ruth, a hugely successful fund-raiser for
worthy causes, taught me to always ask people soliciting donations for good causes to reveal the precise percentage of funds
raised that went to the actual cause and what percentage to
"administration." (Incidentally, Ruth and I discovered one can
often deliver more money to the cause by donating the value of
a single ticket rather than attending yet another supremely boring fund-raising dinner or dance.)

During the era of recurrent polio epidemics, a nurse from
Australia proposed a new treatment for children paralyzed by
poliomyelitis. She had her own unique theories about polio and
how the disease could be treated and preached her message with
religious fervour. In her view, the loss of muscle function that
followed an attack of polio was due to a process, never anatomic-
ally or physically defined, which she termed "mental alienation."
She claimed polio victims had simply forgotten how to use their
affected muscles and recommended nurses and physiotherapists
retrain them in how to use them. She also asserted the muscle
spasm seen during the early, acute phase of the illness could be
relieved by the intensive, repeated application of wet hot packs
applied to the affected limbs. She declared publicly she'd been

sent by God to save children with polio, toured the world preaching her gospel and was haughtily dismissive of any critics. Parents
of children with polio, captivated by her promises of recovery,
flocked to her like cripples and penitents to a holy shrine.

Some physicians, and many physiotherapists and nurses, also
subscribed enthusiastically to her theories and treatments for a
while. During polio outbreaks at many hospitals, including the
Montreal Children's, the physiotherapists, aided by hordes of
enthusiastic volunteers, soaked blankets in boiling water, wringing
them out at the bedside and applying the moist hot packs to the
youngsters' paralyzed muscles. Physiotherapists treated the purported "mental alienation" by encouraging paralyzed children to
focus their minds on making their muscles contract again. Children
long past the acute phase of poliomyelitis were kept in hospital
for months on end, receiving hot packs and exercises in "muscle
memory." Why so many well-trained, well-intentioned folks were
suckered into such hocus-pocus theory remains a mystery.

The nurse eventually paid a kind of state visit to the Montreal
Children's Hospital and was greeted by acolytes with a reverence
normally reserved for cardinals and rich philanthropists. One
of the few people singularly unimpressed was my father, whose
description was colourful and unflattering. He labelled her "a
menopausal virgin with a messianic complex." Following the
advent of polio vaccine, fewer and fewer people could even recall
the meteoric rise and equally precipitous fall of the nurse, her
bizarre ideas and the quasi-religious fervour with which she was
briefly received.

Understandably, people afflicted with serious or incurable
disease grasp at *any* treatment whose proponents hold out the
prospect of dramatic improvement or even cure. There was the
brief mania for vascular surgery for Down's syndrome and the
suggestion of megavitamin treatments for all sorts of conditions.
Only time will tell whether the so-called liberation treatment for

the unfortunate victims of multiple sclerosis will be added to the list of transiently fashionable interventions for serious conditions.

The intermittent triumph of faith and hope over reason and scientific evidence will undoubtedly continue forever. But we should *never* blame or ridicule the victims of a condition or their families for clinging to the hope that some new treatment, however illogical or lacking in validation, will offer benefit where other interventions have failed. At its root, this is another unresolved conflict between science and religion; the former is evidence-based, the latter faith-based.

No one has written more eloquently on this issue than the late, great Dr. Lewis Thomas, one-time dean of medicine at Yale University, a great humanitarian and a superb essayist. Thomas published many essays on medical dilemmas. One of his most compelling pieces, entitled "On Magic in Medicine," was published in 1979 in a collection of essays called *The Medusa and the Snail:*

> *It is much more difficult to be convincing about ignorance concerning disease mechanisms than it is to make claims for full comprehension, especially when such comprehension leads, logically or not, to some sort of action. When it comes to serious illness, the public tends, understandably, to be more skeptical about the skeptics, more willing to believe the true believers. It is medicine's oldest dilemma, not to be settled by candour or by any kind of rhetoric; what it needs is a lot of patience, waiting for science to come in, as it has in the past, with the solid facts.*

We doctors are an incredibly resilient lot. When research produces new cures, or, even better, develops effective preventive interventions for conditions that used to occupy much of our working days, we are incredibly resourceful in diagnosing, naming and treating "new" conditions. You might have expected the extraordinary progress we have made in preventing so many diseases through immunizations and new treatments, such as effective antibiotics and drugs, would have freed thousands of previously busy doctors' office hours for other more languid medical pursuits. That has not happened.

Doctors never run out of "new" conditions to define and treat. Diphtheria, whooping cough, scarlet fever, polio, meningitis and rheumatic fever are, to most young pediatricians, relics of a forgotten past. Our office days are now largely filled with patients suffering from what my pediatric colleague Dr. Robert Haggerty called "the new morbidity," the host of psychosocial, educational and behavioural problems that affect so many youngsters whose parents come to us for help. I have more than once complained to my pediatric colleagues that if it wasn't for ADHD and behaviour problems, I'd be starving.

Pediatricians are not alone in demonstrating such remarkable compensatory remunerative resilience in response to scientific progress. Among our colleagues in ENT (ear, nose and throat medicine), routine tonsil and adenoid removal (T&A) began to go out of style, partly because it was shown youngsters who had previously had a T&A during the polio era developed increased susceptibility to the most damaging (and life-threatening) form of polio, which attacked the brainstem and could paralyze nerves required for vital functions like breathing and swallowing. But as routine T&A fell into disrepute, otolaryngologists rediscovered a procedure already almost a century old, inserting "ventilating tubes" through the eardrums to relieve pressure in the middle ear and release fluid collected there. Parents and doctors were often impressed with the results, partly because most youngsters who undergo the procedure hear better immediately after. This has been interpreted by many parents and doctors as "proof" of the benefit of the procedure (the "immediate pleasure" principle).

Two developments that followed the initial task force report justified the effort and confirmed the validity of its approach. First, the US Preventive Services Task Force, established a few years after the Canadian group, adopted the Canadian methodology intact and has applied it ever since with powerful effect. Second, the two task forces worked in very close collaboration. As chair of the Canadian task force, I attended all meetings of the US group, sometimes along with other Canadian colleagues. My US counterpart, Dr. Robert S. Lawrence, a superb, dedicated, modest physician whose intellect and judgment were stellar, attended meetings of the Canadian group regularly. Finally, when each of the task forces published its national *Guide to Preventive Services,* there was significant binational exchange and collaboration in the authorship of many chapters of both books. Why we didn't simply produce a single task force and a single North American guide escapes me, but issues of national pride (and funding!) were undoubtedly involved. One rather surprising general observation emerged from both task force reports. Remarkably few ostensibly preventive manoeuvres received an A rating (good evidence to include in the periodic health exam), and most of the few A-rated procedures were either newborn screening tests or childhood immunizations.

A few important preventive health examinations deserve special mention because they continue to be the subjects of heated debate, with emotion and "experience" often trumping scientific evidence: the screening mammogram for breast cancer; PSA screening for prostate cancer; and the treatment or prevention of obesity.

You might imagine the number of research publications on each of these important topics might serve as an indicator of how much our knowledge has improved and to what degree our current practices have been justified. To examine this supposition, I recently checked the Pub Med database on the number of relevant articles published over a three-year period (2008 to 2011) in the English-speaking scientific literature on three of the most hotly debated issues in preventive health care. Here are the results:

Obesity: 25,186 publications

Prostate cancer screening: 8,688 publications

Mammography: 3,195 publications

As far as these three topics are concerned, it could be argued the sheer number of publications may be inversely proportional to the advancement of knowledge.

If I Were King

I often wish I were a king,
And then I could do anything.

— A. A. Milne

Most of us daydream periodically about how we would improve the world if granted absolute power. I too am not immune to that fantasy.

Because most of my working career has been spent in children's hospitals, that environment has been the main focus of my daydreams. Over the years, a few of those dreams have come true, though still far too few to suit me.

My limited success began when I arrived in Halifax in 1967. Children requiring hospital care were then admitted to the small antique Halifax Children's Hospital. One of the first issues to catch my attention was visiting policy. Visiting hours, which were restricted to parents — who were called "visitors" — were for just two hours (5–7 p.m.) daily. Each evening, at 7 p.m. on the dot, the stern, commanding voice of the telephone operator boomed throughout the hospital: "Visiting hours are now over. Will the visitors please leave the hospital *immediately!*"

When I asked about recreation programs for the children and about how their educational needs were being met, I was told the former were provided by one elderly woman known as the "play lady"; the latter, by an equally ancient retired schoolteacher. Worse, these two women had not been on speaking terms for some time. When the "play lady" left each day at 5 p.m., all toys were *locked up* for the night! When I asked why, I was told it was to ensure none of the toys would be "stolen" or taken home by the children! I expressed surprise the police were not involved.

Nowadays, several committees usually have to be involved in instituting even small changes in hospital procedures. But in those days, as physician-in-chief, I had considerable freedom to make changes. As a benevolent dictator, the first two policy changes I implemented were that parents were no longer to be referred to as "visitors" in verbal and written communications — only as "parents" — and visiting hours would be unrestricted.

Not all hospital staff supported these "radical" changes. There were dire predictions visitors would spread infection throughout the hospital, and the presence of parents on the wards would interfere with doctors' rounds and patient care, and on and on.

As time went by, I became aware that a couple of pediatric hospitals in the United States — one in Lexington, Kentucky, the other in Indianapolis, Indiana — were experimenting with implementing a radical new concept called "care-by-parent." The underlying concept was that in most families, parents were the most skilled and competent people when it came to caring for their own children. Care-by-parent could also help alleviate the guilt feelings many parents experience (but rarely verbalize) when their child is admitted to hospital.

To learn more about this innovative style of hospital care, I travelled to Indianapolis, where one of my most revered colleagues, Dr. Morris (Morrie) Green was chief of pediatrics. From my first exposure to care-by-parent, I was hooked. Maximizing parents' involvement in the care of their hospitalized children was obviously the way of the future. Parents loved it, as did their children, and the increase in their confidence in their own care-giving skills was blatantly obvious. I returned to Halifax resolved to "go forth and do likewise."

The hospital agreed to establish a six-room Care-by-Parent Unit (CBPU) on a section of one of the wards. The rooms were larger than average, with comfortable bed accommodation for one or both parents, a private bathroom, and a notice board where parents could record the treatments they had provided, medications they had given and so forth. In a reversal of trad-itional practices, we (that is, doctors and nurses) learned to *knock* on the door and ask the parents' permission to enter!

Now it would be historically inaccurate to suggest the majority of my medical and nursing colleagues immediately clasped the concept to their bosoms with religious zeal. Several did, but when we established the unit, a few of my colleagues silently boycotted it and never admitted a patient.

Interestingly, the nurses who staffed the unit absolutely adored the work. All of a sudden, their role had morphed largely from direct caregiver to teacher, and their job satisfaction took a giant leap.

Suddenly, parents were maintaining records of their child's medication and learning to perform complex technical pro-cedures of all kinds, procedures whose performance by parents in hospital (and, after discharge, at home) had previously been unthinkable. Parents were introducing nasogastric tubes, inserting contact lenses in their infants' eyes and so on. Once they had learned the necessary skills, none of us could do the pro-cedure as well. It was, after all, *their* child, and no one knew that child better than they did, and whom did the child trust more?

Eventually, the hospital authorities generously decided to append my name to the unit. I was flattered, but only briefly, because as the "space crunch" for hospital beds gained momentum, the CBPU ceased to exist. My sadness, however, was short-lived, because the story had a happy ending. Care-by-parent lives on in full glory, because today *all* patient rooms in the recently constructed in-patient wards are twice the size of their earlier counterparts. All rooms include private bathrooms en suite and comfortable overnight accommodation for one or both parents. Parents' participation in the care of their hospitalized children is now the norm rather than the exception, and care-by-parent is no longer a radical, mushy-hearted aberration in hospital care for children. For most hospitalized children it is now the norm.

Perhaps the sole relic of tradition overwhelming patient needs in these new structures is in the design of nursing stations, which are, too often, oversized. On numerous occasions, walking through these wards, I have conducted a silent "body count" of nurses in the nursing station compared to those in their patients' rooms. Invariably, the former far outnumber the latter, and the nurses in the station often appear to be having a meeting, chatting with each other or doing paperwork.

When I visited the newly built Children's Hospital of Minneapolis, where my elder son, Alan, happens to be president and CEO, I observed a striking contrast. On the in-patient wards the nurses' stations occupied only a tiny fraction of the space allotted in Halifax. But on the wards themselves, between each pair of patient rooms, there was a small nurses' desk where electronic patient records can be maintained and nurses can maintain frequent eye contact and close physical proximity with the children under their care. Such a design should be the number-one choice for any children's hospital, or for adult hospitals, for that matter!

Certain other subtle and not-so-subtle trends in how pediatric hospitals currently operate give me concern. One is the increasing imbalance between the role and influence of physicians in hospital operations paralleled by a progressive increase in the role of non-caregivers and former caregivers, nurses and administrators in determining how hospitals operate. Let me be clear. I do not believe we should try to resuscitate the era in which the doctor ruled supreme. During my internship, specific doctors — especially surgeons — virtually owned their own wards and ruled them with dictatorial authority. But the reaction to such medical authoritarianism may have gone a bit too far, linked to the adoption of a corporate model of hospital administration.

In 1985, when I stepped down as physician-in-chief, director of research and head of the university Department of Pediatrics, certain subtle changes occurred. I recognized the significance of those changes only with the wisdom of hindsight. First, the title "physician-in-chief" quietly disappeared, and my subsequent successors have been designated simply as "head of the Department of Pediatrics." During my tenure, almost everyone in the community, the hospital and the university knew, for better or for worse, who was head honcho of pediatrics. Nowadays, I suspect that many in the community *and* some in the hospital would be hard put to name the head of the department.

In parallel with the decline in prestige, title and authority has been a steady growth in the role of hospital administration. When I arrived at the Children's Hospital in Halifax, the chief executive was known simply as the hospital administrator. He was paid less than most physicians, and everyone knew his mandate was chiefly to save money by every conceivable penny-pinching measure. As that position was filled by a succession of individuals, the title underwent progressive changes — through executive director, to CEO and, finally, to president and CEO — each grander title presumably accompanied by a progressive increase in remuneration and perquisites. These changes were linked to a gradual adoption of the corporate model of governance in which board members had little or nothing to do with or say about the day-to-day running of the institution. In parallel, physicians too were involved less and less.

The picture was further complicated by a proliferation of the layers of administrative personnel and the introduction of a system in which anyone with either a problem or an idea for improving the system was obliged to navigate a hierarchy of authority, starting at the bottom and working his or her way up, each step involving, of course, a meeting of at least one hour's duration.

The enormous proliferation of meetings was a dramatic result of adopting a complex corporate system. Virtually no change of any kind could be adopted or implemented without one, or often several, meetings. Meetings are usually scheduled to last one hour and always seem to fill the time available. One side-effect is it is virtually impossible to talk with key people without waiting, often for a long time. If you call someone, you are often greeted by an annoying recording, stating cheerfully, "I'm away from my desk right now . . ." and suggesting that if you want to leave a message, "please press one and speak to my assistant, Ms. Blotz." There are no more secretaries. When you do dutifully press 1, you receive yet another recorded announcement from the lively Ms. Blotz, who is also "away from my desk right now." If any recorded voice tells me that "your call is important to us," I will inflict severe bodily harm on the nearest "assistant."

As newly crowned Monarch of Health Care, by appointment to the Queen, I will issue a ukase requiring, on pain of death — or worse — that during daytime hours *every single* telephone in the entire institution must be answered by a living, caring human being, who smiles every time he or she answers the phone.

Without question, the most important individual any family member or visitor meets in a hospital is the *first* person he or she meets. But, in real life, that first contact is often either a volunteer or one of the lowest paid members of the hospital staff who, aside from providing guidance on navigating the hospital corridors, may have had minimal or no training in the fine art of person-to-person contact. Sometimes no one is there to greet the anxious visitor or parent. As I have entered the hospital each day over many years, I have been struck by how few of those at the reception desk, whether paid or volunteer, would greet me with a smile or call me by name.

Operation Smile: I have unabashedly stolen this name from that of a marvellous international program in which plastic surgeons travel all over the world repairing cleft palates and harelips in children who would otherwise be denied such services. In this case, though, I refer to the desperate need for formal training of all hospital personnel who meet the public to smile *immediately* when they encounter any patient, parent or visitor, and then ask how they can help. All of us could benefit from intensive training from the wonderful folks at Disney World, who have refined the process of welcoming strangers to an art.

Under my not-so-benevolent dictatorship, that obligation to smile will be extended to include everyone whose job involves speaking to the public or staff, either in person or on the telephone. All such individuals will be required by law to smile every single time they answer a phone. Penalty for noncompliance will be deportation for one year of postgraduate training at Disney World.

Meetings: Upon my ascension to the throne there will be an immediate ban on *all* meetings (possible exception, the hospital board). My son David, a psychiatrist and a man of profound insights, has written what I consider to be the definitive word on this issue in an article in the *British Medical Journal* from his perspective as physician-in-chief of a large teaching hospital. The title is "Meeting Mania 2004."

He cites the case of a colleague of mine who accepted a position as head of a US department of pediatrics, only *on condition* he would be required to attend no meetings whatsoever. David offers practical suggestions on how the epidemic of meetings might be controlled: Meetings should be conducted standing up rather than sitting down; they should never be held until after lunch, so people could get their work done first; their duration should be reduced from one hour to fifteen minutes; and all leaders should document the total amount of time spent in meetings each month and ask themselves if that time could be better spent.

PowerPoint: Aside from implementing all of David's recommendations, I would add several other dictates on my first day in office. The first is a hospital-wide ban on the use of PowerPoint in public meetings and grand rounds – a weekly gathering of hospital medical staff for a presentation on a specific topic. Over the proscenia of all hospital auditoriums and teaching rooms would be emblazoned the immortal words (author unknown): "Power corrupts — and PowerPoint corrupts absolutely." No one, staff member or visitor, would be permitted to *read* lectures. Laptop computers would be banned from all podiums, and speakers would be required to maintain eye contact with their audiences for at least 85 per cent of their allotted speaking time.

Dress Code: The next imperial proclamation to be issued within forty-eight hours following my coronation would be the imposition of a strict dress code and personal identification system for all physicians, nurses and laboratory personnel. To understand the basis for this proclamation, we need to remember Myth #3: "White coats scare children."

Follow-up: As we move down my list of mandatory reforms in health care, another will be the institution of systematized, hospital-initiated follow-up for patients discharged from hospital and from emergency departments.

Nowadays, many recent medical graduates gravitate toward work in emergency departments. The work has its undeniable attractions, though some of the elements that attract young doctors may not serve patients and their families as they should. It is shift work, after all; and as doctors complete their shifts, they head for home, often with little thought of the patients and families they have treated, sent home or admitted to hospital. By its very nature, such a system tends to preclude ongoing emotional attachment to patients and their families.

Under my New Order, all this will change. Doctors and nurses who work in emergency rooms will be obliged, as part of their job descriptions, to make a certain number of follow-up phone calls every day to the parents of children they have seen and treated the previous day and to record a follow-up note in the child's chart. I guarantee such a system will greatly increase parent satisfaction with their child's care by a factor of more than 2.5 and have extraordinary educational benefit to the caregivers, who will learn valuable lessons about how their patients have responded (or failed to respond) to treatments they prescribed.

Hospital Discharge: Finally, it would be mandated that, when a child is discharged from hospital, parents would be given a written summary of their child's illness and treatment, written in language they can understand. This written summary would be reviewed with the parents verbally as part of the discharge process to ensure they fully understand their child's condition and the plans for further home management.

Between now and my coronation I'm sure I can come up with a few more royal decrees. But those listed here offer an opportunity to raise the quality of health care by a quantum leap with a single wave of my sceptre. I have spoken. *Pax vobiscum.*

Flattery Got Me Everywhere

One day in 2009 I received a telephone call from the chair of the board at the IWK Health Centre. Could I please come down to the lobby of the research pavilion right away? There was something she wanted to speak to me about. I reported as requested, and she began to discuss a couple of issues that seemed peculiarly inconsequential. I began to wonder what could be so important when she finally confessed her phone call had merely been a ruse to get me down there. The hospital board members were waiting to meet with me in an adjoining conference room.

When she ushered me in, I was greeted by a round of applause from the assembled board members. Then the hidden agenda was revealed. They wanted to affix my name to the newly built Clinical Care and Research building, calling it "the Dr. Richard B. Goldbloom Research and Clinical Care Pavilion." I was stunned but thrilled by the extravagant honour and couldn't help but reflect on how far we had come as a hospital, not only since 1967, but beginning even earlier. My predecessor, Dr. Bill Cochrane, was keenly aware of the importance of research in developing a department of pediatrics of international stature. Several years after arriving in Halifax, I was able to persuade our hospital board to commit an endowment of $1 million toward establishment of a vigorous research program at the hospital.

When the day for the dedication ceremony arrived, I walked over to the lobby of the pavilion, where an elevated stage with curtained backdrop and lectern had been erected. A large crowd of colleagues, board members and staff attended. I was touched by the kind words of appreciation by colleagues, especially Dr. Robert Bortolussi. Bob Bortolussi, whom I was lucky enough to have recruited many years earlier from the University of Minnesota, is a distinguished researcher in pediatric infectious disease who is now the hospital's director of research.

Finally it was my turn, or so I thought, until the hospital's CEO, Anne McGuire, touched me on the shoulder and said into the microphone: "Before you say anything, Dr. Goldbloom, we have one more little surprise for you." And with that, she drew back the curtain behind me to reveal one of my longest-standing, favourite patients, a young woman named Angela ("Angie") Elsinga, from Prince Edward Island, accompanied by her mother, Nancy Douglas.

As is so often the case, the patients and families to whom we become most closely and mutually attached are those for whom we have had the least to offer by way of cure — which, I suppose, offers the ultimate evidence that our job description has at least as much to do with caring as with curing.

From earliest childhood, Angie's life had been marked (but rarely impeded) by the effects of an extremely rare syndrome characterized by recurring intestinal polyps throughout the entire length of the intestinal tract and by multiple internal hemangiomas (overgrowths of small blood vessels). Angie had required surgical removal of a large portion of her intestine and construction of a rectal pouch. The intestinal polyposis in this syndrome is combined with multiple localized overgrowths of small blood vessels, called angiomata, which can develop anywhere in the body, including the lung and brain. Never complaining, she had undergone innumerable endoscopic examinations to remove recurrent intestinal polyps. But despite her recurrent, serious health problems, her courage and zest for life never waned. (As I write this, Angie is an inspiring, highly popular teacher of young children in Edmonton, Alberta. She maintains regular contact with me by e-mail and never fails to visit when she is in Halifax.)

When Angie and her mother were unveiled as the mystery guests at that dedication ceremony, I came perilously close to losing my composure. Angie spoke with great sincerity and feeling about our long association, and her words meant far more to me than any spoken by the dignitaries or than having my name inscribed on the new building.

As always, our own three children were quick to prevent Ruth and me from taking our own publicity too literally. On the stage, our son David whispered to me that the letters of my name, affixed in stone above each of the building's porticos, were actually put on with Velcro.

Teetering on the age of eighty-eight, I concluded, with some reluctance, that perhaps the time had come to give up my consulting practice and vacate the office I had been graciously assigned at the hospital for more than two decades. I knew I would miss the stimulation of daily contact with young people and their families and the interactions with old friends and colleagues. But I remembered my father's saying that dated from his early days in vaudeville: "Always leave 'em wanting more," surely one of life's most valuable guidelines.

My decision to retire was endorsed by our three children, most pointedly by David, who reminded me his older brother Alan would turn sixty-five in another eighteen months. He hinted, with no great subtlety, "It might not look right if Alan was to retire before you did." That convinced me I was doing the right thing at the right time.

Despite my protestations, my colleagues at the hospital decided I would not be allowed to "go gently into that good night." They dedicated a weekly pediatric grand rounds to my retirement and invited our three children and our pediatrician granddaughter Ellen to Halifax for the event. My dear friend and long-time colleague Dr. Sarah Shea reassured me they would keep it light. Both our sons spoke eloquently. Alan presented me with a leather-bound copy of every article I had ever published, the earliest dating from my medical student days at McGill, including a few papers I had (mercifully) forgotten. Predictably, David effectively staved off any tendency for anyone, including me, to take my so-called accomplishments too seriously. Here is the text of his sermon, entitled "Growing up Goldbloom . . . a Patellar Perspective":

I am here today on this special occasion, like so many of you, because I need the CME (Continuing Medical Education) credits before the December 31 deadline. As this is an academic grand rounds, I should begin with the usual conflict of interest declaration: I have had no funding from drug companies in the past two years. However, I'm a Goldbloom, a product of nature and nurture (despite my brother Alan's efforts to convince me at age eight that it was only nurture . . . that I had been rescued by my parents from an orphanage; he shrewdly pointed out that I bore no resemblance to either of them).

I am grateful for a chance to talk to you about lessons learned from my father.

The first and most important thing I learned from him was about comedy. Under his guidance, by age six or seven I had memorized comedy LPs and we would recite them to each other, convulsed with laughter. Of course, I thought all families did this. Similarly, as a boy, when I came home from school and walked past my mother tap dancing in the living room, I assumed all mothers tap danced in mid-afternoon. From a very early age, I was awakened by my father whenever a Marx Brothers film came on the late show on TV.

But today I want to talk to you about what I learned from him about being a doctor. It never involved discussion of either the science of medicine or exposure to things medical. The closest I got to an apprenticeship was sitting in the back seat of our car, late for school, while he made morning house calls.

And in the pre-medicare days, we occasionally went as a family to the east end of Montreal for a delicious Italian meal with a family we had never met before . . . grateful patients who fed us in a warm and hospitable way in lieu of payment. I learned more from him about music and medicine in terms of exposure, telling me that a real life goes beyond one's professional pursuits, and it's relevant that one of his first papers, written as a medical student at McGill, was on music and physicians. From an early age he worshipped at the shrine of Apollo, god of both medicine and music.

He never encouraged me to go into medicine (and Alan actively discouraged me, wanting the field to himself), but gave me one piece of advice when I went off to university: "If you're even thinking of becoming a doctor, don't major in science as an undergraduate; learn about the rest of the world." This was wise counsel, as was the only advice I got from another physician . . . my father-in-law, Nate Epstein, a Dalhousie medical graduate, a Cape Bretoner, a psychiatrist, and one of the pioneers of family therapy. When Nancy and I got married thirty-five years ago, he advised me to "live a minimum of five hundred miles from both sets of in-laws." We always have.

Some of the important lessons learned for me have come from his published papers. There are about 140 peer-reviewed publications, not counting his prolific editorials, cheap jokes, and clinical pearls that festooned many years of the weekly newsletter Pediatric Notes . . . *a publication that beat him to retirement last year.*

I've reviewed these papers carefully and committed most of them to memory in order to provide a dramatic recitation today. Many are, of course, unreadable now, anachronistic, or simply factually wrong. But I've singled out five from the last four decades that exemplify why he has been an inspiration to me and to countless others.

1. The Lost Art of Consultation . . . A Plea for the Return of Striped Trousers (Pediatrics, 1975)

He describes the pediatric consultations he witnessed in his father's home office on Crescent Street in downtown Montreal. Beyond the Edwardian formality, it was all about physician-to-physician and face-to-face communication. The referring and consulting physician met in person beforehand, examined the patient together, conferred, presumably took snuff, and then jointly presented the results to patient and family. I think they earned about $12 per day. He contrasted this with the non-collaborative and impersonal reality of modern consultation . . . a mailed blank form that states simply, "please assess and treat." I have learned that even a five-minute conversation with a referring doctor before and/or after a consultation often changes the focus and outcome, but we rarely teach the importance of this to our students.

2. Science and Empiricism in Pediatrics (Pediatrics, 1984)

This may be the first time he used in print the expression "comedy equals tragedy plus time" . . . and I've thought of it often in chuckling about the way my brother Alan treated me as a child. It reflects my father's healthy skepticism about scientifically unsubstantiated but commonly accepted clinical practice . . . a reminder that "experience" has been defined as "making the same mistake year after year with increasing levels of confidence."

In discussing the common pediatric problem of nausea and vomiting, sometimes triggered by sycophantic academic promotion letters, he alludes to the "fecal fascination" of his colleagues in managing intestinal problems. Intravenous rehydration, tonsillectomy and adenoidectomy, tympanometry and ear tubes, colic treatment, screening that does more harm than good, advocacy that precedes evidence . . . all these are on his chopping block. They all underline his belief that "today's dogma is tomorrow's malpractice." And his long view, from a practice that began shortly after the Boer War, has seen every pediatric fashion come and sometimes go, long after the epidemics of pediatric infectious disease has subsided. He worked through many of them, such as polio, scarlet fever, measles, and possibly bubonic plague.

3. Headhunting in the Jungles of Academia . . . A Recruiter's Guide (ACMC Forum, 1985)

Another of my father's peccadilloes (although my mother says he has only one and she hasn't seen it in a while) is the process of recruiting faculty to an academic department. I share his jaundiced view of search firms who happily charge for the offloaded responsibility, functioning as pimps trying to get their johns laid as quickly as possible. But the pearl of this paper is about search committee qual-

ity trumping representativeness and inclusiveness. He notes: "Each search committee should be handpicked . . . superior academic and clinical qualities and sharp judgment in committee members is mandatory. All should be keen judges of academic horseflesh. Remember the ancient adage: 'First class people pick first class people and second class people pick third class people.' He also places value on the phone call over the reference letter to find out the truth about candidates. There is nothing more ominous than a letter or e-mail from a colleague saying, "Call me." And he encourages a prolonged and planned visit by the candidate and spouse, with opportunities for socializing, anticipating the broader life needs of the person and his/her family — again, a far cry from some modern academic practices, like the lost art of consultation.

4. *Interviewing: The Most Sophisticated of Diagnostic Technologies (Annals or, rather, the ANALS, as he never tired of calling the journal while convulsed with laughter at his own joke . . . of the Royal College of Physicians and Surgeons of Canada, 1993)*

This probably stands out as one of my favourites because of its relevance not only to my specialty but to every specialty. I know from my wife, Nancy, an ophthalmologist, that she constantly has to reinforce this skill with her residents. He reminds us that the unchanging and primary need of patients and their families from their physician is the relief of anxiety. And doctors provide this through devoting time, providing clear explanations, and offering hope. It's no wonder that his textbook, Pediatric Clinical Skills, *is all about improving and examining and nothing about technology and treatment. Now in its fourth popular edition, it was recently translated into Greek . . . although any royalties will be part of a comprehensive EEC bailout package.*

It emphasizes the importance of sitting down to talk to patients and families, reading non-verbal cues and understanding family dynamics, family psychiatric illness and hidden agendas, as well as unexpressed fears. He questions how well we are training our students to be communicators. And it's a question well worth posing in 2011.

Of course, he's not opposed to treatment . . . and I remind him from time to time of the important aphorism — not by Osler — that "whoever said laughter is the best medicine never had gonorrhea."

This paper came almost fifty years after his very first paper as a medical student in 1948 on music and medicine, and you will see from his opening paragraph that the die was cast early:

"When the tyranny of the test tube threatens to rob medicine of its reason, those who still believe that the art of healing is something more than ignorance of facts begin to clutch at straws to bolster their hypothesis . . . The heartbeat, respiration, gait, nervous impulses and electrical discharges from the brain . . . in all of these, man is the musician. He is conscious of the rhythm of ovulation" — although my brother Alan believes that over-reliance on belief in this rhythm explains my arrival as a third, unwanted child — "and fertility, though perhaps the musical allegory is a little strained in this respect, since the tempo is a rather protracted adagio, the performer having to wait 28 days between beats. As in medicine, it is the simple procedures in music which are the most important, the most difficult to do well, and the most often neglected. How often does the student of music overlook the simple percussion and auscultation of Bach for the intricate laboratory machinery of Liszt?"

5. Reflections of a Slow Learner (Pediatrics and Child Health, 2010)

Just last year, he reflected on a lengthy career with his perennial enthusiasm for the new . . . "one reward for a lengthy career in pediatrics is that you never stop seeing children with problems you've never encountered before, and if you're lucky, you continue to enjoy the satisfaction of trying to help children and their families."

He has been a lucky man . . . in work, in marriage, in health and in friends. His self-description as a slow learner is ironic and unduly modest, except for the areas of home repair, barbeque assembly and personal finance. In these three categories, he is actually the subject of a Health Canada advisory.

While this last paper incorporates earlier themes, it also draws attention to the low-tech interventions he always values, like:

1. Making the time for family dinners, free of phones and TV.

2. Promoting literacy as an antidote for poverty and misery.

3. Following up by telephone with patients you've seen in cross-sectional assessment (I recall his daily telephone hour from 0700 – 0800 when he took breakfast in the dining room with a phone on the table while we kids ate in the kitchen and my mother slept in, by popular demand).

4. Getting involved in your community as an activist to improve the lives of children.

5. Not preaching to the underprivileged or trying to impose middle-class values.

There are many more lessons I've learned at his knee . . . such as almost no joke is too tasteless if it's really funny and that good speakers use less than their allotted time . . . but his lessons about being a good doctor are really about being a good person. With or without his white coat, he's the same person . . . and to be in his orbit for the last fifty-eight years is the greatest experience of love, laughter and learning that I could have ever hoped for.

Odd Jobs and Music

Moonlighting

For some years, Nova Scotia employed only one full-time citizenship court judge. Then the rules were changed so officers of the Order of Canada could be invited to officiate at citizenship courts to administer the Oath of Allegiance to new citizens and to present them with their citizenship certificates.

Several years ago I was asked if I would officiate at such ceremonies and I accepted eagerly, partly because of Ruth's central role in the revitalization of Pier 21 as Canada's National Museum of Immigration — about which more later — as well as my awareness of the significance and value of Canadian citizenship as the grandchild of four immigrants. The experience of officiating at citizenship courts invariably moves me deeply and increases my sensitivity to the strengths and weaknesses of our systems for attracting and receiving our new immigrants, who are so essential to the future of our country.

On average, thirty to forty individuals (several with children of all ages) take the oath of citizenship at these ceremonies. They come up to the stage to receive their certificates and be congratulated by the various dignitaries present, including members of federal and provincial legislatures.

Although I am always given a precooked script for the ceremony I try to inject a personal touch wherever possible and speak to the audience in both official languages. I want the new citizens to understand *all* Canadians are immigrants (except for First Nations, and there is some evidence that, long, long ago, they too may have come from elsewhere). I point out if my grandparents had remained in Europe and not had the good luck to come to Canada when they did, they and/or their children would almost certainly have perished in the Holocaust and I would never have been born. I stress the complete equality of *all* Canadians, whether their great-grandparents arrived more than a century ago or whether they themselves arrived yesterday.

The average ceremony includes individuals or families from more than twenty different countries. Most of them are visibly moved by the significance of such a powerful moment in their lives.

I have also observed that the civil servants in the Department of Citizenship and Immigration seem to maintain some degree of detachment from the new citizens. This may be a job requirement, just as physicians are supposed to avoid excessive emotional attachment to their patients, lest it blur their objectivity. In contrast, I believe a significant degree of emotional involvement is essential to *both* jobs.

Because of her long-standing involvement with the revitalization of Pier 21, Ruth (and I, by association) have heard innumerable first-hand stories of people whose parents or grandparents or who themselves had come to Canada to escape persecution, to flee conflict or simply to seek a better life. Attending a Canadian citizenship court is a wonderful, moving *and* educational experience for everyone there. Anyone who can remain detached must have a heart of stone.

Over more than a decade, Ruth spoke to many large audiences about Pier 21 and its significance in Canada's history. Together, we cooked up an audience participation exercise that invariably had a powerful educational impact on every member of the audience. She would begin by asking: "How many of you were born outside of Canada?" Usually 15 or 20 per cent would raise their hands. "Please keep your hands up. Now, how many of you have at least one parent who was born outside of Canada?" This would bring the proportion of raised hands to at least 50 per cent. "Keep your hands up," she would say. "Now, how many of you have at least one grandparent born outside of Canada?" By this time, most of the audience had hands in the air. "You see," she would point out, "we are a nation of immigrants. But we have never paid adequate tribute to our immigrant population."

Periodically, small groups of refugees from the other side of the earth have crossed our broad oceans at great personal peril, and sometimes unbelievable cost, to land on Canadian soil. In many quarters, their arrival has been greeted with more paranoia and disdain than empathy. Whether it was the more than 170 Sikh refugees fleeing persecution who were literally dumped in the sea off the shore of Charlesville, Nova Scotia, on July 12, 1987, or, more recently, the Tamil refugees who landed in Vancouver, the reaction in Canadian officialdom and among many ordinary Canadians has been anything but sympathetic. On the cocktail party circuit, I have more than once heard well-heeled people complain, "These people are jumping the queue." "What queue?" I ask, but I never receive a satisfactory answer. I assume they are referring to some rank order of importance of different categories in government files of routine applicants for immigration to Canada.

When such heartless opinions were expressed, Ruth would often ask: "Have you ever looked into the eyes of an immigrant?" The question usually went unanswered and the respondent would quickly change the subject.

Canada has always welcomed immigrants in the "entrepreneurial" category — those who can prove they have $800,000 or more to invest — with open arms. How quickly we forget our entire country was built by immigrants, most of whom, like my own grandparents, came here with little or no money, little or no education and certainly nothing to invest (except, in my Grandpa's case, in a poker game). In perhaps a majority of cases, it was not they, but their children who built this marvellous country of ours. Today, much of Canada remains underpopulated, with enormous areas of unoccupied, unproductive land that cry out for energetic people to work the land, grow the crops, milk the cows and contribute not only to their own success and happiness but also to ours. But once Canadian families get to be three or four generations past the arrival of their forebears, it is easy for them to become victims of what Alfred Doolittle, the unforgettable dust-man of Shaw's *Pygmalion,* referred to as "middle-class morality."

Admitto Vos ad Gradum

In 2001, I received an unexpected phone call from the office of Dalhousie University president Tom Traves. Could I drop in to his office for a brief meeting? When I arrived, the chair of the board, Jim Cowan, was also present. The two of them presented me with a totally unexpected proposal: would I become chancellor of the university? When I asked them for a job description I was told there wasn't any. They explained they *hoped* I would attend and officiate at the university convocations (twelve in the spring, three in the fall). Beyond that, I would be welcome to attend university board meetings if I wished and could participate in such meetings whenever I felt it appropriate.

I was, of course, flattered by the invitation and decided, on impulse, to accept. I knew the chancellor got to wear a glamorous, gold-encrusted gown and to sit on a "throne" at centre stage during convocation ceremonies. All in all, it sounded like an enjoyable occupation.

I prepared for my new role by reviewing Dr. Peter Waite's engaging two-volume history of Dalhousie University. My first discovery was that Dalhousie had inexplicably managed to survive and even thrive for its first 137 years without the benefit of a chancellor, which raised some interesting questions about the importance of the post!

In *The Lives of Dalhousie University, Volume Two - 1925-1980,* "The Old College Transformed", Peter Waite recorded the events of 1957 as follows:

> *In the meantime Dalhousie collected ideas about what chancellors actually did, from McGill, Toronto and Western. The duties were laid down in the Dalhousie board minutes in December 1957. The chancellor was elected by the board for a term of five years. If present, he or she presided at convocation. The chancellor was a member of the board but not the chairman. In effect, the office was what the chancellor chose to do with it.*

To my amazement, I realized I had at least a passing acquaintance with each of my four predecessors. C. D. Howe spent three years in the position before he retired from it. He was succeeded in 1968 by Lady Dunn, who later became Lady Beaverbrook. She remained in the office until 1990, a total of twenty-two years! She was followed by New Brunswick industrialist H. Reuben Cohen (1990–94) and my immediate predecessor, Sir Graham Day (1994–2001).

My contacts with Clarence Decatur Howe, Dalhousie's first chancellor, were brief but unforgettable. Before Ruth and I were married, she had joined forces with three of her university classmates to rent an apartment in a venerable Sherbrooke Street apartment building called Haddon Hall. One of her roommates was Elizabeth ("Liz") Howe, daughter of C. D. All four girls had steady boyfriends. As a result, the apartment was a high-traffic facility. None of the four girls could have been called a good housekeeper. When the front door was opened, the air current generated would often cause dustballs to float silently across the living room like tumbleweed across the pampas in a Western movie. On one occasion, when I opened the front door, I bumped into a rather large lady, down on her knees with a bucket of soapy water, scrubbing the floor. I assumed the girls had splurged and hired a cleaning woman. But Liz Howe appeared seconds later and said to me: "Dick, I'd like you to meet my mother!" Mrs. Howe, a woman whose mind was rarely clouded by doubt, was mortified by the lack of cleanliness in the girls' apartment. During that era, C. D. visited Montreal fairly often and would stop by the apartment to visit his daughter, often accepting some food and drink for lunch. After her assessment of the girl's apartmental hygiene, however, Mrs. Howe issued her husband strict instructions not to consume "a single morsel" of food that emanated from the girls' kitchen. Their sole permissible contribution to his lunch was to boil water for his tea! Soon after that episode, I dropped by the apartment at noon one day. There was C. D. Howe, sitting on the girls' tattered couch, eating his meal from a workman's black tin lunch box! Ruth and I subsequently met Mr. and Mrs. Howe in their Ottawa home when we attended Liz's wedding.

When Ruth and I moved to Halifax, we arrived just in time to attend a large dinner in Sheriff Hall, the women's residence, in honour of Lady Beaverbrook. After she was introduced by the university president, Henry Hicks, she got up and gave the briefest, most pointed and disarming speech I have ever heard. She said, "I know why you've appointed me to this position, so let me know what you need, and I'll see what I can do." It was all over in less than two minutes, and the audience responded with a group gasp.

Lady Beaverbrook apparently considered the chancellor's gown she had inherited from C. D. Howe insufficiently ornate to suit her high office. She therefore arranged to have a much fancier, heavily gilded robe designed for her, and she wore it to sit for her official chancellor's portrait. But, despite the glamorous new robe, she would never officiate at a Dalhousie convocation. I was told Henry Hicks had hoped her appointment would lead to major gifts of money to the university. Ultimately Dr. Hicks had to travel to the UK to see Lady Beaverbrook and perform the surgical procedure some wag referred to as the "wallet biopsy."

Lady Beaverbrook's successor, H. Reuben Cohen, was an outspoken New Brunswick industrialist. Reuben's blunt comments from the podium during convocations sometimes left the audience a little short of breath. The episode I remember best occurred during a convocation ceremony for graduates in the Faculty of Medicine. An attractive female medical graduate appeared before him to receive her degree. He announced to the assembled audience: "This is the young woman who examined my prostate!"

Since 95 per cent of my chancellor's responsibilities involved officiating at convocation ceremonies, I tried to make the experience more personal than I had previously observed at several universities, where graduates would traverse the stage (sometimes in pairs!) in just a few milliseconds, receiving little more than a perfunctory handshake and one or two words of congratulations, and then they were gone.

Thanks to the strong hand of President Tom Traves, Dalhousie convocations became models of split-second timing and efficiency. While the sheer number of convocation ceremonies might have seemed excessive to some, they had the virtue of allowing each ceremony to be more memorable for the graduates and their proud parents. I felt the graduation experience might be made a little more meaningful if I took a moment to greet each graduate by name and address a question or comment to each, to treat each one as an important individual of whom we were genuinely proud. I took it as a personal challenge to elicit a smile from each graduate and awarded myself a 95 per cent success rate!

During my years as chancellor, I officiated at all the convocations each year. The ceremonies were exhilarating and sometimes even fun. I often asked the young graduates about their plans for the future, or at least for the subsequent year. Some had a clear-cut career path. Others hadn't a clue. One young woman's response was especially frank: "Oh God, don't ask me that. I only got out of bed a half hour ago!" A couple of young graduates to whom I put the career question glanced at my gold-encrusted robes and said: "Well, I'd like your job!" (They were probably under the impression I was receiving a salary commensurate with the stately costume.)

But among many unforgettable moments, the most memorable was at a convocation when I was conferring degrees in business administration. As always, I held a copy of the program in my left hand, so that by the time the graduates approached my throne I could address them by name and knew their town and country of origin.

I glanced toward stage left where the dean stood at his lectern and microphone. There, to my utter horror, stood the next degree candidate and, so help me, he was *talking on a cell phone!* How could any graduate be so disdainful of the occasion to be carrying on a conversation on his cell phone? On the stage? As he walked toward me, I had abandoned my characteristically warm, welcoming smile. I recall, however, that he looked somewhat older than most of his classmates; and as he approached me, he apologized for using his cell phone on stage, explaining he had been speaking to his eighty-five-year-old mother, who lived in British Columbia and was not well enough to make the trip to attend his graduation. He was simply trying to involve her in the ceremony.

Without admitting it, I felt like the world's number-one misanthrope for having prejudged him so unfairly. To this day, I don't know why I did it but, as he stood before me, I asked him: "Do you suppose I could have a quick word with your mother?"

He looked thunderstruck but trotted out his cell phone and dialled her number. By this time, the entire audience had figured out what was happening. I spoke to her for about a minute, told her how proud we were of her son and predicted a fine future for him. I suppose my reflex response was a kind of atonement for having been upset with him and for having misinterpreted his act of love and sensitivity as an expression of disrespect for the occasion. That is forever engraved in my memory as a highlight of my chancellorship.

My only other reflection on my term in that high office was the impression that students in certain faculties exhibited particular group characteristics of personality and demeanour. These views are undoubtedly unjust generalizations, for which I apologize. Math majors seemed to be on another planet; medical graduates seemed especially full of hope and promise; and people in business administration seemed particularly joyless.

I completed my term as chancellor with a degree of regret, as one should at the end of any job that gives pleasure. My successor is another friend, Fred Fountain. He and his wife Elizabeth are exemplary human beings, and both are keenly interested in the students and their futures.

Moments Musicaux

The man that hath no music in himself
Nor is not moved with concord of sweet sounds
Is fit for treasons, stratagems and spoils;
The motions of his spirit are dull as night,
And his affections dark as Erebus:
Let no such man be trusted.

— *Shakespeare,* The Merchant of Venice

Beginning prenatally, and to the present day, music has played a central role in my life. The relevant genes came from both sides of the family. My father had a fair tenor voice and had sung on stage during his vaudeville days. He was a regular concert goer and a rabid opera fan. From our earliest youth, he took my brother and me to regular Sunday afternoon concerts of the Montreal Symphony, then a far cry from the world-class orchestra Montreal boasts today. My father was also a regular aficionado of the Saturday-afternoon broadcasts of the Metropolitan Opera. He would sing along enthusiastically with the tenor soloists, sometimes drowning them out. His brother Tevye was a keen amateur violinist who played in community orchestras in Vancouver. My uncle Harry and aunt Florence played for a time in several chamber groups and orchestras, including the Dubois Orchestra.

Florence also performed as the cellist in the Dubois Trio. My mother's younger sister, Ellen, was the only family member who pursued a lifetime career in music, and her story deserves special consideration.

Although she died forty-three years ago, I remember Ellen Ballon as a curious mixture of extraordinary talent and of great promise never fully realized. Her career had begun when she was just four years old! She auditioned at the Conservatorium of Music at McGill University, which had been established in 1896 by Donald Sutherland, Lord Strathcona, then principal of McGill. She auditioned before the entire music faculty, which then consisted of a single individual, Madame Clara Liechtenstein, a pianist who was "a former pupil of Franz Liszt."

Soon after taking Ellen under her wing, Madame Liechtenstein accepted another promising Montreal Jewish girl as a pupil. Her name was Pauline Lightstone, who became an opera singer of considerable distinction and sang leading roles at the Paris Opéra Comique, several times opposite the great Enrico Caruso. In those days, there was a widespread assumption you could make it in opera only if you had an Italian name, so Pauline Lightstone changed hers to Pauline Donalda. Montrealers who knew her in later years when she returned to her native city referred to her as "Madame Donalda" or simply "Donalda." I came to know Pauline Donalda in her later years, after she had returned to Montreal. She taught singing but kept one foot in the opera world, producing a single opera each year at Her Majesty's Theatre, for which she usually imported one or two Metropolitan Opera stars to perform leading roles.

Ellen gave her first public concert in Montreal at five, lifted onto the piano stool by the mayor of Montreal. Two years later, Madame Liechtenstein, deciding this extraordinary child needed a higher level of instruction, moved Ellen to New York to study with Rafael Joseffy, one of the world's greatest pianists of that era, and harmony with Rubin Goldmark. She made her New York debut in 1910, playing with the New York Symphony under the baton of Walter Damrosch. At that concert she played not one but two concerti, the Mendelssohn G-minor and Beethoven C-major! Around 1914, at the age of sixteen, Ellen moved to Switzerland to study with Josef Hofmann. She also studied with the great pianist Wilhelm Backhaus in Vienna and Alberto Jonas in New York.

An important omission from her various biographies is that, as a very young *Wunderkind*, she was patronized by several extremely wealthy families in New York, including members of the Vanderbilt and Whitney families. In those days, it was not unusual for the very wealthy to latch on to child prodigies, pamper them, support them financially and introduce them to lavish lifestyles unaffordable even to the most successful soloists. Aunt Ellen went through her entire life supported and cosseted by a succession of obscenely wealthy patrons, living a lifestyle most people experienced only in the movies. She cultivated friends among the famous and well-to-do, including Somerset Maugham, Edna Ferber, Nelson Eddy, Morton Gould, and many others. Luigi Ferragamo kept a plaster cast of her feet in his Italian studio, so she could (and did) regularly order shoes in the latest style that fit her to perfection. Her gowns were created by Valentina, and I had the impression she may have been the principal support of Elizabeth Arden's super-chic Fifth Avenue salon.

She performed for the rich and famous, for crowned heads and potentates. She played for Sir Wilfrid Laurier, then Canada's prime minister, and Lady Laurier in New York in 1909. She played three times at the White House, for Presidents Taft (1912), Roosevelt (1934), and Eisenhower (1954), and gave private recitals at Kensington Palace for members of the British royal family. In addition to recurring concerto performances with the New York Philharmonic, she also appeared with the

Vienna Philharmonic, the Berlin Philharmonic and the Concert-gebouw Orchestra of Amsterdam. She also played on numerous occasions with the Montreal and Toronto Symphony Orchestras.

I have a wonderful portrait of her as a young woman, decked out in the glamorous prescribed attire then *de rigueur* for all women being presented at court at Buckingham Palace, including a headdress of white ostrich plumes and an elegant white dress with a long, flowing train.

During her young adult years, Ellen moved to London, where she rented a mews flat in a small courtyard called Lyall Mews, off Sloan Square. I was ten or eleven when my parents took us on one of many trips to Europe and we visited Ellen. Although I have forgotten many details of my childhood and youth, the glamour of her London flat is indelibly imprinted in my memory. The interior was monochromatic: walls, carpet, furniture and Steinway grand all in purest white. I felt I had strolled on to the set of a Hollywood musical.

Aunt Ellen took us next door to a twin mews flat to meet her newest and dearest friend, an extraordinarily talented twenty-one-year-old sculptor named Sally Ryan, known as Tammie.

Aside from her extraordinary talent as a sculptor, she was — important to Ellen — a humongously wealthy heiress, a grand-daughter of Thomas Fortune Ryan, who had made his fortune in public transit, becoming one of the great railroad barons of the late nineteenth and early twentieth century.

In 1940, Ellen and Tammie returned to New York where Tammie purchased two mirror-image, side-by-side flats at 2 West 67th Street. One served as Tammie's studio and apartment, the other as Ellen's. Each apartment had a striking Hollywood-type two-storey-high living room, with an enormous two-storey window offering a fabulous view of Central Park. The second storey housed two bedrooms with a French door that opened on to a tiny, indoor Juliet balcony overlooking the living room below.

Ellen's apartment was elegantly furnished, with a Steinway grand framed by the huge, imposing living room window. In contrast, Tammie's "living room" served as her sculpture studio. I am led to believe there was a somewhat secret door between the two apartments to allow for "dangerous liaisons."

Some time after, Tammie purchased a 200-acre "farm" estate they called High Perch Farm near Silvermine, Connecticut, complete with a gaggle of servants, a caretaker, a marvellous cook, a beautiful outdoor swimming pool and a couple of Bedlington terriers. She built a magnificent two-storey, naturally lit sculpture studio a little distance from the main house. Although Tammie was the owner, she left the running of "the farm," as they called it, to Ellen.

In a biography of sculptor Sir Jacob Epstein, Tammie is described as his student and Ellen as her lover. In my youthful naiveté, I considered them just "close friends." The possibility of a lesbian relationship never entered my mind. (At that age I probably thought that lesbians were people who came from Beirut.) In any case, in those days, "nice" people never discussed deviations in sexual orientation, and even with the infinite wisdom of hindsight and maturity plus a medical education, I still have some difficulty in distinguishing Ellen's "true" sexual orientation. Unquestionably, Tammie was lesbian. She wore thoroughly mannish clothes (I don't believe she owned a dress), had a rather masculine haircut and treated Ellen as one would a marital partner.

To complicate matters, Ellen kept a kind of permanent boarder through much of their lives on Central Park West, the promising Canadian poet Ralph Gustafson. He later returned to Canada where his poetry became well known and, years later, he married. It was, by any measure, an unusual ménage à trois. Tammie Ryan eventually died of laryngeal cancer, having been a heavy smoker all her life.

Late in life, Ellen encountered an extraordinary man who confessed he had been worshipping at her shrine since he had first heard her play when both were young. He had then been a music critic for a local newspaper and had attended one of her concerts. He fell madly in love with her. Now, many decades later, they met again and his ardour was undimmed. His name was Theodore Lafleur ("Ted") Bullock, a former Lieutenant-Colonel in Quebec's distinguished Royal 22nd Regiment (the "Van Doos"), who had been awarded the US Medal of Freedom in 1946. He also served as Director of the Canadian Pavilion at the 1958 Brussels World's Fair. Soon after he reconnected with Ellen, he proposed, she accepted and they married at Temple Emmanuel in New York. As a prelude to this union, for reasons now lost in history (his decision or Ellen's insistence?) he converted to Judaism. The conversion could hardly have been described as *pro forma;* he actually underwent a circumcision! I could only conclude: "greater love hath no man."

Ruth and I dined with Aunt Ellen and Uncle Ted on numerous occasions, usually at the Ritz Carlton Hotel in Montreal, where Ellen maintained a suite, complete with a Steinway baby grand she played only occasionally. Dinner was memorable. Ted was always impeccably dressed, often in black tie. His sense of protocol may well have reflected his military background. He had a careful seating plan, always held the ladies' chairs and was generous and diplomatic in steering the conversation. His generosity, like Ellen's, was undoubtedly facilitated by Tammie Ryan's seemingly bottomless bank account.

Aunt Ellen died in 1969, after which Ted Bullock moved to a seniors' colony in Hemet, California, not far from Palm Springs. Sometime after moving to Halifax, I reconnected with him, partly as the result of a conflict between him and McGill University. Ted had offered the McGill Faculty of Music Ellen's large collection of musical memorabilia. The collection included original scores by famous composers and signed photographs of famous musicians.

Whoever was spokesperson for McGill had told him (or so he told me) they would be delighted to accept Ellen's collection *providing* Ted would also donate a building in which to house it. Ted became enraged and promptly withdrew the offer. I have no way of knowing whether he was drunk or sober during these negotiations, but I received a phone call from him: "Dick, what's the name of that university you're attached to in Halifax?" he asked. He then told me about his altercation with McGill and said he had decided to donate the entire collection to Dalhousie. I spoke to the president, Dr. Henry Hicks, a colourful man who had been Liberal premier of Nova Scotia from 1954 to 1956. He quickly agreed to accept the gift unconditionally. Ted came to Halifax, met Henry Hicks and completed arrangements for formal transfer of the collection.

During that same visit, Ted took me aside and told me he had "a small favour" to ask. Would I serve as sole executor of his will? I told him I had zero experience as an executor of anything. He explained his will was simple and uncomplicated and that my duties would give me no problems whatsoever. How could I possibly refuse? Two weeks later, to the day, I received a phone call from Montreal informing me Ted had been found dead, possibly from a heart attack, in his room at the Ritz Carlton. Late in Ted Bullock's life, it had become clear he had a major problem with alcohol addiction. Whether this played a role in his demise remains a mystery.

My duties as his executor turned out to be far more complex, convoluted and time-consuming than I could have imagined, notwithstanding his reassurances. The will had to be probated in both the United States and Canada. More than two years later — after one trip to California, two or three to New York and multiple consultations with lawyers, accountants and notaries on both sides of the border — his estate, which was not all that large, was finally settled.

When he cleared out his California prefab home in Hemet, he sent me several gifts. I treasure these gifts. They include a museum-class collection of miniatures my aunt Ellen had accumulated as a hobby throughout her career. It includes a dining room table, about fifteen centimetres long, set with tiny, perfect sterling flatware and a minuscule Royal Crown Derby china tea service. Other treasures included three bronze sculptures created by Sally Ryan. One is a bust of Ellen. Two are portraits in bronze, one of a black woman wearing a bandana. Her eyes are closed, head turned to one side, her chin resting on her hand, a superb study in repose. The other is the head of a young black boy, looking modestly downward, eyes half-closed. (The models for these marvellous portraits were, in fact, Aunt Ellen's cook and her young son.) Both are deeply moving. My sons now have two other Ryan busts of people in her social circle: John Gielgud around the time he played Hamlet in London, and Somerset Maugham, a frequent visitor to High Perch Farm.

Aunt Ellen herself was "a mystery wrapped in an enigma." I mourn for the career as pianist she might have had. Ellen had the misfortune of having been a child prodigy in an era when *Wunderkinder* were often "adopted" and indulged by wealthy patrons, much as one might adopt a cute animal as a pet. Had she learned at an early age that talent alone was not enough, and that even the most gifted soloists must work daily, often for hours on end, to perfect, maintain and improve their performance, and had she not been seduced by a lifestyle of great opulence, who knows what she might have achieved?

In the end, Ellen died of a gastrointestinal cancer, a mere mortal once again. As often happened during that era, no one told her what was actually wrong with her. When she became deeply jaundiced, her doctor said she had hepatitis. Like most patients, she probably knew the truth but went along with the charade.

Nowadays, few people, even in the musical world, remember her. But in ways musical and nonmusical she played an important role in my life. She shaped my musical tastes but also — through negative example — taught me to distinguish what is really important in life from what is not.

Intermezzo

Paul Robeson

My first meeting with Paul Robeson, the distinguished bass-baritone, took place in Sally Ryan's studio in Lyall Mews, where she was doing a plaster bust of him. Robeson and my aunt Ellen had shared the bill in a concert tour of Scandinavia under the auspices of the International Artists Series, which often sponsored European concert tours featuring two soloists on the same program.

Paul was larger than life: big, broad-shouldered, his head seeming too big for his body. His speaking voice (like his singing voice) sent shivers down your spine. He spoke very softly and gently, with a natural *vibrato,* like the sound of distant thunder. Those old enough to remember Paul Robeson will associate him with one song in particular, "Ol' Man River," which he sang in the original 1928 production of *Showboat.* Audiences invariably demanded he include this song in his recital programs, usually as an encore.

Whenever he was in Montreal to perform, Paul came to my parents' home for dinner. His last visit to Montreal, as an actor rather than a singer, was when he appeared in the title role of Shakespeare's *Othello* opposite Uta Hagen, who played Desdemona. The historic importance of that production may seem ludicrous nowadays, but it was then a truly big deal. Not only was a black man playing the role of lover to a white woman, but (horrors!) he actually kissed her on the stage, a first in the history of the English-speaking theatre!

Of all my memories of Paul Robeson, the most vivid was when my maternal grandfather, Samuel Ballon, was terminally ill with a severe pneumonia. We mentioned his illness to Paul, who was in Montreal for a recital. He said he would like to visit him, out of friendship for Ellen and the family. My grandfather was barely conscious then. Although Paul should have been at the theatre to begin his recital, he pulled a chair up to the bedside, sat down as though he had all the time in the world, took Grandpa's hand in his and quietly crooned a Yiddish folk song to him. My grandfather seemed to relax and to be at peace. He died a couple of days later, but that deathbed scene, which I witnessed from the doorway, stayed with me, a valuable lesson in palliative care.

Oscar Levant

During the mid-thirties, a remarkable pianist, wit and world-class neurotic made a brief but spectacular appearance in our lives. His name was Oscar Levant, and he had almost certainly been told to contact my father by their mutual friend, playwright Sam Behrman. Sam had been my father's closest boyhood friend in Worcester, Massachusetts. He and Oscar Levant were members of a small group of extraordinarily creative individuals, including George and Ira Gershwin, playwrights George S. Kaufman and Moss Hart and actress Ruth Gordon.

Oscar was generally acknowledged to be the foremost interpreter of Gershwin's music. He played Gershwin's two best-known works, the *Rhapsody in Blue* and the Concerto in F, better than the composer himself.

I felt a particular affinity to Oscar Levant because at that time

I was hugely attracted to Gershwin's music, and as an under-graduate at McGill, had played both the *Rhapsody in Blue* and the Concerto in F in public concerts.

Oscar had also acquired a remarkable reputation as a genius and wit, largely through appearances as a regular guest on a popular radio quiz program *Information Please*. Members of the audience submitted questions to the show's three panelists. They received two dollars if their question was used and *five* dollars if the panel was unable to answer it, lavish rewards in those days. Each of the three panelists had an encyclo-pedic knowledge of innumerable arcane topics, so it was hard to stump them. Oscar's own knowledge was extraordinary, extending far beyond music. Coupled with his knowledge was a wit that has rarely been equalled.

For all his musical talent, intelligence and wit, Oscar was a deeply tragic figure, his life haunted by an assortment of demons. He could be literally paralyzed by superstitions (the number thirteen, anything vaguely connected with death and an assort-ment of other fears and phobias). He was a chain smoker who consumed up to forty cups of coffee per day. He spoke openly about his mental health problems, but even then, his acerbic wit never abandoned him. Having had several admissions to what were then called "mental hospitals," he reported such hospitals now refused to admit him "because I depressed the patients."

When Oscar telephoned my father on arrival in Montreal, my father invited him up to the house. Oscar said he wanted to practise, and we had a pretty decent Steinway baby grand. Whatever composition I mentioned, he dove into it and played it, note-perfect. Toward the end of the afternoon at home with Oscar, we took him back to his hotel and arranged to pick him up before the concert, scheduled for 8 p.m. At about 7 p.m. Oscar telephoned, saying he was sick and was cancelling the concert. (He was known for cancelling concerts, often at the last minute, if anything upset his psychic equilibrium.) Being aware of his neurotic tendencies, my father made an executive decision. We got in the car, headed for the hotel and went up to Oscar's room. He was lying in bed. We insisted he get out of bed pronto and managed to get him to the theatre, where he played the full program to an enthusiastic audience. Typically, as an encore, he played the three Gershwin piano preludes, confirming his undisputed status as Gershwin's premier interpreter.

Oscar Levant's life evolved sadly and ended even more sadly. He was admitted to psychiatric hospitals on several occasions and underwent psychoanalysis without much improvement. This was well before the revolution in psychopharmacology that changed the outlook for so many patients with mental illness.

Isaac Stern

I was ten years old and Isaac Stern was fourteen when we first met. My parents, my brother Victor and I were in San Francisco, visiting my father's sister Eva and her family. At Eva's house, we met the Stern family who had immigrated to San Francisco earlier from Russia. Aunt Eva told us then that Isaac was a very talented violinist, but I did not hear him play until several years later. The only benefit I reaped from that visit was that Isaac taught us how to play poker.

When Ruth and I married, we spent several days of our honeymoon with Isaac and his family at a farm he had rented in Vermont for the summer. After that, we got together regularly, mostly in New York or Montreal.

On one memorable occasion, a year or so after Ruth and I were married, Isaac and his faithful accompanist, Alexander ("Shura") Zakin, came to visit. They had been touring US military bases in the sub-arctic and had flown to Montreal to play a recital. Knowing I had a decent piano, they asked if they could come to our apartment for the morning to practise. Ruth offered to make lunch. Now, it's fair to say Ruth had not yet reached the apogee of her culinary skills. Given a limited range of options, she offered them a lunch of scrambled eggs, which they accepted. After finishing their home-cooked repast, as they were leaving and kissing Ruth goodbye, Shura paid her the ultimate compliment: "You know, Rootie," he cooed, kissing her on both cheeks, "you are only voman I know who can take *real* eggs and make them taste like powdered!" We quoted him for decades thereafter.

Over a lifetime of friendship, I (or Ruth and I) took unfair advantage of our friendship with Isaac only three times, but always for a good cause. The first was when, at age seventeen, I organized a series of student subscription concerts at McGill. I was a sophomore at the time. Since our resources were very limited, the fees we offered to guest soloists were, to put it mildly, meagre. The best we could offer was $600 for *both* Isaac and Shura, a fee that wouldn't even begin to cover their expenses. They agreed to play — as a gesture of unadulterated friendship — but Isaac warned me if I was *ever* to reveal the fee for which they had performed, they would have to have me killed.

The second time I took unfair advantage of our friendship was for the opening of the Rebecca Cohn Auditorium, a brand new concert hall at Dalhousie University. In response to whining and cajoling, Isaac agreed to come and perform in a concert to celebrate the opening. The concert was a huge success.

My third imposition came in 1992. Ruth and I had agreed to lend our names to a gala event to raise funds to establish an endowment fund for Symphony Nova Scotia. The event, called Pure Gold, featured a gala banquet and a concert the following night. Ruth and I again took serious advantage of not one, but two of our musician friends (both, sadly, now deceased), Isaac Stern and the great Canadian contralto, Maureen Forrester, for whose children I had been pediatrician for many years in Montreal. Both agreed to come and spoke eloquently at the banquet. The following night's concert was a huge success, and the event initiated an endowment that has since grown to over seven million dollars.

Maureen Forrester

Maureen Forrester was a superb Montreal-born contralto who achieved a world-wide reputation. She married Eugene ("Jack") Kash, a violinist and teacher, and together they produced five fine children. Typically, Maureen would perform right up to the final moment of each of her pregnancies, and I remember sitting in the audience wondering whether I might be called out at any moment to provide newborn care backstage.

When Maureen married Eugene Kash she converted to Judaism, and she attended her very first Passover Seder at our house. Between my own bad (but loud) piano playing and the performances of many musical friends, music was always an important element of our family life.

The Soviet Invasion

In 1956, Isaac Stern and Shura Zakin became among the first American musicians to perform in the Soviet Union, where both had been born. The fact both spoke Russian fluently enhanced the huge success of their tour.

Ruth and I never dreamed their Soviet tour would have the slightest impact on our lives, but it did, and in a lasting way. Following that tour, the USSR opened the tiniest chink in the Iron Curtain, allowing a few Russian musicians — and at first, only a handful of the *crème de la crème* — to travel to North America to perform, always under rigidly controlled conditions.

Since Shura and Isaac were among the few personal friends the Soviet musicians had in America, and since their North

American tours often included performances in Montreal, Shura would phone in advance whenever musician colleagues from the USSR were due to come to Montreal and beg us to "take care of them." We were more than happy to oblige.

Since their performance fees were paid to the official Soviet government music agency, the performers could keep only a small portion of their fees. Many became compulsive shoppers with that money, hungrily snapping up material goods difficult or impossible to buy in the USSR. On an early North American tour, violinist David Oistrakh purchased a large refrigerator and had it shipped back to Moscow. Someone who later visited the Oistrakhs' Moscow apartment told us the refrigerator occupied a place of prominence in their living room.

The earliest Soviet luminaries were accompanied by minders, KGB operatives assigned to ensure they didn't try to defect. A single bad performance, one poor review, or the slightest political *faux pas* could spell *finis* to further permission to tour in the Wicked West. Wives who accompanied their musician husbands on tour could be particularly vulnerable to this kind of paranoia. Oistrakh's wife, Tamara Ivanovna, was a sweet, gentle woman in our home. But when her husband was performing, she became so agitated she was incapable of sitting in the audience and usually hid out in a backstage bathroom until it was over.

David, Tamara and their son, Igor, also an outstanding violinist, had repeatedly been feted by the rich and famous during their first North American tour. Probably as a result, Tamara concluded North Americans were waited on hand and foot by servants. When Ruth produced a beautiful roast of beef for Sunday lunch, Tamara began to speak excitedly in Russian to David and Igor. Igor explained his mother assumed the beautiful luncheon had been prepared by unseen servants. Hearing this, Ruth beckoned her into the kitchen to peek in the oven, proving beyond any shadow of doubt the meal was entirely her own work. Tamara was so impressed she presented Ruth with a large brooch given to her by the queen of Belgium.

Before the Oistrakhs left our home to return to their hotel, Igor took Ruth aside to beg a special favour. His mother was very embarrassed by the dark moustache on her upper lip. Could Ruth do anything about it? The next morning, we visited them at their suite in Montreal's Windsor Hotel, Ruth carrying what seemed to me to be a lifetime supply of depilatory cream in a brown paper bag. The two women disappeared quietly into the bathroom. Ten minutes later they emerged. Tamara Ivanovna's upper lip was as smooth as a baby's bottom. Igor took one look and performed a celebratory handstand in the middle of the room. Her husband went through an elaborate charade pretending to be heartbroken, weeping over the dramatic change in her appearance. He spoke rapidly in Russian, while Igor translated: "Father say, when he and Tamara Ivanovna very young and first meet, she have 'leetle' moustache, and he love her ver-r-ry much; then, after they married for many years, she have 'beeg' moustache . . . like Cossack . . . and he love her even more. Now father ver-r-ry sad, because moustache all gone!"

Two other memories of the Oistrakhs' visit stick in my memory. When I walked with Igor along Sherbrooke Street, he would often turn his head and look back over his shoulder, clearly checking whether we were being followed. On another occasion we were walking past a newly completed, multistorey, automated parking garage in downtown Montreal, in which cars were driven onto an elevator and then carried automatically to the appropriate level, where they were taken off and parked automatically. He was captivated by this mechanical marvel. As we watched, he leaned over to me and whispered facetiously: "Capitalism . . . it is terrible, no?"

The Oistrakhs were only the first of a series of famous Soviet musicians to visit us, including the marvellous pianist Emil ("Mila") Gilels and his wife Lala. When I suggested during a nice

lunch at Café Martin they should bring their daughter Elisabeth
with them next time he came to Canada, Mila looked at me in
total disbelief. Then he reached over and pinched my cheek, as
you would with a young child. He said: "Baby, you no understand. When Lala come, Elisabeth no come. When Elisabeth
come, Lala no come." I had forgotten momentarily that when
Soviet musicians travelled abroad, at least one member of the
immediate family was required to stay behind, a hostage against
the risk of defection to the West.

During our lunch, Mila seemed keen to confide. At one point,
he looked around to make sure no one was eavesdropping and said
confidentially: "You know, real name Hillel." Presumably, his name
had been changed somewhere along the line to conceal Jewish roots.

The last of our string of Soviet musical visitors was a young
pianist who would become a lifelong friend. Marina Mdivani
arrived on our doorstep in the Montreal suburb of Hampstead
on November 21, 1963. When I opened the front door to welcome her, the vision was unforgettable. She wore a very tall fur
hat, like a Russian Hussar, had a very pleasant disposition and
spoke cautious, Russian-accented English reasonably well. A
pupil of Emil Gilels and a rising star in the pianistic firmament,
she was scheduled to perform in a concert in Montreal the next
evening. But that was the day John Kennedy was shot, and Marina was so devastated she immediately cancelled the concert out
of respect for the murdered US president.

Some years later, Marina immigrated to Canada with her
son, settling first in Hamilton, Ontario, and later moving to
Montreal to join McGill University's Faculty of Music, where
she is now professor of piano. Although our recent contact has
been limited to occasional phone calls, she will always be a part
of my family.

Zubin Mehta

Pierre Béique, the general manager of the Montreal Symphony Orchestra, was in panic mode. His music director, Igor Markevitch, who was scheduled to conduct the gala opening concert of the season in less than two weeks, had just telegraphed from Paris to cancel his appearance. How could Béique possibly find a conductor who would open the season by galvanizing Montreal audiences into new peaks of enthusiasm sufficient to bring them back for the rest of the season?

At that moment, one of the MSO office staff told Béique a young conductor was waiting to see him. His name was Zubin Mehta and he had a letter of introduction from Hans Swarowski. Béique was about to brush Mehta off when he was seized by an impulse. "Look," he said to the young conductor, "I'm going to give you one chance. I'm going to let you conduct our opening concert in two weeks' time . . ."

The concert was an instant howling sensation. That was 1971. The rest, as they say, is history.

Mehta was gifted with extraordinary musical insights, knowing every score by heart. He also had "a good stick"; his movements were clear and meaningful and he had a unique ability to transmit exactly what he wanted his fellow musicians to produce. Zubin Mehta formed an instant bond, not only with audiences, but more importantly, with the orchestra members.

Zubin and his wife Carmen Laski, a young soprano, became close personal friends, and I cared for their two children. Through them, we added many interesting folks to our growing list of friends in the music world, one of the most memorable being the young, hugely talented pianist Daniel Barenboim. I still cherish the bizarre memory of Daniel and Zubin playing (and singing) a compressed version of Puccini's *Tosca* in our living room. Their version concluded with Daniel standing on the piano stool (as Tosca) and leaping off the Castel Sant'Angelo to certain death in the Tiber River below. That performance could have dealt a death blow to Puccini himself, but it remains one of my best (and funniest) musical memories.

Jacqueline du Pré

On a rainy, windy, miserable Sunday morning in the 1960s, I had just begun to unwind after several house calls and was looking forward to a rare day of relaxation. I had a busy pediatric practice at the time with a sign-out arrangement with two pediatric colleagues. Thus, each of us covered all three practices every third night and every third weekend. When we were on call we often worked far into the evening.

I was lying half-asleep on the sofa when the phone rang. It was Zarin Mehta, Zubin's brother. He wanted us to go with them to a performance by an eighteen-year-old British cellist. He had heard her play once before and said she was phenomenal. I was reluctant to give up half my day of rest for anything or anyone, but Zarin was insistent. We *must* hear this extraordinary girl. So we drove in the teeming rain to Salle Vincent d'Indy and took our seats. Moments later, from the wings emerged a stunningly beautiful woman with long, flowing blonde hair. Her name was Jacqueline du Pré. She sat down and smiled at the conductor, and they began to play.

Even in a lifetime of concert-going, the number of occasions when a performance makes the hairs on the back of your neck stand up, catches your breath and completely stills your body are vanishingly few. That Sunday-afternoon performance was one. The physical element of her playing was, in every way, an integral part of the performance and added to the magic of her music-making. Both visually and audibly, her playing had an almost erotic quality. The sound was big and round, and her musicality (how you move from one note to the next, as Isaac

Stern would describe it) was masterful. I have never heard the Elgar concerto played with more conviction or passion. Her body swayed as she played, her blonde mane tossing as if to complement the bravura passages.

We met Jacquie after that performance, and met again periodically thereafter, including a dinner together in Stockholm when she had already become Daniel Barenboim's girlfriend (they later married). Jacquie's development of multiple sclerosis, from which she died in 1987, cut short a brilliant career and deprived the world of a truly great musician.

Yo-Yo Ma

Our son David and Yo-Yo had been undergraduates at Harvard at the same time and then got to know each other a few years after graduation. They have remained good friends ever since. Though I didn't meet him until after his career was established, I had heard Yo-Yo's father's name regularly in Isaac Stern's home, because Mr. Ma had taught piano to the three Stern children. Some years ago Yo-Yo came to Halifax as soloist with Symphony Nova Scotia. Yo-Yo is the least stuffy professional performer in the business. When he appears as a guest soloist with a symphony, he often performs in the first half of the program. After intermission, audience members are amazed to spot him sitting in the very back of the cello section, playing as an orchestra member. It is a rare manifestation of modesty and egalitarianism. That's what happened in Halifax.

After the concert, Ruth and I had laid on a small reception in our home for Yo-Yo, a few guests and a few orchestra members. During the gathering, I suddenly remembered a unique birthday present given to me a few years earlier by Gary Karr, the double-bass virtuoso who lived for several years in Halifax: an embossed sterling silver yo-yo! Deciding our guest of honour would be a much more appropriate owner of that gift, I fished it out of a drawer, called for everyone's attention, made a few extravagant remarks and presented it to Yo-Yo, who seemed pleased to have it. Before the party ended, Ruth asked Yo-Yo if he would sign our guest book. He did so, inscribing two lines, entirely in Chinese characters. Naturally, Ruth asked if he would translate what he had written. He obliged: "It says "*broches* on your *toches*" (in Yiddish, "blessings on your butt").

My Own Brief (but Spectacular) Career as a Maestro

Some years ago, at a fund-raising event in support of Symphony Nova Scotia, Ruth bid on, and won, an opportunity to conduct the orchestra. She presented me with the certificate as a birthday gift. I was delighted because one of my secret lifetime ambitions would finally be gratified — and this just could signal a major career change! My debut was scheduled to take place at "Beer and Beethoven," an annual fund-raiser for the symphony, at which the orchestra plays a few pieces, a few listen, more talk, and everyone drinks a lot of beer.

I consulted with the orchestra's personnel manager to find out how much say I would have in choosing a work that would be sufficiently dramatic to show off my fabled baton technique and captivate the musicians and, of course, the audience. I also asked how much rehearsal time was allotted for my performance. "Six minutes," he replied, deadpan. I realized immediately this unreasonably brief time limit would severely (and unfairly) limit my choice of repertoire and the degree to which I could inspire the orchestra. After reviewing the library of scores to find an appropriately showy piece whose length was within the dictatorially prescribed time limit, I settled on the overture to

Glinka's opera *Ruslan and Ludmilla,* a lively work with sufficient *brio* to show off my podium personality and musical insights. The playing time turned out to be exactly six minutes, meaning I would be allowed only a single run-through, with virtually no time to prescribe improvements in the ensemble's understanding of my interpretation of the work.

When I listened to a recording of the work and followed along in the conductor's score, I realized I would have to wave my baton with my right hand while flipping pages frequently with my left, roughly equivalent to trying to pat the top of your head and rub your tummy in circles simultaneously. Clearly, the only way I could meet this challenge was to commit the score to memory, which I did.

I anticipated some members of the orchestra would not take my conducting debut as seriously as they should, partly because many were personal friends and had never taken me seriously to begin with, and partly because most of them knew this overture by heart. Therefore, when I mounted the podium for the rehearsal, baton in hand, I began by explaining to the musicians that, since I was incapable of flipping pages rapidly with one hand while conducting with the other, I would conduct this work "in the same way that my wife performs the Dance of the Virgin . . . entirely from memory!"

While leading them through Glinka's masterpiece, I had the uncomfortable feeling certain members of the orchestra were laughing at me. But perhaps I was being over-sensitive. For some inexplicable reason, and notwithstanding my brilliant interpretation of the work, I have not been invited to conduct Symphony Nova Scotia again. Undoubtedly, this is an oversight, but it is never too late for the orchestra management to come to their senses and respond to popular pressure. I live in hope.

Shabbat dinner in Montreal at my parents' home. Front row, left to right: Susan, Mrs. Annie Goldbloom, Jonathan, Dr. Alton Goldbloom, David, Michael, Barbie; back row, left to right: Alan, Sheila (wife of Victor), Victor, Richard and Ruth, slightly in front of Richard.

My mother and father, Annie and Alton Goldbloom, with Ruth's mother, Rose Schwartz, in the middle, 1965.

Chatting with a family outside the IWK in the 1970s.

Dr. Sydney Gellis, my mentor and lifelong friend.

Picture of me, *circa* 1977.

The board of directors of the Izaak Walton Killam Hospital commissioned Al Chaddock to depict me in the hospital setting. Admiring the painting are IWK executive director Bernard Lamontagne and Eleanor Lindsay, 7 West head nurse, also depicted in the painting.

Spending a quiet moment with Maria VanBerkel, a surgical patient of Dr. Alex Gillis at the IWK in 1985.

Ruth's mother, Rose
Schwartz, on her
ninetieth birthday.

My father, Dr.
Alton Goldbloom,
Canadian pediatric
pioneer and first
trained pediatrician to
practice in Montreal.

At the naming ceremony for the Goldbloom Pavillion at the IWK,
October 2005.

Ruth in our Halifax home.

In our Halifax home, 2012.

Bruce MacKinnon's tribute to Ruth Goldbloom — a pair of tap shoes hung up on a hook — forever. On the bottom of one of the heels was engraved, simply "RUTH". He had said it all.

With our three children in 2013. From left to right, Alan, Barbie, me and David.

Music has always played a central role in my life.

My Final Chapter

Losses

Mourn not the dead that in the cool earth lie —
Dust unto dust —
The calm, sweet earth that mothers all who die
As all men must;

Mourn not your captive comrades who must dwell —
Too strong to strive —
Within each steel-bound coffin of a cell,
Buried alive;

But rather mourn the apathetic throng —
The cowed and the meek —
Who see the world's great anguish and its wrong —
And dare not speak!

— *Ralph Chaplin*

No life is immune to the trauma of losing family members and close friends. For doctors, there are the irreparable losses of patients, with whose families we have often developed unique, close relationships. Such losses, consciously or subconsciously, play a key role in shaping our feelings toward others and affect how we practice medicine; and they shape our ability to empathize with families in trouble.

Our attitudes toward death and dying mature over time. When I was young, I had aunts and uncles who succumbed to cancer. In those days, the "C-word," as it was sometimes called, was rarely uttered between doctor and patient, sometimes not even in conversations with the patient's family. Elaborate ruses and euphemisms were invoked. I am certain most patients knew the truth, but they too went along with the charade.

Like most others of my vintage, my life has been punctuated by a number of deeply felt, unforgettable losses. During my school days at Lower Canada College, I rode my bicycle to school several kilometres daily along the busy main thoroughfare of Sherbrooke Street. One day, I learned to my horror that a fellow student, a couple of years younger, had been hit by a car while riding his bike to school. He was killed instantly. His family name was Montefiore and we knew the family socially; they were a branch of one of Great Britain's most venerable Jewish families. We were all deeply shaken by his death, and my parents, understandably, worried I might meet the same fate. Whether through sympathy or cowardice (more likely, both), I decided then and there to leave my bike at home and take the bus to school.

The deaths of contemporaries during our younger years become permanently engraved in our memories, since they shatter our youthful illusions of invincibility and immortality. Another of my school friends developed the most severe form of poliomyelitis during one of the several polio epidemics to hit Montreal. Suffering from so-called bulbar polio, in which the virus infects the nuclei in the brainstem that control vital functions such as breathing, he became rapidly and extensively paralyzed, unable to breathe on his own. He was admitted to the Montreal Neurological Institute on a respirator (the "iron lung"). He died after a few days.

Then, two slightly older Selwyn House classmates, Gerry Hanson and Peter Gordon, both close friends, were killed overseas in the line of duty during World War II. Aside from the deep loss, their deaths also instilled feelings of guilt that I was not "doing my bit" for the war effort. Actually, my entire "wartime service" consisted of three years in the Canadian Officers Training Corps (COTC), which included three two-week periods of intensive training at three different army camps in Trois Rivières, Farnham and St. Jean. Much of the training consisted of parade drill, cleaning our rifles and shooting at targets on the rifle range. One member of our group, who will remain nameless, had the uncanny knack of hitting a target fairly regularly, but frequently it was the target belonging to the cadet next to him. He was promptly nicknamed "sniper." The fact some of us never saw active service may have been partly responsible for the Allied victory.

One of my earliest military epiphanies came during my first year at COTC while marching with my brave comrades out of the camp on a foot-blistering five-mile route march. A band — brass, clarinets and drums — played us out of the camp as we left on our body- and character-building marching excursions. They were not seen or heard again until our bedraggled troop marched back into camp three hours later. Looking neat and fresh, they'd play us back in to the camp. When it came to avoiding excessive exertion, I realized immediately the band members had it made. Keenly aware of my own musical gifts, I declared myself a drummer. I was welcomed with open arms and given my own snare drum and sticks. I faked it a bit at first, but my natural sense of rhythm soon kicked in. That musical metamorphosis was the end of my military marching career. I was embraced as a fullfledged drummer, playing poker in the barracks with my fellow musicians for two- or three-hour stretches while waiting for the return of our exhausted comrades-in-arms.

By the time I was old enough to enlist, the end of the war was just over a year away. My professor of biochemistry, Dr. David Thomson (an authority on nutrition, but one of the most skeletal, undernourished-looking men I ever knew), got wind I was thinking of enlisting. He also knew I was applying for medical school. He called me into his office and lectured me to the effect that my duty to king and country would best be fulfilled by entering medical school. Somehow, his chat seemed to assuage my guilt, and I followed his advice.

One of my most keenly felt losses came with the death of my dear friend and pediatric colleague Alan C. Siegel. When I arrived in Boston in 1950 and reported for duty as a senior resident at the Children's Hospital, my first assignment was to the infectious disease ward. Alan Siegel and I hit it off about two minutes after we met. We both laughed a lot, told bad (often ethnic) jokes and shared an unshakable irreverence toward "the establishment." Alan was a marvellous mimic. He did deadly impersonations of several of the Harvard pediatric luminaries, particularly the more pompous ones. His medical knowledge and clinical skills were outstanding, and children loved him. After completing his training, he ran a busy pediatric practice in the Chicago suburb of Winnetka and worked at Children's Memorial Hospital in Chicago. We became virtually inseparable, and our friendship grew to include his wonderful wife, Corinne, and their children.

In 1968, Ruth and I and the Siegels decided to attend an international pediatric congress in Mexico City. International medical congresses are one of the least fruitful sources of new scientific medical information. The programs are typically laden with previously published work and "state of the art" reviews and

are often dominated by folks who seem to devote an inordin-
ate amount of their time attending international gatherings and
hobnobbing with foreign colleagues of similar disposition.

Our hidden agenda in deciding to attend this meeting was
a post-congress excursion to a tiny village of Zihuatanejo, an
undiscovered gem on the Pacific coast. After the meeting, we
took off from Mexico City in a six-passenger Piper Navajo air-
craft for Zihuatanejo. The flight was bumpy, and when the going
got rough, Alan would invoke whatever religious rituals (his
own and others) he could exhibit to calm our apprehensions. He
would make the sign of the cross on his chest, then, moments
later, recite the Kaddish, the Hebrew prayer for the dead. When
we landed on the tiny airstrip, we registered in the village's single
rudimentary hotel and set out for the beautiful beaches.

After a day or so, Alan and I decided to go deep-sea fishing,
engaging a local fisherman to take us out in his boat. Before long,
Alan landed a huge sailfish, of which he was justifiably proud.
The fisherman made us a delicious *ceviche* and we headed back
to the village at noon.

When Alan and Corinne left us for a beach a short boat
ride away, Ruth and I agreed to follow soon after. As our boat
approached the beach, we spotted a large man, clearly Alan,
standing unsteadily in shallow water, being helped ashore by several people. By the time we reached the beach, he was in serious
trouble, with acute heart failure and pulmonary edema (fluid
filling his lungs). I immediately started resuscitation, mouth to
mouth and vigorous chest compressions. I asked a bystander
to bring some oxygen. After what seemed forever, he returned
with the community's entire oxygen supply, a small, globe-like
canister, about the size of a small bowling ball, that might have
sufficed to keep a cat alive, but only briefly.

Alan's tragic death and the difficult days that followed are
etched forever in my memory. As if in tribute to Alan, even those

awful three days had a strangely comical aspect. There was no mortuary in Zihuatanejo. Embalming was impossible, and it was blisteringly hot. Then there was the question of how to get Alan back to Chicago for burial.

This turned out to be an almost insurmountable problem. Since officials would not transport the body in the Piper Navajo that had flown us in, we had to find some means of transporting the body over the very rough, 250-kilometre dirt road to Acapulco where we could arrange transport on a larger plane. Only one person in Zihuatanejo had a vehicle large enough to accommodate Alan's body. It was a station wagon owned by the one and only local physician. I found out where the doctor lived, went to his house — it was now night — and knocked on a shuttered window. He was not pleased at being disturbed. He refused to come out, speaking to me in broken English through the shutters. I explained our predicament and, after some consideration, he volunteered, reluctantly, to transport the body — for a fee of $1,500!

Time was moving on, and we had an unrefrigerated, unembalmed body on our hands in a stiflingly hot climate. I asked myself what I would wish for, had I been the victim, and knew immediately I would have been more than happy to be buried on the spot. With great apprehension, I presented the options to Corinne. She agreed the only logical and practical solution was to bury Alan in Zihuatanejo. This was the beginning of the next bizarre chapter. I was told I had to obtain a death certificate at the mayor's office. As with the doctor's "offer" of transport, every phase of dealing with the local bureaucracy was payola-dependent. The mayor's office was a tiny, streetfront, partly open-air establishment, where a local functionary blew a huge cloud of dust out of the depths of an ancient typewriter, inserted a large form and began to ask me innumerable questions about the deceased, including the colour of Alan's hair, eyes and skin and the shape of his nose and ears. He made it clear my failure to provide specific answers to any of his questions would result in his inability/refusal to complete the required death certificate. I quickly learned to fabricate what I didn't know for sure. At this point, it seemed as though there would be no end to the process. Fortunately, a Montreal pediatric colleague, Dr. Hugh Brodie, was also staying in Zihuatanelo. Hearing of the tragedy, he offered to help. I accepted with enormous relief.

The next task was to arrange for a grave to be dug in the local cemetery. I was informed I would have to hire no fewer than *five* gravediggers at exorbitant pay, which had to be supplemented with a generous supply of tequila. Since there was no choice, we complied. With the grave only half dug, the gravediggers went on strike, laying down their shovels until we provided more pesos and tequila. There followed further extortionate demands for money to pay for the launching of fireworks, a regular feature of the committal ceremony. At this point my Jewish heritage clicked in. I drew the line at the fireworks.

Despite the bizarre circumstances of that entire tragic event, all of us, including Alan's widow, Corinne, appreciated the extent to which it was in character, a curious kind of tribute to Alan. One year after Alan's death, Corinne brought her children to Zihuatanejo to visit their father's grave. Even that visit also had its comical aspect. The family was directed to the graveyard, where they asked to be shown Alan's grave. The local guide did not seem to know where it was. None of the Siegels was fluent in Spanish, but one managed to produce the query, "Gringo?" At that, the guide experienced a sudden epiphany and immediately escorted them to the gravesite of the only gringo interred at Zihuatanejo, my dear friend, Alan Siegel.

The death of a patient is always painful, and trying to help a family to come to terms with such a terrible loss is difficult at best. I've seen it done with great skill and, rarely, with no skill or empathy whatsoever. In the latter category, I recall when my long-standing, faithful secretary faced the possible death of her father who was undergoing major cardiac surgery at a nearby hospital. She was going to see him right after his surgery, and I offered to accompany her for support. I joined her and her family in a small shared waiting room where families of other patients also sat anxiously. The surgeon suddenly appeared in operating room greens. His face was expressionless. *He never sat down!* He stood over the waiting family and simply said, "I'm sorry, he died," and then turned on his heel and left. I still cringe as I recall that awful moment. Obviously, he had never been exposed to even the rudiments of how to break bad news or chose to ignore them, or possibly any humane instincts he might have possessed had been surgically removed at birth.

The basic principles of how to break bad news are well known to most doctors. They include sitting down in a completely private, quiet setting — *never* standing over family members — allowing plenty of time, answering the inevitable questions and never allowing that difficult moment to become the final contact with the family. For physicians and nurses who have cared for a patient of any age, including the smallest pre-term infants, having at least one member of the care team attend the funeral and write condolence notes is a small but vitally important gesture that means the world to the family of any deceased patient, irrespective of age.

Far too often, these simple, crucially important gestures are neglected. It is not unreasonable to suggest most such practices should be institutionalized. Their importance increases, of course, in inverse proportion to the age of the patient. Where infants and children are concerned, the loss is not mitigated by the predictability of a child's death. When a child dies, it is doubly important for caregivers to give tangible expression to the fact they have not forgotten the child or the family, and they share the family's sense of loss. All of a pediatrician's patients are (or should be) special, but some are more special than others, usually because of their particular personal qualities rather than what we can do to be helpful. During my years at the Montreal Children's Hospital, I received a call from an internist I knew at the Montreal General. Would I please see a toddler who had been flown in from Newfoundland? He told me he had no idea what was wrong with the youngster but said that the boy had been referred with a diagnosis of celiac disease and seemed very ill. I told him I would see the child right away. The boy, named Clark, was severely malnourished. He had a very distended abdomen and a frequent cough. I asked the parents if he tasted salty when they kissed him, and they answered with some surprise, "Yes, he does!" This is a well-recognized clinical tip-off to cystic fibrosis, in which the concentration of sodium and chloride (salt) in the sweat is strikingly elevated. I admitted Clark to hospital. We confirmed the diagnosis within hours and instituted intensive treatment, antibiotics and chest physiotherapy, directed mainly at his lung infection, and measures to improve his nutrition. Thanks more to his resilience than my skills, he responded dramatically to treatment, gained weight and was soon transformed into a happy, lively, outwardly normal youngster.

He grew up to be a remarkably healthy young man. I saw him regularly, because his parents insisted on bringing him from Newfoundland to Montreal for all his follow-up. When I moved to Nova Scotia in 1967, Clark's parents contacted me in a state of high excitement because they were moving to Nova Scotia too, and I could therefore continue to care for him. They insisted on taking Ruth and me to dinner the evening we arrived in Halifax, and we became close friends.

Clark became an admirable, enthusiastic young man who rarely allowed his illness to impede his enjoyment of life. I once admitted him to the respiratory ward of the Children's Hospital for a few days of intensive treatment, even though he was in his early twenties. He pointed out to me he was "the only kid on the ward with a beard!"

Clark called me one day and said he wanted to come and see me and was bringing a friend. The friend turned out to be a very attractive young woman. They told me they wanted to get married, but his parents had serious misgivings. I listened to the two of them for a long while and came to appreciate that both were knowledgeable and accepting of the realities of Clark's illness and his long-term prognosis. They were also aware that since males with cystic fibrosis are usually sterile, their prospects of producing children were slim to nil. Their understanding of the situation was thoroughly realistic, and I supported them. Clark's parents were, understandably, less convinced, so I met with them separately and suggested all of us should support this fine young couple in their marriage plans. The couple enjoyed several happy years together until, eventually, Clark died of his disease. He and his family were living examples of how the quality of life can have far greater value than its duration.

While the death of a child or young adult from any cause can be devastating and can illustrate how much we have yet to learn about curing disease and alleviating suffering, one kind of death is by far the most difficult to bear — death by suicide. Suicide can occur at any age, but it is most painful and shattering when it involves teenagers and young adults. Few, if any, deaths are more deeply engraved in our memories. Like teenage pregnancy, suicide has far too long been part of a hidden epidemic, concealed under cover of euphemisms. In my younger days one would hear stories such as "Mary Jane has gone out of town to live with her aunt for a few months . . ." Everyone knew Mary Jane was pregnant, but everyone went along. Similar systematized denial existed for a long time with suicide. Everyone suspected suicide when they read the age of the deceased in the paper, accompanied by words like "suddenly" or "unexpectedly," or "after a brief [unspecified] illness," followed by an appeal for memorial gifts to a mental health association. But it is a sure sign of maturation that the reality of suicide has begun to be accepted and discussed, as is now the case with most forms of mental illness.

Recently, Ruth and I attended the sad funeral of a twenty-year-old son of good friends, a promising university student who had committed suicide. At the funeral, for the first time in my memory, I heard the boy's father, mother and sister and the minister speak openly and frankly about the fact his death had been self-inflicted. And as I write this, we recently attended a visitation for the bright and beautiful granddaughter of a close pediatric colleague. She had hanged herself while still a university freshman, having made a previous unsuccessful suicide attempt at age twelve.

On reflection, I am amazed at how often my life has been touched by suicide among family, friends and acquaintances. When I was a second-year medical undergraduate at McGill, one of my classmates walked up to the top of Mount Royal one evening and shot himself. We asked ourselves the usual questions. To this day, I have no answer.

Sometime after that event, a high school classmate of mine did the same. He was a German Jewish boy who, like a small number of other German Jewish citizens, had escaped to Canada during World War II and had been placed in a Canadian internment camp as an "enemy alien." He was later released and joined my class at Lower Canada College. The wisdom of hindsight did not help me understand him better. He had been a quiet fellow, but nothing had suggested to me he was troubled, though, given his life history, he had had every reason to be.

Two of my first cousins committed suicide. One, a highly competent radiologist, and his wife, a Holocaust survivor, both in their sixties, got into their car in their garage and turned on the engine with the door closed. Both perished. No one had seen it coming. The other was a physician who had never shown any signs, at least not to me.

For some suicide victims whom I knew well, the mode of self-destruction assumed an almost theatrical quality uncharacteristic of their "normal" personalities. A colleague and onetime resident of mine who headed a department of pediatrics in the United States went up one day onto the roof of the hospital where he worked and jumped to his death in the hospital parking lot.

Georg Tintner, a remarkable musician who served from 1987 to 1999 as music director of Symphony Nova Scotia, also ended his life. He was a superb musician who lived a spartan lifestyle; a vegetarian, he wore no animal-related clothing, and he was strikingly self-effacing. Tintner developed a malignancy late in life that gradually impaired his ability to conduct. One day, in deep despair, he leapt from the balcony of his apartment in downtown Halifax. The depression resulting from his illness may well have led him to such a desperate act, but the dramatic manner in which he chose to die seemed uncharacteristic of the man.

Despite increasing openness about the problems of depression and suicide, and in spite of bringing mental illness out of the closet, it seems fair to ask how much measurable progress has been made in suicide prevention. More than twenty years ago (as told in an earlier chapter), when I joined forces with the admirable Dr. Robert Lawrence to produce the joint US-Canadian book *Preventing Disease . . . Beyond the Rhetoric,* we had individual chapters written by experts in their respective fields, members of either the Canadian or the US task forces we chaired on disease prevention. We included two chapters, however, on the preventability of suicide, one providing a US perspective, the other a Canadian one. Part of the reason for this rare separation of Canadian and US perspectives was the very different situation in our two countries regarding access to lethal weapons, a factor that could affect comparative suicide rates.

Dr. M. Alfred Haynes, director of the Drew/Meharry/Morehouse Consortium Cancer Center in Los Angeles, provided the American perspective. In an editorial comment on Dr. Haynes's chapter we pointed out that "preventing suicide turns out to be more a matter of speculation than of reliable scientific evidence." There are hints of genetic predisposition to suicide, including studies of twins and a Danish study in which adoptees who committed suicide were more likely than control subjects to have had relatives who committed suicide. The problem is anything but simple, and the perspective on prevention is exceedingly complex. Contributing factors may include genetic factors, a family history of suicide, real or perceived losses, previous suicide attempts, exposure to other suicides, access to lethal weapons and social factors. Depression, though, remains the most important single risk factor, and for that disorder effective treatment is available, both pharmacological and electroconvulsive. Whether counselling has any direct value in prevention remains a matter of speculation, and its measurable effect is still being debated.

The Canadian perspective was provided by Jane McNamee and the late Dr. Dan Offord, a superb child psychiatrist and humanitarian. They pointed out that in 1985 the suicide rate in Canada was higher than the homicide rate, being highest in twenty- to twenty-four-year-olds and in people over the age of seventy. Suicide rates in people with fatal illness ranged from four to sixty-six times those of the general population. Their evaluation of the documentary evidence for the effectiveness of suicide preventive interventions was chastening. They pointed out that "very few Canadian suicide intervention programs have been formally evaluated," including crisis centres. They found no firm evidence suicide rates for the population as a whole declined following introduction of community psychiatric services. But, notwithstanding the clear need for solid, objective epidemiological evidence on the effectiveness of efforts to prevent this awful tragedy, two facts remain: Most physicians get to treat only one patient at a time; and for many patients with depression, one of the most common human afflictions and a frequent fore-runner of suicide attempts, effective treatment is available and should always be used when appropriate, with careful follow-up of vulnerable patients. If such interventions were to prevent even a minority of suicides and help *some* young people achieve productive, happy lives, they would be more than worthwhile. Bringing mental illness out of the shadows is a healthy start. Realistically, regardless of the statistical picture, each patient needs to be treated as if that treatment will make a difference.

One violent, non-suicidal near-death experience altered my life dramatically. It involved a man I never met.

The story begins in my early childhood, when I spent a lot of time playing with my first cousin, Henry ("Hank") Nevard, the youngest son of my mother's oldest sister, Miriam. Hank and I shared a love of mimicry and a sense of the ridiculous. At one point in our youth, we discovered a stash of our Grandfather Ballon's favourite cigars hidden in the back of a linen closet and saved for very special occasions (as we later found out). We hid in the dark recesses of our grandparents' backyard, where we lit up our cigars and tried to blow smoke rings like a couple of wealthy bankers. Predictably, we became acutely nauseated. We were unmasked, Grandpa discovered the theft and we were severely punished.

As a young man, Hank moved to New York, where he became seriously ill with ulcerative colitis. He was cared for at Mount Sinai Hospital by no less a luminary than Dr. Burrill Crohn, who had described the intestinal inflammatory disease that bears his name. The disease dogged Hank throughout his life, eventually leading to his death in his forties. Meanwhile he had married a woman who herself had an intriguing lineage. She had been born to an unwed young Jewish mother, fathered by a married Irish-Canadian lawyer. Then, as now, Jewish babies available for adoption were virtually non-existent. To fill the unmet need, a certain Jewish doctor who never made it into the Canadian Medical Hall of Fame for ethical supremacy was in the habit of getting unwed mothers to sign themselves into his clinic with fictitious Jewish-sounding names; he then sold the babies to families desperately wanting to adopt a child. This little girl was literally sold to a couple named Rosenstone for the then princely sum of $2,000.

She had been given the name Sheila, but her doting adoptive father, Moe Rosenstone, observed that she "sparkled," and afflicted her with the nickname "Twinkle," the name by which she is known to this day. Twinkle led a charmed life, her every whim indulged beyond imagination. On her graduation from high school, I was told, her father promised her a trip to Europe if she got an "A." Second prize, for lower marks, would be a trip to California. She couldn't lose. After she married my cousin Hank, they produced two fine children, a boy and a girl, who joined my growing list of patients. By 1966, though, the marriage had soured and they divorced. Soon after, Twinkle began dating a young engineer and developer, Dan Rudberg. They married in 1969.

On September 8, 1972, Twinkle and Dan were driving in downtown Montreal, en route to dinner with friends at a local Greek restaurant. Dan took a wrong turn onto City Councillors Street, where they stopped in traffic. Suddenly the back door of the car in front of them flung open, a barefoot teenager jumped out of the back seat, ran to the sidewalk, knocked down an elderly woman, snatched her purse and began to run away. Dan got out of his car, chased the boy and caught him hiding in a clump of bushes. Suddenly, the boy produced a large knife and stabbed Dan in the chest. He died on the spot.

The sheer cruelty of this catastrophe stunned everyone. Twinkle went into a deep depression and hid from all social contacts. Twenty years after Dan's death, she still had no idea of what she was going to do with the rest of her life. But she began to think about the teenager who had murdered her husband and what might have led him to commit such a horrible act. She decided to find out more about the boy and discovered he had been only fourteen when he murdered Dan. He was the child of a single mother and had lived a life of continuous neglect. He ran away from his home in Baltimore to Montreal, where he joined a street gang. He had purchased his knife on the morning of the day of the murder, when he displayed it proudly to his fellow gang members and told them, "This will be for some hero."

As Twinkle began to emerge slowly from her feeling of total devastation, she wondered whether anything could be done to counteract youth violence. She took the first step when she realized that, like herself, the boy who killed Dan was also a victim.

To explore what might be done to prevent violent acts, she convened an informal gathering at the McGill School of Social Work. About twenty-five people attended, including the late Michel Proulx, a wise family court judge, his wife, Brenda Zosky Proulx, an experienced newspaper reporter and teacher of journalism, police officers, child psychiatrists, social workers and others. They reviewed several existing programs designed to benefit young people whose lives had been touched by violence, either as perpetrators or as victims.

Among the programs they discussed was one established in Washington, DC, by a former newspaper photographer. It was called Shooting Back. Youth participants were each given a camera and asked to photograph places and things that were important in their lives. In another program, King of Survival (KOS), initiated in New York's notorious South Bronx, young people were taught literature and art. They also learned to process their own photographs. Both programs seemed to have turned around a number of their youthful participants and seemed like good models. But in the course of these discussions, Brenda Zosky Proulx, the former newspaperwoman, suggested that in addition to a photography program, it might be valuable (as in KOS) to teach young people to *write* about their lives.

They called the new program "LOVE," an acronym for "Leave Out ViolencE." Its central thrusts were photojournalism and nonjudgmental discussions, in groups and individually. Every young person was given a camera, taught how to use it and how to develop, print and enlarge photographs. (This was before the digital age.) The participants were also taught to write prose and poetry. The Montreal program grew and flourished, boasting a remarkably high retention rate. Referrals came from a wide range of sources, including social workers, psychiatrists, the police and schools. Eventually, LOVE programs were established in Montreal in both English and French. Before long, programs were established in Toronto and Vancouver.

In the summer of 1998, Twinkle Rudberg came to Nova Scotia for a visit. She asked if I would be willing to establish a LOVE program in Halifax. At the time, I had more on my plate than I could handle but promised to help in any way I could. It was a great idea, and there was no shortage of youth violence in Halifax.

For many voluntary organizations, the surest guarantee of success in the early stages is charismatic leadership. That quality was deeply rooted in the character of the young woman who would become the program's director in Halifax. Her name was Sarah MacLaren, and her ability to relate to troubled youth was truly remarkable. She was patient and nonjudgmental but also had an uncanny knack for challenging young people to improve their lives and themselves.

Under Sarah MacLaren's leadership, the LOVE program was established in Halifax in 1999. Youth are referred to the program from a variety of sources — schools, social workers, the police and so on. The first year of the program focuses on photojournalism. By a stroke of good luck, the twice-weekly sessions are held in the facilities of the School of Journalism at the University of King's College. Many of the young people, at the time of their entry into the LOVE program, could never imagine themselves in a university environment. But after their first year, any intimidation they feel has pretty well evaporated. In fact, a good many LOVE alumni have gone on to enter university or community college.

Youth who complete the year of photojournalism successfully proceed to a second year, devoted to leadership training. This year includes an intensive four-day summer program at a camp in Northern Ontario.

LOVE is one of the most successful programs anywhere for helping troubled youth. The hard evidence is overwhelmingly convincing. It has maintained a very high retention rate. Furthermore, practically all youth entering the program come from families receiving social assistance, but very few LOVE alumni are on social assistance. Several graduates have gone on to enter university or community college. (During my tenure as chancellor at Dalhousie University, my greatest thrill was conferring a degree on a young woman who was an alumna of LOVE.)

Also, the program has now been extended to two First Nations reserves, where it has been very successful.

In effect, the LOVE program is all about the *prevention* of losses. It has proved, dramatically, that youth whose lives have been scarred by violence are *not* a lost cause.

The Book of Ruth

Whither thou goest I will go.
Where thou lodgest I will lodge.
Thy people will be my people
And thy God will be my God.

— *Ruth 1:16*

On my first visit to Ruth's New Waterford, Cape Breton, hometown, her family welcomed me with a warmth and enthusiasm normally reserved for the Second Coming. Later on, I learned why.

When Ruth was an undergraduate at Mount Allison University, she invited a succession of boyfriends to visit. Their family names were Fraser and MacDonald, and Ruth's Granny, a marvellous, tiny Russian Jewish woman with a devilish wit, was mortified at the thought that one of these liaisons with a "*sheygetz*" (gentile) might become permanent. When her Granny quizzed her as to whom she was bringing home that summer and was told it was a guy named Goldbloom, she declared her unequivocal love for me, sight unseen. When I did meet Granny, that love was reciprocated in full. She spoke a little English but was most comfortable in Yiddish, which I spoke a little but understood pretty well.

Granny had two contemporary "buddies," Jewish women of the same vintage: Ruth's aunt, Mrs. Conter, and Mrs. Medjuck. They loved to sit on Mrs. Conter's front balcony in rocking chairs, the perfect setting for observing (*and* commenting on) passersby. My friend, psychiatrist Nate Epstein, referred to the balcony quite correctly as "the reviewing stand." The three women also liked to go to the movies at the ill-named Majestic Theatre. All three were so deeply absorbed in the movies they would talk back to the actors on the screen, a scene right out of Woody Allen.

Their views of the world and everything in it were rarely clouded by doubt. When Mrs. Conter was watching TV during the first moon landing, one of her sons came into the room and said: "Look, Ma, men are walking on the moon!" She was unimpressed: "A bunch of actors!"

Whenever Ruth's mother asked Mrs. Conter how she was feeling, the answer never changed: "I didn't sleep last night, maybe not five minutes." Rose Schwartz doubted it; Mrs. Conter never seemed to *look* tired. Her insomniac mantra ended abruptly late one night when the store's burglar alarm, which was housed in Mrs. Conter's house and was loud enough to wake the dead, went off. People tried in vain to awaken her by pounding on her door. Ultimately the firemen had to be called. They broke the door down and turned off the alarm. After, Rose Schwartz confronted Mrs. Conter with "You didn't sleep, maybe not five minutes, eh?" the complaint was never repeated.

When I first met Ruth's mother, Rose, I gained some insight into the gene pool that had produced the vivacious, dark-haired creature who was to become my wife. Having come to Canada from Russia when she was thirteen years old, Rose Schwartz (née Claener) refused to set forth on Russian soil for the rest of her life. Even when Ruth and I offered her the opportunity some seventy years later, she flatly refused. She said she would not give a nickel to the country that had treated her and her family so miserably.

As a young woman, Rose met a handsome young man, Abe Schwartz, from Sudbury, Ontario. Abe opened a small general store in New Waterford. I was told he had once sold a radio to a local coal miner *before* reliable radio transmissions had reached New Waterford. The man returned a few days later, complaining he could hear nothing but noise on his brand-new radio. Abe explained to him how lucky he was because the "noise" he was hearing was actually the sound of the war in China. The man seemed satisfied and never complained again.

When Ruth was only five years old, her father came home from the store one day for lunch. He told Rose he had a terrible headache. He lay down on the couch and closed his eyes. Moments later, he was dead. He was thirty-five. In retrospect, he had almost certainly suffered a ruptured cerebral aneurysm.

He left a wife with five young children (the eldest just seven) and pregnant with the sixth. Rose had no choice but to take over management of her husband's store. She had absolutely no business experience but was a quick learner. She marched down to the T. Eaton Company (her husband's main business competitor) and approached a man named Carmen Hughes, manager of the men's department. "How much do they pay you, Mr. Hughes?" she asked him. "Twenty-five dollars a week," he replied. She told him: "I'll pay you five dollars more a week to manage our men's department, but you have to report for work at nine o'clock Monday morning." He accepted, and remained manager of the men's department for the next forty years. When he finally retired, Rose gave him and his wife a four-week tour of Europe.

Rose did far more than merely sustain her husband's business. She built it into a hugely successful department store, ultimately with a couple of branch stores. All but two of her children worked there when they were young, eventually developing highly successful businesses of their own. None ever failed to give their mother full credit for their successes; they would say proudly that they were graduates of the Rose Schwartz School of Business. Rose was regarded by many as the matriarch of New Waterford, a town she loved dearly and unequivocally. She spent very little time in the office of her store, instead staying on the floor to greet customers and their children by name and make sure every single one was receiving dedicated attention. Aside from walking home every day at noon to make sure her children were getting a healthy lunch (plenty of coleslaw), she was always in the store. Many members of her staff had begun to work there as teenagers and spent their entire working lives in the store. It is hard to imagine any business with so little staff turnover or with such of lifetime loyalty from its employees.

Rose was never ill until the final days of her life. She regarded illness as a kind of character defect, a perspective Ruth inherited despite marrying into a family of physicians. There was an unwritten, unspoken agreement among her staff that they *never* complained to her of not feeling well, even if they thought they were dying.

She was a superb saleswoman who never allowed a customer to feel pressured. Nevertheless, a favourite family story tells of the night a coal miner (I'll call him McKinnon) awakened her around 1 a.m. with a phone call. His wife had just died. As was then the custom in Cape Breton, he wanted to make sure she was nicely attired so she could be laid out in the living room first thing next morning for friends and neighbours who wished to pay their respects.

"Missus Schwartz, do ye s'pose ye could open up the store so I could come down and buy a dress for her to get laid out in?" he asked. Such requests were not unusual. Rose got up and went to the store to meet Mr. McKinnon. She told him she remembered his wife loved the colour blue. She knew her size, so she picked out a blue dress and told him his wife would look lovely in it.

"Well now, Missus Schwartz, how much is that there dress?"

"Twenty-five dollars, Mr. McKinnon."

"Jeez, Mrs. Schwartz, that's a lot of money."

"But, Mr. McKinnon, it's *washable!*" she explained.

Rose's children never tired of retelling that story.

Rose never lectured her children. She encouraged them to learn by experience and to profit by their mistakes. When her son Irving was only fifteen and already working in the store, he suggested they buy an entire railroad car full of furniture in Montreal and have it sent to New Waterford and pulled onto a town railroad siding. He would then conduct a giant sale, selling the contents directly from the freight car. Rose agreed to let him proceed with his plan, which his siblings considered a harebrained scheme that could result in a major loss. They told Rose so, but she defended her decision: "If it works, it will be a wonderful thing for the store, and if it doesn't, he will have learned a lesson he'll never forget." In the event, Irving sold every last stick of furniture over a couple of days. Thus began his own remarkable career as an entrepreneur.

Rose Schwartz's business was so successful she sent every one of her six children through university. Edna, Ruth's older sister, became the women's fashion buyer for the store. She eventually left New Waterford, moved to Toronto, and opened a hugely successful ladies' dress shop — Edna Schwartz of the Colonnade — at a swanky address on Bloor Street. Like her mother, Edna was deeply committed to customer service. If she felt a particular dress did not look right on a customer, she would not allow the woman to buy it.

Only her eldest son, Joseph ("Joey") broke the family business mould and became a physician. The quietest and most studious of a rowdy brood of boys, Joey was extraordinarily well read. He eventually became a radiologist, married a girl from England who was a painter and became staff radiologist at St. Martha's Hospital in Antigonish, Nova Scotia, working in a semi-rural setting so he could have easy access to hunting and fishing. One rainy night he was driving back from another nearby hospital in the little red MG sports car he loved. Joey ran into a truck parked on the highway with no lights and was killed instantly. Rose never set foot in a synagogue again; her belief in a protective God shattered forever. The third terrible loss she endured was when her eldest daughter, Edna, died of a brain tumour in 1979.

As an adult, Ruth achieved a national reputation as a successful fund-raiser for an endless succession of worthy causes that included universities, social support services such as the United Way and Kids Help Phone and her greatest fund-raising triumph, almost single-handedly raising the many millions needed to restore and revitalize Canada's last remaining immigration shed, Pier 21 in Halifax.

But many of her admirers were unaware that Ruth's first philanthropic fund-raising experiences were as a tap dancer, raising funds for various worthy causes in New Waterford. For years, Rose treasured a printed invitation to a United Mine Workers' fund-raising social. It read as follows:

UMW Social
Friday night at 7 pm
Ruth Schwartz will dance.
(Police protection provided)

Ruth had shown a remarkable aptitude for tap dancing. Her mother would put her on the bus from New Waterford to Sydney once a week to take lessons from a woman named Vivian King.

Rose was on a buying trip to Montreal when she was taken to a pseudo-Russian night club on Peel Street called The Samovar. One of the dancers appeared in a costume Rose thought would be perfect for Ruth. She went backstage after the show, introduced herself to the dancer and bought her costume on the spot. Back in New Waterford, she had the store's dressmaker, Elizabeth Deveaux, cut it down to Ruth's petite size.

Thanks to Ruth, Elizabeth ("Eliza") Deveaux later achieved a moment of unexpected fame in the Montreal social register. During the 1950s, Ruth and I were members of the Montreal Symphony Orchestra's Junior Committee, established to stimulate interest of young adults in the symphony. Our major fund-raiser was a ball held aboard the *S.S. Homeric*, a classy ocean liner scheduled to spend a couple of days docked in Montreal. It was a super-elegant affair, and young women from Montreal's haute monde purchased designer gowns for the occasion. One day Ruth received a phone call from the *Montreal Star*'s society editor who wanted a description of the gown Ruth would wear to the ball *and* the name of the couturier. Ruth had never received such a request, so she stalled and told the editor she would get back to her.

She had gone to one of the dress factories where her sister Edna ordered dresses for the store, picked out a dress she liked and had it shipped promptly to the store in New Waterford. A young woman on the store's staff was exactly Ruth's size, and Ruth used her regularly as the model when any of her clothes had to be adjusted. Faithful Eliza Deveaux did the alterations and the dress was shipped back to Ruth. It arrived a week before the ball. As promised, Ruth phoned the society editor. She described the gown she would be wearing in rather extravagant terms. "Who is the designer?" asked the editor. "Eliza Deveaux," replied Ruth.

"Eliza Deveaux?" said the editor. "I don't think I've ever heard of her. Where does she work?" Ruth replied: "She's in the Far East," and that was the end of the conversation. The best part of the joke was that the description with Eliza Deveaux's name appeared on the *Montreal Star*'s social page in the report of this glamorous ball. Ruth delighted in telling the story. It pretty well summed up the down-to-earth perspective of a small-town girl on what some considered high society in the big city.

During much of our life together, Ruth kept a pair of tap shoes in the trunk of her car, ready to perform at the slightest suggestion. She taught our granddaughters to tap (though none achieved her virtuosity) as well as several great-nieces. In her mid-eighties, her ancient, worn tap shoes mysteriously disappeared from the trunk of her car. She repeatedly accused me of having thrown them out, but I was genuinely innocent. In Florida, in the winter of 2010, she reiterated her longing to tap dance again. I was skeptical, but to honour her wishes, we drove to a little shop specializing in dance paraphernalia. There was a bin full of half-priced items. I rummaged through the contents and triumphantly withdrew a brand-new pair of silvered leather tap shoes in *exactly* her size. When I showed them to her she could not have been more excited. The last video recording of her art was made six months before she died. She was dancing while holding on to the back of a chair for stability, but the old sparkle was still there.

I was a twenty-one-year-old first-year medical student at McGill and Ruth was twenty-two when we were married on June 25, 1945, in the chapel of Shaar Hashomayim Synagogue, in the presence of family and a few close friends. After a lovely reception at the now long-gone Windsor Hotel, we departed for our honeymoon. In those days, newly married couples couldn't wait to hit the road and consummate their union at the nearest "No Tell Motel." (I have often reflected on those days when attending weddings in recent years. Typically, the principals have been "shacking" — as Cape Bretoners used to call it — for months or, more often, years. As a result, the newly legally united couple show not the slightest sign of wanting to escape the party, and next day their lives continue much as before.)

My father had very generously loaned us a pale blue Ford convertible for our honeymoon. We set out on a road trip that would take us across the northern United States, through the badlands of South Dakota and north to Vancouver to visit my Goldbloom relatives. Then we drove down the coastal highway, through Oregon to San Francisco, stopping to visit my father's sister Eva and her children. There began one of the more memorable events of our honeymoon. We had stayed at San Francisco's venerable Palace Hotel and were leaving to drive south to Carmel and Monterey. I called downstairs for our car and a bellhop picked up our luggage. We jumped into the car and drove off to Carmel, where Aunt Eva and her husband had booked a room for us at a delightful resort hotel. I signed the register and went outside with the bellhop and opened the trunk of the car to retrieve our luggage. To my horror, the trunk was empty! Reconstructing the crime, we guessed, correctly, that the bellhop at the Palace Hotel in San Francisco had brought our bags down from our room and left them beside the car. We had jumped into the car from the other side and driven off, leaving our bags on the curb.

My explanation to the hotel desk clerk fell on unbelieving ears. He demanded we pay in advance. We phoned the Palace Hotel. They retrieved our bags and loaded them on a bus to Carmel, where they arrived the next day. Ruth and I decided this temporary glitch was not worth mourning and treated ourselves to a good dinner. Ruth was wearing a black cotton dress with a large white front panel. While enjoying dessert and coffee, we started to giggle over our tragicomedy and its *sequelae*. In the midst of hysterical laughter Ruth managed to spill the entire contents of her coffee cup down the white panel on the front of her dress. We solved the problem in the only sensible way — by going to bed.

Our transcontinental honeymoon was unforgettable. We drove back via the California redwoods and Yosemite National Park. Tanned and happy — decades before UV exposure began to get a bad rap — we returned to our two-room Montreal apartment and to the realities of second-year medical school.

In our early years together, Ruth supplemented our income by working as a physical education teacher. Her initial experience in seeking a teaching job turned out to be one of the darkest events in a long, happy life. Ruth had done well in phys ed at McGill, leading her class in practice teaching. In those days, the English-speaking public schools of Montreal were divided by the school board: one Protestant, the other Catholic. Jewish students were treated as "technical Protestants"; those who attended public school did so at one of the schools under the Montreal Protestant Central School Board.

When Ruth started job-hunting, Dr. Lamb, head of the Phys Ed Department at McGill, urged her to apply for an advertised position with the Protestant board. He told her she was a natural for the position and he would give her the highest possible recommendation. She applied, and waited. Finally, at the end of June 1946, she received the following letter from J. D. Lang, supervisor of physical education for the Montreal Protestant Central School Board: "I have to inform you that the Education Committee will not grant you permission to teach Physical Education in one of our schools," he wrote. "Why they have discriminated against your race is very disappointing to me, and

I am sorry if I have given you the impression that there would be no barrier at this time."

After I began to practise pediatrics in Montreal, we made a down payment on a lovely, small house at 108 Thurlow Road in Hampstead, a quiet, residential community in western Montreal where, incidentally, until just a few years earlier, home ownership had been denied to Jews.

Ruth became a regular door-to-door canvasser for worthy causes such as the United Way. She discovered, by accident or by design, that having a young child by the hand (our youngest, David, was frequently drafted) greatly enhanced the likelihood of getting a contribution.

When our two younger children enrolled at St. George's School (known in some quarters as a progressive school), Ruth was appointed a member of the board. The school needed a gym, and Ruth cooked up the idea of raffling a new car to raise a good portion of the funds. She buttonholed the owner of an automobile agency on Decarie Boulevard and sweet-talked him into donating a brand-new car.

Since those early days, Ruth has championed one cause after another, including the Montreal Symphony Orchestra (later renamed l'Orchestre Symphonique de Montréal, OSM for short) and an assortment of hospitals and universities.

As chair of the board of Halifax's Mount Saint Vincent University, she raised several million dollars for a new building. At one point, she wrote a letter to the Montreal-based J. W. McConnell Foundation asking for a significant contribution for the university, which had been founded by the Catholic Sisters of Charity. She received a written response saying her request would be considered. At the bottom of the brief reply was a handwritten note saying, simply, "Cynthia sends her love." I realized that Cynthia was Cynthia McConnell, wife of David McConnell, a long-standing schoolmate of mine at Selwyn House. Eventually, the formal response arrived. It read:

Dear Mrs. Goldbloom,

Until we received your request we had never heard of Mount Saint Vincent University. However, we figured that if a nice Jewish girl could be Board Chair of a Catholic University, it couldn't be all bad. Please find enclosed our cheque for $150,000.

Sincerely yours . . .

Ruth established the first gift shop at the Children's Hospital in Halifax, named it the Gift Horse, staffed it with volunteers and turned it into a major fund-raiser for the hospital. Not content to run it as a typical hospital gift shop, she stocked high-end merchandise such as Ginori china and recruited prospective brides to list the Gift Horse as a source for wedding gifts. She kept a calendar of the wedding anniversaries of members of the medical staff and the dates of their wives' birthdays, and sent them not-so-subtle reminders to buy a gift. She hand-picked Christmas gifts for physicians and residents (who were invariably delighted with her selections). She recruited a staff of about forty volunteers for the shop, which netted the hospital auxiliary a handsome profit every year.

One of Ruth's most distinguishing characteristics was the conviction that you had to believe deeply and passionately in the cause for which you were working. Sometime after we moved to Halifax she was invited to chair the annual campaign for the Halifax-Dartmouth United Way. She agreed to do so

but decided she should educate herself about why she was asking individuals and corporations to donate. She visited each of
the fifty-two agencies supported by the United Way. No United
Way campaign chair had ever done that before. In later years,
whenever she spoke publicly about philanthropy, she invariably underlined the word "passion," stressing it was difficult or
impossible to convince a donor if you did not believe passionately in the cause.

Her philanthropy was formally recognized in many ways,
notably by her appointment as an Officer of the Order of Canada
and a member of the Order of Nova Scotia and by the conferral
of no fewer than five honorary degrees, from McGill, Dalhousie,
Mount Allison, Acadia and the University of King's College, as
well as other honours and awards.

But her greatest achievement, and the one that brought her
greatest satisfaction, was her pivotal role in rescuing Canada's
last standing immigration shed, Pier 21, then, as she would often
say, "a rat-and-pigeon-infested, crumbling building on the Halifax waterfront."

In 1989, Ruth was called by a man she didn't know. His name
was John P. LeBlanc. He asked if she would join the Pier 21
Committee, which he had established to do something to ensure
that the significance of Pier 21 in Canada's history would not
be lost. John had written a little book about its history. He had
been the last officer in charge of immigration when the building
closed, presumably forever. At that time, the plans of the Pier 21
Committee were, to say the least, modest. They wanted to install
a bronze plaque on the front of the building to mark its significance in Canada's history.

In the years that followed, the revitalization of Pier 21 took
on a far more ambitious perspective. Ruth never spoke publicly
about the project without beginning by acknowledging her personal debt, and the country's debt, to John P. LeBlanc, who was

the "still, small voice" who spoke out about the building's crucial importance in Canada's history.

After she had served for several months on the Pier 21 Committee, John took her to lunch one day and confided he had cancer and that his prognosis was grave. He asked her to assume his position as chair of the Pier 21 Committee. She felt she had no choice. She managed to persuade then-provincial premier John Savage to give her some unused downtown government office space and furniture. She reported Savage had told her: "I'll give you anything you want — except money!"

Soon after John P. LeBlanc died, Ruth decided Pier 21 deserved more than a bronze plaque to regain its proper place of honour in the hearts and minds of Canadians.

On July 12, 1987, even before LeBlanc's call to Ruth, something happened that would change Ruth's plans for Pier 21.

Early that morning, Vernon Malone, a fisherman in the tiny community of Charlesville on Nova Scotia's south shore, awoke, looked out his window and saw an extraordinary sight. Wading ashore through the fog were more than 170 men and one woman, wearing costumes the like of which he had never seen before. They were Sikhs who had left the Punjab in India to escape religious persecution — just as Ruth's ancestors and mine had left Russia. They had been put ashore that morning from the fifty-nine-metre Costa Rican ship *Amélie*, which had sailed from Rotterdam eighteen days earlier.

None of the strangers spoke English. Nevertheless, Vernon Malone welcomed them ashore. Vernon bought and borrowed bedding, and friends and neighbours loaned trailers to accommodate the visitors. Later, when asked by a reporter why he had given these strange people such a generous welcome, he quoted from Hebrews 13, verse 3: "Be not forgetful to entertain strangers, for thereby some have entertained angels unawares."

Malone rounded up several fellow citizens, among them a woman named Rosalie Stoddard. She took the strangers to the church hall and fed them peanut butter sandwiches. None had ever tasted peanut butter before.

The story of the Sikhs' flight from persecution — and Vernon Malone's and Rosalie Stoddard's roles in helping them — would become a major source of inspiration for Ruth's plans to revitalize Pier 21.

Most of the Sikh refugees who had left India to escape religious persecution and violence have since gone on to become successful Canadians. Seventeen years later, more than seventy of them, together with their wives and children, returned to Charlesville to express their gratitude, offering to build a community hall for the people of the town.

In 1995, a G7 Conference of leaders of the seven richest industrialized countries was scheduled to take place in Halifax. Ruth learned it was traditional for the leaders to make a commemorative gift to the host city. Always the consummate schmoozer, Ruth spoke to a friend. He encouraged her to submit a formal proposal to the G7 and stressed she should incorporate the word "legacy" as often as possible.

One day before the end of the G7 conference Ruth received a phone call from someone in the prime minister's office requesting her presence in the audience for the closing ceremony the next day. In the final sentence of his farewell address, Prime Minister Jean Chrétien announced the legacy of the G7 conference to the host city of Halifax: a gift of $4.5 million toward the revitalization of Pier 21 — contingent upon the Pier 21 Society raising the other half of the $9 million needed for the project.

The very next morning, Ruth descended on the head of the Atlantic Canada Opportunities Agency (ACOA) with a request for major support for the project. His initial response took the form of a challenge: "Prove to me you can raise $50,000 in the next twenty-four hours." Ruth left his office and went directly to the office of Clay Coveyduck, vice-president of the Royal Bank of Canada. She knew that regional banks could make donations of up to $10,000 without seeking approval of their head office. He quickly gave her a cheque for $10,000. She successfully repeated the performance at four other regional banks and obtained additional funds from a couple of wealthy private donors. At precisely 10:30 a.m. the next day she was back in the ACOA president's office, the challenge met. "He nearly fell off his chair!"

To secure the remainder of the $9 million, she criss-crossed the country, knocking on board room doors and speaking to wealthy potential donors. Harry Steele, a close friend and then president of Canadian Pacific Airlines, gave her free travel anywhere in the country. Ken Rowe did the same on his airline, CanJet. Before long, she had raised the required $9 million. In what may be a national record, I am told, her expenses to raise this amount came in at 3 per cent!

Since that time, Ruth has always asked every fund-raiser how much of every dollar raised actually goes to the cause. In many cases, the proportion that finds its way to the cause is alarmingly small. Both of us were convinced Canada needs legislation making it mandatory for all appeals for charitable funds to indicate the exact percentage of every dollar raised actually ends up serving the cause.

Many people have told me they hate asking other people for money. By contrast, Ruth regarded it as an honour, a responsibility, a challenge and a privilege.

As time went by, she received many requests to speak publicly to audiences on one of two topics: fund-raising and Pier 21. She often asked me to help put her thoughts down on paper, which I would do only occasionally and reluctantly, because I knew she always expressed herself best spontaneously. Even if she had a scripted talk in front of her, she would always depart from it after one or two lines to speak extemporaneously, articulately, passionately and convincingly. Her passion was blatant and infectious. Invariably, she would finish her talks on the same note: how lucky and privileged she was to have been able to work for such worthwhile causes. More often than not, she would conclude with a story, probably apocryphal, that she felt illustrated her own great fortune in life. When she was a little girl, growing up in New Waterford, Cape Breton, the following sign appeared on a notice board in the town post office:

LOST:

Brown and white puppy. One ear missing;
tail cut off;
left hind leg broken, badly reset. Recently castrated.
Answers to the name of "Lucky."

Ruth believed she had a lot in common with that pooch.

Even when she was in her eighties, hardly a week went by without a telephone call, often from someone she had never met, asking for a few minutes of her time to seek her advice on how to raise funds for their particular cause, often a charity or institution of which she had never heard. She always agreed to meet with them, hear about their plans and offer suggestions. But aside from specific suggestions about potential donors and ways to make the appeal more appealing, she would always stress how essential it was for them, as fund-raisers, to have passion for their cause.

The last cause to which she lent her time and energy, even as her final illness overtook her, was to raise funds to establish an endowed chair in Jewish Studies at Dalhousie University. The campaign had been kick-started by a gift of $1 million from a single donor, but $3 million was required to fully endow the chair. Her staff partner in this venture was a bright, sensitive young man named Ben McIsaac from Dalhousie's Department of Development. Ben became a frequent visitor to our condo, often accompanied by a toasted Montreal bagel and coffee. After Ruth took ill and was no longer able to work on the project, Ben sent her a note saying, "It would take only one more Montreal bagel to make me convert."

To family and friends, Ruth, then eighty-nine, seemed ageless and indestructible. But like a thief in the night, what would be her final (and almost her only) illness crept up on her. She seemed to have lost a couple of pounds but had no particular symptoms. She was checked by our devoted and skilled family physician, Dr. Victoria ("Vicky") Mitchell, who examined her, did some tests and found nothing abnormal. However, she remarked: "You know, Ruth, the one thing we haven't done is a chest x-ray." She ordered it, and I took her to the Children's Hospital to have it done.

I waited in the adjacent room when the image first appeared. I knew immediately we were in trouble. There in the central portion of her right lung was a large round mass, obviously a tumour. We consulted a chest surgeon who performed a needle biopsy, revealing a malignant growth known as a non-small-cell adenocarcinoma of the lung. He recommended radiation therapy, holding out the possibility of a cure. She underwent thirty sessions of radiation therapy, hardly turning a hair, keeping the technicians entertained with her good humour and slipping them candies at every opportunity.

For these radiation treatments, pinpoint tattoo marks were made on her chest and a closely fitting mould of her upper body was used to guide the radiation beams precisely toward the tumour mass. She wore a hospital gown for these treatments, after which one of the female technicians would always help her by hooking up her bra. On one particular day, the female technicians had disappeared, leaving only one young male technician. With no alternatives evident, she asked the young man: "Are you any good at hooking up bras?" He replied promptly: "Well, actually, I'm better at unhooking them." Both laughed and he succeeded at the first try, after which they became the best of friends.

At the conclusion of her cycle of radiation, another chest radiograph showed all traces of the tumour had miraculously disappeared! We were delighted. For the next several months, Ruth remained symptom-free until one day she told me she could sometimes see "something funny . . . like a red fan" turning in her peripheral field of vision. Soon after that, while attending a meeting, she bumped directly into someone she had obviously not seen, nearly knocking the man over. When I told our daughter-in-law, Nancy, a superb ophthalmologist, she thought Ruth should have an MRI (magnetic resonance imaging) of her head. I took her back to the Children's Hospital and sat in the control room, watching her slide in and out of the huge MRI machine as the images of her brain appeared on the screen in the control room. There were several large metastatic lesions of the tumour in her brain, and the explanation for her visual disturbances was obvious. There was no escaping the fact the outlook was grim and inevitable.

We decided to move to our country home on Second Peninsula, Lunenburg County, on the shores of Mahone Bay. This turned out to be the best possible decision from every perspective. She was surrounded at various times by our three devoted children and their equally devoted spouses, plus grandchildren and great-grandchildren, every one of whom adored her unreservedly.

Care workers arrived at the house every day at 8 p.m., spending the entire night tending to her every need and bathing her each morning. She became progressively more debilitated, able to come to meals in a wheelchair but unable to stand alone, and sleeping for sixteen to eighteen hours per day. Miraculously, Ruth remained completely free of pain through much of her inexorably downhill course. She knew exactly what lay ahead and accepted her destiny with equanimity.

Ruth wanted to be sure she left a significant remembrance for each of her grandchildren and great-grandchildren and for several other people who had played special roles in her life. She gave away many of her worldly possessions to relatives and friends: attractive items of clothing and pieces of jewellery; and she gave many of her possessions to charitable causes she loved, such as Adsum House, a refuge for abused women.

She talked openly about her funeral arrangements. She also instructed me that after her death I was to deliver a huge gold cardboard cylinder filled with Werther's candies to her radiotherapy technicians. About a week after her death, I obeyed her instructions and all of us had a good cry. It was just another of the innumerable instances of her generosity toward those who had been especially kind to her and whose good work had too often gone unrecognized and underappreciated.

Ruth made it clear she wanted to die at home — in our country home, an idyllic spot. I cannot imagine anyone receiving more loving or more skilled care at the end of life. Her physical deterioration was gradual but progressive, beginning with inability to walk independently, using first a walker and then a wheelchair.

Finally, she was confined to a hospital bed loaned by the local pharmacy.

Such consistent, loving or expert care could not have been equalled anywhere else, certainly not in a hospital. A wonderful organization, aptly called Heart to Heart, supplied marvellous caregivers every day and each night. They heard Ruth's every move or sound via an intercom and were at her side in a split second. Nurses from the Victorian Order of Nurses visited daily to prepare her medications; most valuable of all, her palliative care physician, the incomparable Dr. Jeff Dempster, visited her, and all of us, at least once daily, often twice. He assessed her and ensured she received enough analgesics to keep her pain-free and, in her final days, to let her sleep peacefully, free of anxiety. If there is such a thing as a "good" death, Ruth's was one of the best.

During the last months of her life I slept in our bed, placed tightly against hers, so I could reach out and hold her hand or check her pulse. Her muscle weakness increased progressively, and she gradually lost all ability to move voluntarily. We knew the end was near.

On the morning of August 29, 2012, our daughter Barbara, son Alan and I sat by her bed. She had been showing so-called Cheyne-Stokes breathing, a type of breathing often seen within hours before death: increasingly deep breaths followed by short periods of apnea (no breathing). As we sat by her bed, I held her wrist and hand, feeling her pulse as it became thready and irregular. Then it quietly stopped forever.

Nothing prepared us fully for the finality of her that moment. But it brought a kind of relief, because she had no longer been aware of her surroundings and had lost all ability to move.

Knowing Pier 21 would be far too small to accommodate the number of people that would likely attend her funeral, we arranged to hold the ceremony at the Cunard Centre, a very large facility adjacent to Pier 21.

More than 3,500 people from all walks of life attended. My children and I met with Rabbi Ari Isenberg, a good friend of Ruth's and mine. He knew we were secular rather than observant Jews, and we told him we wanted the focus of the service to be Ruth and her life. He was entirely sympathetic. He opened the service with a brief prayer and then turned the ceremony over to our children and grandchildren. Our three children spoke first, and their individual eulogies captured Ruth and her spirit as no one else could have done. Finally, after each one spoke so meaningfully and honestly about their mother, all seven of our grandchildren ascended the stage and stood in a line, while Stephen, aged twenty-seven, stepped to the microphone to speak on behalf of them all.

Dozens of those who attended told us they had never been to a funeral ceremony that was as personalized or meaningful. Many funeral ceremonies I have attended have been so formulaic they were highly forgettable for everyone but family members. But everyone who attended this memorial ceremony for Ruth was deeply moved. No matter how well they had known her during her life, they left that ceremony knowing her even better.

After her death, both local and national newspapers printed moving editorials and eulogies. But to me, one of the most moving tributes was a nonverbal one, in the form of a cartoon by Bruce MacKinnon, the extraordinary cartoonist of the *Halifax Chronicle Herald.*

It showed a weathered pair of tap shoes hung up on a hook — forever. On the bottom of one of the heels was engraved, simply "RUTH." He had said it all.

The Final Word

In writing this book I've depended heavily on the instrument known as the "retrospectoscope." But in this case, I am pretty confident in the accuracy of my recall.

My entire life has been hugely enriched by music and musicians and by children — by my young patients and, most of all, by my own three children. Someone once asked: "Did those three kids of yours come fully grown and successful, or did you and Ruth have a hand in the end result?" Well, perhaps we did. Perhaps we made a difference. We encouraged our three children to do well in school, to eat three square meals a day and to engage in productive activities. I imagine they picked up on the message that laughter is the best medicine, since all three have a highly developed sense of humour. They also realize they should take their work, but not themselves, seriously. They learned, by parental example perhaps, to be inquisitive and to expand their horizons. In their eulogies to Ruth, Alan mentioned his mother's "abhorrence of prejudice and intolerance"; Barbie spoke of how her "mother and father made her feel that she was beautiful, talented and supremely lovable"; and David learned from his parents, among other things, that "marriages matter; families matter."

Alan was an excellent student from day one and enjoyed a parallel, profitable career as a child actor. At six, he attended a performance of *Jack and the Beanstalk* by the Montreal Children's Theatre, whose Montreal performances in Victoria Hall were favourite entertainments for children's birthday parties. Alan, a bright, quick study who followed directions well, frequently performed leading roles in Children's Theatre productions. When advertising agencies required child actors to perform in television ads or movie roles, their first stop was usually the Montreal Children's Theatre. Alan appeared in TV ads for an assortment of products, such as peanut butter and cough medicine. The former TV ad employed trick photography. Alan, age eight, was tarted up in classical elf costume, pointed Robin Hood hat, knickers and high boots. He jumped out of a giant bottle of peanut butter and launched into his spiel extolling the virtues of the sticky delicacy.

Although he received $150 for the shoot, the real profit came from residuals, the royalties paid to the performers every time the ad was shown on TV. Over a few years, Alan accumulated enough income to underwrite the cost of a final year of high school in Switzerland, at Neuchatel Junior College, where he perfected his French, skiing and social skills, though not necessarily in that order.

His appearance as the peanut butter elf generated a story that gained a special place in our family folklore. A couple of months after the ad was filmed I was driving him to school when he mentioned he had not yet been paid for filming the peanut butter ad. I suggested he be patient, but he announced he was writing to the advertising agency requesting an explanation for the delay. I suggested he might show me the letter. It read as follows:

Dear Sirs,

On September 15th I appeared in your advertisement for Barbour's Peanut Butter. I am still patiently awaiting your cheque.

Signed,

Alan Goldbloom, Elf

To me, the designation he had appended to his name was, in pediatric terms, roughly equivalent to a PhD.

Alan also starred in a bilingual film series broadcast on CBC Television's National School Telecast entitled *Visite au Québec.* The series was designed to foster bilingualism in young people. The film documented the adventures of two boys, one francophone, the other anglophone (Alan), travelling together throughout various regions of Québec.

Alan's thespian career somehow mirrored that of his paternal grandfather, who had begun his stage career as a child actor in Worcester, Massachusetts, and continued for many years as a professional actor until he decided to study medicine. Like him, Alan grew up to enter the "family business." He attended medical school at McMaster University, then a newly established and radically different medical school that had opened one year earlier. Like me, he trained in pediatrics at Children's Hospital in Boston. He not only developed exceptional skills as a pediatrician but, in the process, snared the wonderful young woman, Lynn, who would become his wife and co-progenitor of two further generations.

Lynn was then a play therapist at Children's Hospital. Her father was a highly respected pediatrician, practising in Johnstown, Pennsylvania. In Boston, Lynn had an active social life, but her parents were concerned because none of the boys she had been dating was Jewish. When Lynn finally informed her parents she was dating "a nice young Jewish doctor," they were ecstatic and asked her to send them a picture of the lucky guy. The letter reached them in late December after, as he had done many times before, Alan had played Santa Claus at the hospital. Lynn sent her parents a photograph of herself sitting on Santa's lap with a note announcing this was the "nice Jewish doctor" she was dating. Lynn and Alan were married at her family home in Johnstown.

They produced three children, all of whom have become highly successful adults: Ellen, the eldest, is a pediatric endocrinologist (fourth-generation pediatrician) at Ottawa's Children's Hospital of Eastern Ontario. Married to a successful real estate developer, she now has three children. Amy, next in line, is an economist and a vice-president in the institutional investment division of the Royal Bank of Canada. Stephen, the youngest, graduated from Dalhousie University and then spent three years as a researcher for the Washington-based television program *PBS NewsHour*. He later moved to San Francisco to take up a new post as manager of business development for a media company. Thus, Alan and Lynn's children have all been hugely successful in their vastly different occupations. Far more important, they are all superb human beings whose wisdom is reflected in their choice of a partner.

Barbara ("Barbie") is the second of our three children. An extraordinarily insightful and effective teacher, her destiny as an educator was sealed by age fifteen when she initiated and ran an after-school homework program for Grade 11 children from St. Henri, an economically disadvantaged area in Montreal. The program was held in the study centre of a local church. Word of its success reached the Montreal Children's Hospital, and Barbie was invited to come and present the weekly grand rounds on her program, the sole occasion the speaker at grand rounds was of pediatric age. Barbie remembers being "nervous as a kitten" about speaking to a large audience. I reassured her that only a handful of people would show up. But when the day came, the auditorium was packed to the rafters. Barbie had also made me promise *not* to come to her presentation. I agreed — but I lied — and sneaked in to the back of the auditorium, hiding behind one of my colleagues.

Barbie is a *rara avis,* a born teacher with uncanny ability to capture the attention and imagination of young people. She obtained a BEd from Boston University, followed by an MA in Education at Harvard. Having taught in various settings and served for a time as a school principal, she ultimately evolved into a highly skilled educational consultant, evaluating and remediating children experiencing learning difficulties in school.

Barbie has been married twice. She was only nineteen and attending Boston University when she met Bob Issenman, also a Montrealer and son of friends of ours. They married in Halifax. During their early years of marriage, Barbie suffered two successive ectopic pregnancies, one of which nearly cost her her life and ended her capacity to reproduce. With the help of an obstetrician friend and through private adoption, she and Bob fulfilled their desire for children of their own. Barbie and Bob became the proud and happy parents of two newborn babies: Michael and Kate.

Their marital relationship later deteriorated, ending in divorce. It often happens that once the complex emotions surrounding a marital breakup have gradually subsided — the anger, blaming, disappointment and feelings of failure — it is eventually possible for divorced parents to commit to the best interests of their children. Fortunately, this is what happened. Both remarried, Bob to a social worker and Barbie to a fellow teacher from the large private school where she had taught. Her husband, Tony Hughes, a Welshman, taught art and design and is a highly creative graphic designer and stunningly talented photographer. Most important of all, he and Barbie are deeply devoted to each other and to their children and their two grandchildren. And Barbie is a devoted daughter, never more so than during Ruth's final summer in Second Peninsula. She moved in to take charge of our home, our family and the many visitors. Not only is she super-organized, a master at multitasking, but she is also an astonishingly good cook, our very own "Barefoot Contessa"! She nourished and nurtured us all.

Barbara's two children, Michael and Kate, each reflects a wonderful combination of natural talent and skilled parenting. As a pediatrician, I see Michael as exhibit A in underlying the importance of nourishing children's strengths rather than dwelling on their perceived shortcomings, which every child has. From early childhood, Michael was a poster boy for hyperactivity. He investigated everything that came within his reach and ran when others walked. His academic performance could have been generously described as "borderline." But, at the same time, he exhibited characteristics whose significance we only appreciated fully much later, including a remarkable talent for building or repairing mechanical and electrical or electronic equipment previously abandoned as irreparable; a highly developed quality of generosity; and a love of children.

As I have observed repeatedly in pediatric practice, our education system often tries to squeeze all children into the same channel, inadvertently highlighting their perceived shortcomings and failing to celebrate and nourish their strengths and talents.

Michael is a case in point. After finally escaping from the education system, he evolved into a computer geek and is now a partner in a firm that builds and repairs complex computer systems for large corporations.

Kate, a mother of two, is, like her mother, an inspiring teacher. The qualities that make her a truly great teacher include a unique ability to capture the imaginations of young children and inspire calm and commitment in the very young. As always, some youngsters can be defined by a single incident. In one unforgettable instance, when Kate was a schoolgirl, she was having difficulty understanding a math problem in her homework. Her mother tried to help her, but she wasn't getting it. Finally an exasperated Kate blurted out: "Listen, Ma, what do you expect from a kid who was conceived in the back of a pickup truck?"

David, our youngest, is also one of a kind. A character from his toddler years, he loved nothing better than dressing up in a wild assortment of costumes and disguises. As a young boy he was incredibly naive, and his older brother, Alan, made him the butt of innumerable practical jokes. When David was about ten, Alan sent him a typewritten letter informing him he had won a one-week trip to Hollywood for a screen test; David, like Alan, had gone to acting school and had thespian aspirations. The fact Alan signed the letter "O.Y. Vésmire"[¶¶] went completely over David's head. David informed most of the civilized world of his good fortune until the ugly truth was revealed about ten days later.

David was a born entertainer, always in demand as a performer and mimic. He was also a good student who attended Oxford University as a Rhodes Scholar. Between first and second year, he married Nancy Epstein. Later they both ended up in medical school at McGill. Their union seemed to have been preordained and was as close to being incestuous as you can get without actually sharing DNA. During family vacations in Cape Breton, Nancy Epstein, her parents and grandparents occupied a cottage about twenty-five yards from the Schwartz bungalow. David and Nancy were constant playmates. Both graduated in medicine from McGill, in the same class, and practise in their

---

¶¶ A thinly disguised word-play on the Yiddish phrase"Oy vay is mir" (literally, "Oh, woe is me").

respective fields, David in psychiatry and Nancy in ophthalmology. David has also managed simultaneously to sustain his keen interest in music. He is a very good pianist and in his younger days did a brief stint as a barroom pianist at a Vermont ski resort. Nancy is an accomplished flautist, and she and David play together from time to time (not often enough). David also inherited the family's love of theatre. He is a compelling speaker who can maintain a brilliant balance of wit and wisdom, all of which has kept him frequently in the public eye. He and Nancy have produced two bright and witty sons. Daniel, the elder, has graduated in law and begun a legal career. Will, the younger, is a first-year law student at the University of Toronto.

As a family, we never get enough of each other's company. We celebrate each other's successes and are always first responders when anyone is in trouble.

But, by any measure, the crowning piece of good fortune was discovering my extraordinary wife, Ruth, in whose shadow I invariably appeared larger and smarter than I really was. I have often been asked, "What made your marriage tick — and why was it so successful?" Luck may have played a part, but it takes more than that to traverse sixty-seven years together with smiles on your faces. Our "secrets" included warm, open communication, the ability to laugh at ourselves (and others) and never taking ourselves too seriously.

More than anyone else, Ruth provided much of the glue that binds us together so tightly as a family, and I anticipate her influence will endure for generations to come.

As I progress through my eighty-ninth year, it is an unending source of satisfaction and contentment that the family's future is in such capable, talented hands. By any measure mine continues to be . . . a lucky life.

As I was putting the finishing touches to this manuscript, I received an e-mailed gift from my dear friend and fellow pediatrician Jane Hailey. It contained a poem, written by her late father, the prolific novelist Arthur Hailey, about five years before he died. His heretical views on his own mortality and on the mythology of the sweet hereafter are identical with my own.

A Last Request

by Arthur Hailey

> *Over my helpless, mute remains,*
> *Please do not play barbaric games,*
> *Nor cast a superstitious nod*
> *Toward some non-existent god.*
> *Instead, respect my intellect,*
> *Which made me, thoughtfully, reject*
> *Man's wishful, vain, deceiving scrimmage*
> *Creating gods in his own image.*
> *I've relished life: on earth, found "heaven,"*
> *Known love and joy, received and given.*
> *I do not need Elysian vales —*
> *The stuff of flimsy fairy tales!*
> *I'd much prefer that you, my friend*
> *Conclude my story with "The End."*

No one could have had a luckier life than mine.

Acknowledgements

This book reflects the work of many people whose continued efforts have made me appear far more articulate (and wiser) than I really am. Top of the list of in-house editors have been Ruth, my dear wife of sixty-seven years. Without her support and encouragement I would never have completed this task. Close on her heels were our three children, Alan, Barbara and David and their wonderful spouses, Lynn, Tony and Nancy.

I also acknowledge with gratitude the following: Michael Levine, Stephen Kimber, James Lorimer, Eleanor Wachtel, Vicki Grant, Rod Ziegler, Liz Crocker, Alan Stern, Bernice MacLellan and the staff at the IWK Foundation. These friends and colleagues helped to make this book possible by reading drafts, offering wise counsel, making creative suggestions, editing, proofing and providing words of encouragement along the way.

My final words of thanks go to my dear friend, Tia Cooper. She began by typing the manuscript but as the book progressed she became my amanuensis and shepherded me through the maze of the book publishing world. I can never fully repay her, so I won't even try.

Richard B. Goldbloom
OC, MD, FRCP, D.Litt (Hon.)

Index

About the Author

Richard Goldbloom, the first physician-in-chief and director of research at the Izaak Walton Killam Hospital for Children in Halifax, is one of Canada's pre-eminent pediatricians. Under his leadership, the IWK became one of Canada's leading centres for pediatric care, teaching and research. But the scope of his interests and contributions has extended far beyond the usual boundaries of his medical specialty. He was founding chair of Halifax's Waterfront Development Corporation and, for many years, chaired the Rhodes Scholar Selection Committee for the Canadian Maritime provinces. An accomplished amateur musician, he also served as honorary director of Symphony Nova Scotia. Dr. Goldbloom was appointed an Officer of the Order of Canada in 1987 in recognition of his pioneering work in regionalization of pediatric care in Nova Scotia. He has received honorary degrees from four universities including his alma mater, McGill University. Dr. Goldbloom was married for sixty-seven years to his college sweetheart, the former Ruth Schwartz of New Waterford, Cape Breton, Nova Scotia. Their marriage, which produced three children, seven grandchildren and five great-grandchildren, was a lifelong love story that ended, sadly, when Ruth died of cancer in August 2012.